Eng
cati
mu
of
app
Na
sub
the
cris

Ho
and
pro
wi
po
co
ro

Th
th
is
cat

Th
H
Simon Shepherd, Ann Thompson, Nigel Wheale.

SHAKESPEARE IN THE CHANGING CURRICULUM

Edited by
Lesley Aers and Nigel Wheale

London and New York

First published 1991
by Routledge
11 New Fetter Lane, London EC4P 4EE

Simultaneously published in the USA and Canada
by Routledge
a division of Routledge, Chapman and Hall, Inc.
29 West 35th Street, New York, NY 10001

Phototypeset by Intype, London
Printed by T J Press (Padstow) Ltd
Padstow, Cornwall.

British Library Cataloguing-in-Publication Data
Shakespeare in the changing curriculum.
1. Educational institutions. Curriculum subjects. Drama in
English. Shakespeare, William, 1564–1616
I. Aers, Lesley   II. Wheale, Nigel
822.33

Library of Congress Cataloging-in-Publication Data
Shakespeare in the changing curriculum/edited by Lesley Aers and
Nigel Wheale.
p.   cm.
Includes index.
1. Shakespeare, William, 1564–1616—Study and teaching—Great
Britain. I. Aers, Lesley. II. Wheale, Nigel.
PR2987.S484   1991
822.3′3—dc20   90–24469

ISBN 0–415–05392–7
ISBN 0–415–05393–5 pbk

Contents

CONTENTS

Plates

(between pages 180 and 188)

List of Contributors

Lesley Aers was Head of English at King Edward VI Upper School, Bury St Edmunds, Advisory Teacher for English to Suffolk LEA, and is currently Specialist Inspector for English with Durham Education Authority.

Bob Allen teaches English and Drama at Deben High School, Felixstowe, Suffolk and he is the Open University tutor for Shakespeare in Suffolk and Essex. During 1989 he was seconded by Suffolk County Council to research developments in 'The Arts in Suffolk Schools'.

Sarah Beckwith taught in the School of English and American Studies at the University of East Anglia, and she now lectures at Duke University, North Carolina. She is writing a study of late medieval crucifixion piety.

Elaine Hobby is a socialist and lesbian who has been active in the women's movement since the mid-1970s. Her work experience includes A-level, WEA, Access and degree-level teaching. She is now Lecturer in Women's Studies at Loughborough University. Her main research interests are in seventeenth-century women's writing, and she has published *Virtue of Necessity: English Women's Writing 1649–1688* (London: Virago, 1988), and co-edited *Her Own Life: Autobiographical Writings by Seventeenth-Century Englishwomen* (London: Routledge, 1989).

Fred Inglis has taught in secondary modern, grammar, and American high schools, a College of Education and the Division of Advanced Studies, Bristol University. He is now Reader in Arts Education at the University of Warwick. His most recent publications include *The Management of Ignorance: A Political*

Theory of the Curriculum (1985), *Popular Culture and Political Power* (1988), and *Media Theory* (1990), all published by Basil Blackwell, Oxford.

Peter Reynolds trained as an actor at the Central School of Speech and Drama and the London Academy of Music and Dramatic Art. He worked in the theatre in Britain and the United States before going to Sussex University to read English. He was closely associated with the 'Shakespeare and Schools' INSET project at the Cambridge Institute of Education, and his latest publication, *Practical Approaches to Teaching Shakespeare* (Oxford: Oxford University Press, 1991), is based on his experience with the project. Peter Reynolds lectures in Drama and Theatre Studies at the Roehampton Institute.

Val Richards has taught English and Drama in secondary schools, at the Laban Centre, Goldsmiths' College, and Middlesex Polytechnic. She is now a practising psychotherapist.

John Salway is a former English teacher. From 1986 to 1988 he was Research Associate to the 'Shakespeare and Schools' project, involved throughout the United Kingdom in developing fresh approaches to teaching Shakespeare with schools, LEAs, theatre companies (including the RSC), and the BBC. He is now Artistic Director of 'Chalk and Talk' Theatre Workshop.

Simon Shepherd teaches English Drama at Nottingham University, which includes regular production work as well as history and theory. He is part of the editorial collective of Nottingham Drama Texts. His publications include: *Marlowe and the Politics of Elizabethan Theatre* (Brighton: Harvester Press, 1986) and *Because We're Queers: The Life and Crimes of Kenneth Halliwell and Joe Orton* (London: GMP, 1989).

Ann Thompson is a Senior Lecturer at the University of Liverpool, England. Her major publications are: *Shakespeare's Chaucer* (Liverpool: Liverpool University Press; New York: Barnes & Noble, 1978); and edition of *The Taming of the Shrew* (Cambridge: Cambridge University Press, 1984); *Shakespeare, Meaning and Metaphor*, as joint-author with John O. Thompson (Brighton: Harvester Press; Iowa: University of Iowa Press, 1987); *'King Lear': The Critics Debate* (London: Macmillan, University Press of America, 1988); *Teaching Women: Feminism and English Studies*, as joint-editor with Helen Wilcox (Manchester: Manchester University Press; New York: St Martin's Press, 1989). She is currently working on *Which Shakespeare?*, a guide to the competing editions, to be published by the Open University Press, and is editing *Cymbeline* for the Arden Shakespeare.

Nigel Wheale lectures in English at Anglia Higher Education College, Cambridge. His doctoral dissertation examined the popularization of 'Humanist' discourses in the European renaissance. He is an editor of *Ideas and Production*, a series in cultural studies (Buckingham: Open University Press), and author of *Postmodernism: A Theory in Practice?* (London: Pinter Press, 1992).

Acknowledgements

The following friends and colleagues have contributed in myriad ways to this book: Paul Allit, Tim Cribb, Nora Crook, David Dabydeen, Ed Esche (who argued late into many Stratford nights with the Revd Sinmore), Helen Falkner, Richard Fredman, Rex Gibson, Russell Jackson, Barbara and R. F. Langley, Rod Macdonald, Sorley Macdonald, Brian Musgrove, Kevin Nolan, Shirley Prendergast, J. H. Prynne, Charlie Ritchie, Rick Rylance, Robert Smallwood and the Shakespeare Institute, Stratford, the staff at the Shakespeare Centre, Stratford, and Richard Spaul. Thanks also to Anglia Higher Education College for timetable remission towards producing the book, and colleagues in the Department of English, Drama and Performing Arts and School of Humanities for their help and interest.

Thanks to the National Film Archive, London, for supplying production stills reproduced in Peter Reynolds's article, and to the Rank Organization and Sovscope Films for permission to reproduce them. Thanks to the Tate Gallery for permission to reproduce John Everett Millais's *Ophelia*, and to Oxford University Press for permission to quote extensively from the Folio text of *King Lear* edited by Stanley Wells and Gary Taylor, *The Complete Works* (Oxford, 1988). The quotation from John Williams's *Stoner* in Fred Inglis's article is reproduced by permission of the author and the University of Arkansas Press. For use as cover materials, James Gillray's *Shakespeare-Sacrificed; – or – The Offering to Avarice*, 20 June 1789, is taken from Gillray's *Works*, 2 vols (London, 1847), by permission of the Syndics of Cambridge University Library, and thanks to the Photographic Department for their excellent work. The frame from 'Judge Dredd' is taken from *2000 AD*, Prog. 570, 16 April 1988, script by Wagner and Grant,

ACKNOWLEDGEMENTS

art by Jim Baikie, lettering by T. Frame, by permission of Fleet-
way publications. We are extremely grateful to Jane Armstrong,
Helena Reckitt, Moira Taylor and Beth Humphries at Routledge
for their efficiency and encouragement throughout.

Introduction

Nigel Wheale

FINDING SHAKESPEARE

What is your substance, whereof are you made,
That millions of strange shadows on you tend?
(*The Sonnets*, 53.1–2)

Good teachers don't write enough about their skills and successes;
they are too busy, and classroom communicative skills are not
necessarily the same as expressive written skills. Good teaching
is knowledge plus enthusiasm, together with love and clarity;
these can't all be legislated for, but the conditions for their
efficient use can be encouraged. We constructed this book with
three contexts in mind: first, the debate over the resourcing and
objectives for education in Great Britain during the later 1980s;
second, the debate about the nature of English Studies as a coherent subject discipline during the same period; and third, the
unique and fiercely debated position that Shakespeare's writing
occupies within the two previous arguments. The chapters in this
book articulate a variety of views about the value of continuing
to teach Shakespeare as a compulsory element of secondary and
further education. Fred Inglis makes a vigorous defence of studying Shakespeare from what he takes to be the intrinsic appeal of
the dramatic poetry which may captivate students 'From the most
able, to [those] that can but spell'. This was the confidence of
Shakespeare's earliest editors, John Heminge and Henry Condell,
when they addressed the First Folio 'To the great Variety of
Readers' in 1623. From a more adversarial position, Simon
Shepherd is sceptical about the status generally given to these
plays and poems, and he rewrites the Sacred Name as anything

but 'Shapesphere', which was James Joyce's version of the reputation.

Only one emphasis unites all the essays in their approaches: that careful attention in the classroom to Shakespeare's language, whether from the point of view of a theatre workshop, film or video adaptation, the politics of gender, psychoanalysis, or a discussion of the plays' textual history, can generate enthusiasm and constructive argument. What the students take away from that discussion is much less predictable, ranging from a passion for the plays which will be explored through a lifetime's reading, theatre-going, perhaps even acting, to a lively scepticism about the uses to which canonical authors are put by national and educational institutions. After intensive study of the *Sonnets* for A level, the wit on the back row may still dismiss them as no more than a 'renaissance Chat Line'. Our chapters report on some current attempts which try to take full account of developing political and educational contexts in order to apply contemporary approaches to the teaching of Shakespeare, the great shibboleth of Eng. Lit.

At this point we reach for our dictionary, just to make sure. '*Shibboleth*: word used to distinguish the true-hearted from the weak-spirited, and more crucially, those of the tribe from those who cannot pronounce the word.' Reaching now for the Authorized Version: 'Then said they unto him, Say now Shibboleth; and he said Sibboleth: for he could not frame to pronounce it right. Then they took him, and slew him at the passages of Jordan: and there fell at that time of the Ephraimites forty and two thousand' (Judges 12:6). *Sashpierre*: a word used for detecting foreigners; *Shaxbee*: a secret password identifying members of a party or sect; *Shakeschafte*: mode of speech characteristic of a profession or class.

Shakespeare's family name is recorded in over eighty variants during the medieval and early modern period, one radical instability among many more which encourages us to question every aspect of the reputation which attaches to this unstable name. As an insecure shibboleth, the idea of these plays and poems grouped under the generic heading 'Shakespeare' represent: a national totem; a rite of passage that has to be negotiated within education; and, having demonstrated competence in the mystery, the name then becomes a fetish which identifies an elite (Garber 1990). And what else?

Let's try to locate some of the kinds of existence that we grant to a name like 'Shakespeare', the national poet of a language which has become a world language in our own period. During the late sixteenth century English was spoken by perhaps five million people, and restricted to a provincial corner of Europe. Today some things haven't changed, but the number of English-speakers is nearer 500 million and Shakespeare is no longer simply a national poet, but a world contender. This status replicates the name across many kinds of context. 'Hamlet' can be found on packets of cigars, Danish stripped pine furniture, and – we swear – tins of guava halves in syrup; there is a selection of his heroines labelling a range of body sprays in Sainsbury's; the author's statue is engraved on the £20 note (four Rockets make one William), and did you hear about the cheque-card thief who was disappointed to find his face didn't match what he thought was the security photo of the bearded owner on the Bard Card hologram? Collecting Shakespeareana during a term from the newspapers and airwaves will decorate a wall very effectively. So we have established the daily presence of a reputation within the mass culture, a name from a cultural register being transposed to the cash register (Holderness 1988).

Here the image has become a guarantee of financial meanings, distinct from, but related to its meanings in education or the theatre. If we take a school trip to Stratford we might buy a Shakespeare hologram, visit The World of, or take a bus and tour The Country of. This is the circulation of Shakespeare as cultural capital within the voracious patterns of social consumption. As an effect of popular culture, Shakespeare is also big in the movies, and not just on the Art House circuits. Sigourney Weaver confessed that in creating the role of Ripley, the heroine of *Alien* and *Aliens*, she took inspiration from some pretty traditional male role models, and a leading contender was Henry Five (her phrase): and this creates anomalies in the screen fantasy we are offered (Penley 1989: 133). The debt works in the opposite direction too: there is a secret connection, not known to many, between Laurence Olivier's performance as Richard III and the Big Bad Wolf in Disney's *Three Little Pigs* (Hawkins 1990: 115). Most people encounter Shakespeare in the context of lager adverts, Comedy Aid routines (that Balcony Scene again, with Frank Bruno as a memorable Juliet), or in the puerile and vicious parodies of 'popular' journalism: 'Beware the AIDS of March' (the *Sun*, April 1989, exploiting research on the subject of homosexuality in the plays).

These incarnations of Shakespeare are reasonably tangible; we can watch them and be exhilarated, bored, or outraged; we can read and study them, buy them, or note them as part of the modern image repertoire. The National Author, whether it is Dante, Goethe, Cervantes, Pushkin, or Shakespeare, is peculiarly weighted with meaning. His language (is there anywhere a *female* National Author?) becomes canonical in particular ways, within syllabuses, quoted at moments of national crisis, invoked as talisman to unify the nation behind a single project, often aggressive. This figure is reverentially installed within the high cultural discourses, but then pays a price by being forced to live a more vigorous, parodic existence in mass cultural consciousness, on the streets and in ad-wars on the airwaves, reproduced on beermats and via the million shadows of a hologram. As teachers we can make use of this high/low differential effect in the classroom, where most students will know Shakespeare first as a miasma, a reputation, and then more familiarly as that pack of five cigars.

The aspects of the name-of-Shakespeare which are hardest to define are those airy nothings which are offered as criteria of excellence and forms of belief. An example from the middle shelves of the market: when they banish us to That Island, we are to console ourselves with music plus three texts, two of which are prescribed. In a notorious broadcast from the Desert Island studio (Radio 4, 1 December 1989) Lady Diana Mosley, wife of Sir Oswald Mosley (the founder of the British Union of Fascists during the early 1930s) hoped that she would be allowed her copy of the Bible in the Authorized Version because its 'early seventeenth-century English is so beautiful'. But she added that it is 'rather short on jokes' and in addition selected Proust for light relief. No one has yet said: 'Well thanks, but may I trade in Shakespeare/the Bible for *The Mahabharata* (the world's longest book, a library to keep one distracted under the palms) or Wisden /*The Koran*/William Gibson . . .'. That Island evidently belongs to Prospero: whitely Christian, peopled with blank verse-readers.

But coming over the hypermarket public address system we hear a message with a much more seriously Educational tone. The fiercest arguments are fought over the value and status of Shakespeare's 'language'. In December 1989 the Prince of Wales presented the Thomas Cranmer Schools Prizes, awards made to children for public speaking, and he used the occasion to criticize the teaching of English in schools and lament the decline in standards of the written and spoken language. The competition had been organized by a conservative weekly journal, the *Spectator*, together with the Prayer Book Society, an association for the defence and appreciation of traditional liturgical forms in the Church of England, and it commemorated the 500th anniversary of the birth of Archbishop Thomas Cranmer. Speaking from next to the pulpit in the opulent City Church of St James, Garlickhythe, Charles attacked attempts to revise traditional liturgical language, and linked what he took to be the feebleness of the Church of England's Alternative Service Book with 'a calamitous decline in literacy and the quality of English'.

Inevitably, when he invoked the language of mid-sixteenth-century Anglican belief he could not refrain from invoking the language of early seventeenth-century popular entertainment. The association of Cranmer with Shakespeare is rendered legitimate through this conservative perspective which is trying to establish the history of a supposed linguistic decline. In the early modern period itself, the linking of the two areas of writing would almost certainly have been thought blasphemous. But that is a pedantic and teacherly point. Prince Charles was much more up to date when he offered a slightly witty rewrite of Hamlet's third soliloquy, as if spoken by Mel Smith: 'Well frankly, the problem as I see it/ At this moment in time is whether I/ Should just lie down under all this hassle . . .', and so on. For this he might receive an adequate pass in some current forms of GCSE comprehension exercise. But Charlie's point was to contrast our present 'dismal wasteland of banality, cliché, and casual obscenity' with one of the greatest moments of 'the world's most successful language' (here combine the use-value and aesthetic-value arguments for Shakespeare in mutual admiration). The *Daily Express* columnist Charles Moore, who invited the Prince of Wales to be Patron of the Cranmer Prize competition, glossed the Prince's speech as 'a call to Church and nation to revive themselves in the present by recovering their past' (*Daily Express*, 22 December 1989).

The career of the English literary curriculum as a nationalist agenda has been clearly researched in the work of historians and critics such as Chris Baldick (1983), Raymond Williams (1983), Brian Doyle (1989), Raphael Samuel (1989), and Tony Crowley

(1989). So for example, exactly similar appeals were being made to the saving qualities of the Prayer Book by figures in authority during the late 1920s, another period when national identity was perceived to be in crisis. From *Our Inheritance* by the then Prime Minister, Stanley Baldwin, 1928:

> Fifty years ago all children went to church, and they often went reluctantly, but I am convinced, looking back, that the hearing – sometimes almost unconsciously – of the superb rhythm of the English Prayer Book Sunday after Sunday, and the language of the English Bible leaves its mark on you for life. Though you may be unable to speak with these tongues, yet they do make you immune from rubbish in a way that nothing else does . . .
>
> (Crowley 1989: 254–5)

As students and teachers of Elizabethan-Jacobean culture, what are we to make of these ugent remarks, addressed directly to us by Prince Charles and so many others? We could recognize them as moralistic gestures with no relevance at all to actual educational practice; or we can think more about the kind of appeal which is being made to the use of Shakespeare and his plays' contexts.

The Prince's summons leads us deep into the million strange shadows of ideology, in these forms: the language presented as an ideal cultural institution; an appeal to religious discourse and mystical categories; a version of national history as visionary national unity. And all of this bears down on the text called Shakespeare in the ways in which it is deployed as a national scripture, when it is made equivalent to Common Prayer, as in the Prince's speech. Let's make a scholastic, a religious, and a political response: first, recent historians of early modern English society argue that the Reformation attempt to have the population internalize religious belief as a regulative set of social practices was widely perceived to have failed by the mid to late seventeenth century. Reformed religion, of which Cranmer's Prayer Book was a central element in England, had failed to win hearts and minds, even then (Wrightson 1982). Second, a counter-argument from within faith: Christianity in its origins was only belatedly a text-based religion, and the Gospels are said to be rather ordinary Greek, literary-wise. To worship the language of worship is from this point of view an empty formalism.

Last, a strategic point: we as professors of English literature may have enjoyed the arguments over the death of the canon, and be bravely proceeding to the new forms of subject organization proposed by critics such as Malcolm Evans which are more equal to our students' needs and interests (Evans 1989: 283–5). But other powerful voices still deploy Literature for their own purposes, and the argument must continue with and against them. The worst possible tactic is to refuse to debate questions of value in terms that non-specialists can understand, to abandon Shakespeare's writing without giving good reason; a chatshow discussion in 1988 chaired by Clive James allowed Kenneth Baker, then Secretary of State for Education, to dominate the argument because the representative Radical Academic effectively refused to join debate at all, denying that Hamlet existed (Sec. of State fr Edctn: hhhrump, ghhrrr)´ and offering instead a discussion of some of the evening's TV transmissions. The ground for argument was left vacant, and conservatism expanded as it will to occupy the vacuum, enthused and triumphant. Lesson: the plays cannot simply be abandoned, or the ideology that would be dominant will inhabit them for its own purposes, as heritage, nationalism, pot-pourri (Fr. lit.: 'rotten-pot').

THE EIGHTIES: A LOST DECADE

And folly, doctor-like, controlling skill,
(*The Sonnets*, 66.10)

The debates within and beyond English universities over the status of literary studies have occurred during a particularly dismal period for education in the context of national politics (for some American arguments, see Beehler 1990). Since 1979 Mrs Thatcher's Conservative governments have remorselessly deprived all educational sectors of badly needed resources. During December 1989 inspectors reported that book stocks in primary and secondary schools were seriously inadequate because of under-funding, with parents increasingly expected to make good the shortfall. What they describe as 'literary poverty' was the result in the secondary schools surveyed, with a narrow range of poetry or drama available to students, and very little writing at all available from before the twentieth century. One tenth of teachers changed their jobs or retired in 1989; only 68 per cent of state school posts were filled by permanent staff (compared to 90 per cent in private schools). The urgent need to improve participation rates in higher education, together with consistently inadequate provision of training in skills, have continued the dreary record of Britain's failure to take mass education seriously. The use-value arguments increasingly circulated within educational debates about national decline relative to international 'competitors' and the urgent need to provide a highly literate and numerate workforce can be exactly paralleled with numerous rows from any period during the last hundred years in this country. Our taskmasters (and their mistress) have a very slow learning curve indeed. And here is another ideological fault line: teachers and lecturers have their own aims and objectives for what they want to teach, values or skills which may run counter to the dominant value system. Education is a major process of social conformation, in numbers of ways; but an intrinsic part of the process is the encouragement to question or reject some current social expectations. There have been periods when teachers have had to teach in deep contradiction to the national parameters set for educational practice, as in the late nineteenth century during the experiment of 'payment by results' for teachers, and we may be entering another sustained period of this kind of counter-teaching. This battle for the content and emphases of the curriculum is one of the subjects of the present collection.

The English political elite has cynically administered the decline of public sector education in response to short-term budgetary objectives and for its own narrow ideological reasons. At the same time it has insulated itself from consequent damage through use of private education and the most privileged areas of the university system. And let's be clear: Shakespeare is expensive to teach, because our pupils need to spend time with the language and conventions that are now quite alien, they need a choice of good editions, and they have a right to expect to be able to study the plays in performance and on film and video. But it is not fanciful to imagine a division of cultural knowledge that will widen, as the privileged insist on knowing what they choose to term their heritage, and which they can afford to internalize, while the rest of us are left to cope with life skills and contemporary studies. The continuing divisive effects of the English class-cum-education system will not be solved by the National Curriculum proposals.

Three broad strands in contemporary critical debate help to

define the work in this collection: these are cultural materialism, feminist historiography, and new historicism (the positions are helpfully reviewed in Dollimore 1985 and Cohen 1987). The majority of the essays are influenced to greater or lesser extent by this critical activity, and two contributors (Bob Allen, Fred Inglis) define their approaches by arguing against some of the assumptions of critical theory. But imaginative teaching of Shakespeare from whatever critical perspective is not going to reverse the losses sustained by education during the past decade. To have that kind of expectation would be to reconstitute the grandiose claims for the humanities which critical theory has so persistently criticized. The most we can claim is that the approaches encourage a critical response to Shakespeare in a range of activities which we wish to offer to pupils and students as engaging, relevant, and at times provocative. And that these activities can be used in the new syllabus for cultural studies which must displace the regressions and dilutions of the National Curriculum:

> 'Education' must always be in excess of 'training': it is about a critical, dynamic creation of knowledge, not an instrumental measuring of information.
>
> (Light 1989: 34)

DEVELOPING NEW RESPONSES TO SHAKESPEARE

> If there be nothing new, but that which is
> Hath been before, how are our brains beguiled
> (*The Sonnets*, 59.1–2)

In the teaching of Shakespeare, we use the revaluations of English literature and its institutional formations in the following ways. By:

- taking careful account of the constraints and possibilities of changing syllabuses to locate good teaching and assessment practice (Lesley Aers, Bob Allen, Fred Inglis);
- introducing current scholarship which is re-editing the play texts (Ann Thompson);
- modifying the classroom emphasis on reading as the only way to comprehend the plays by the addition of a variety of drama workshop activities (Bob Allen, Simon Shepherd, John Salway);

- incorporating the politics of gender and its historical representation (Sarah Beckwith);
- countering patriarchal assumptions in the plays through an awareness of lesbian and gay values (Elaine Hobby);
- introducing psychoanalytic approaches to dissolve simplistic assumptions about character (Val Richards);
- drawing on our students' audio-visual knowledge and enthusiasm to study the plays in film and videotape format (Peter Reynolds, Nigel Wheale).

All of these are demanding in physical and intellectual resources; they need more time, more space, more technology, more preparation, and simply better books, than are going to be available in the averagely equipped secondary school. But we make no apology for describing these approaches, many of which were developed in the comparatively better resourced areas of further and higher education – where, we stress, the advantages are only comparative. And we are confident that the ideas offer possibilities for everyone throughout the curriculum, and that they rightly make claims on resources, and indicate what resourcing should be in future. They become part of the new agenda for cultural studies in our schools which must be formulated to take us beyond the present material and intellectual poverties.

Textual scholarship of the most careful sort contributes to the new ways of teaching Shakespeare. Ann Thompson indicates how there needs to be a mutual awareness between textual and theoretical approaches to the plays. The versions which we know of canonical plays like *Hamlet*, *Othello*, and *King Lear* were constructed during the early eighteenth century by editors who established their texts of the plays by conflating the early Quarto and Folio editions. Even then there were voices raised against this patching together of all available versions to produce one apparently seamless script. Does not the reality of theatrical practice make it more likely that the scripts were knocked about, adapted in the light of the successes and failures of performance? And that therefore variant versions of the plays might represent different states as they emerged during their early performance history? But an understandable desire not to exclude any of the lines, and a less pardonable reluctance to allow the possibility of revision by the author (or even worse, company) dictated that the tradition of conflating texts was the accepted editorial method until quite recently. Established contemporary editions such as the Arden Shakespeare (about to be revised) still preserve the tradition of conflated texts. These almost certainly represent no play that was ever performed in the early seventeenth century. But since the beginning of this century a much more scrupulous kind of bibliographical approach has begun to differentiate the variety of texts which actually contributed to the earliest editions of Shakespeare, and this work has recently begun to gain prominence in more generally available versions of the plays.

This scholarship excavates the outlines of revision and excision buried within the conflated texts which are often covered by 300 years' worth of conjecture and speculation. The monumental work of a textual scholar like Peter Blayney in his *The Texts of 'King Lear' and their Origins* (Cambridge, 1982), and of the editors working with Stanley Wells and Gary Taylor to produce *The Complete Works* (Oxford, 1986) offer, for example, the possibility of two quite distinct versions of *Lear*: *The History of King Lear* (from the Quarto text) and *The Tragedy of King Lear* (from the Folio). The Folio may represent a text revised in the light of the experience of performance, or the author's second thoughts. In classroom exercises, based around discussion of a conflated text compared to extracts from a 'revised' text, it becomes possible to explore the implications of revision, even speculate on why and how the changes were made (Taylor and Warren 1983; Werstien 1988).

The Summer 1990 issue of *Shakespeare Quarterly* was devoted to 'teaching Shakespeare', and it reflected no clear consensus among teachers from the United States on how to profess this author – even its editor describes the collection as one of 'apparent disorder' (*Shakespeare Quarterly* [SQ] 41/2 [iii]). The previous issue which focused on pedagogy (SQ 1984) had been dominated by discussions of teaching through performance. Three of our chapters explore the use of workshop-based methods, and two examine the use of film and video in Shakespeare studies. Bob Allen surveys the development of practical drama work within the 'balanced entitlement' curriculum during the last twenty-five years, a rich and varied provision which he perceives to be threatened by the more prescriptive programme of the National Curriculum. John Salway describes how he has used theatre workshop activities to tackle the racist sentiments articulated – or provoked in the audience – by classic texts such as *Othello* and

11

The Tempest. He draws on the growing scholarship which is defining the Black presence within English culture and society, and which provides an invaluable corrective to the blind Eurocentrism afflicting so much of the traditional curriculum. Astonishingly, the American contributors to *Shakespeare Quarterly*'s pedagogy issue offer no discussion of the problems to be encountered in teaching this virulently nationalist author within a culturally diverse, interdependent world. Taking care to examine how the Black presence is routinely defined by exclusions and denigrations within the traditional white male canon is only a part of the vital construction of a culturally balanced and fully responsive curriculum (Gerschel and Nasta 1989; Donald 1989: 23).

Simon Shepherd uses the possibilities of workshop practices to articulate opposition to the repressive conventions prevailing within many educational structures. In good workshop activity (as elsewhere) the relationships between students, text, teacher, and assessment can all be recast. The distracting charisma of Shakespeare's reputation can be critically examined, and the plays staged sceptically in order to experience radical differences in conventions between late sixteenth- and late twentieth-century performance. For Simon Shepherd a central issue here is the assumptions about character that students often bring to the play texts. The commonplace empathetic reaction to the roles can elide troubling issues of domination and subjection implicit in early modern society. The (frequently difficult) process of understanding Shakespeare's language ('often more abstract and tortuous than that of his contemporaries') can be helped by the thrilling, embodied pleasure of collaboration in performance. And as actors in the fullest sense of the word, the students can positively experience the contesting and construction of meanings within the workshop space.

Feminist criticism has made a remarkable contribution to English studies in the last twenty years, and this work has been very valuable in rethinking renaissance literature. Feminist research has supplied new contexts and these create new questions with which to approach the drama. We have seen what is effectively the discovery of the range of women's reading and writing in early modern England (Greer *et al.* 1988; Hobby 1988); the creation within the last twenty years of the systematic study of family organization in the period, allowing us to match the plays' representations of familial affections, antagonisms, and power with what may have been the diversity of experience within the defensive hierarchy of renaissance society (Ezell 1987); there is work on the realities of gendered behaviour as it differed crucially for males and females in the public and the private spheres (Jardine 1989); and there are attempts to reconstruct the assumptions which audiences brought to the symbolic representation of women on the public stage (Howard 1988).

But there is no single 'feminist' reading or interpretation to be made. From within feminism, diametrically opposed positions are taken on Shakespeare's female roles: researching in renaissance assumptions about gender, Lisa Jardine argues that a pervasive misogyny and repression of female character informs the plays, even in scenes where twentieth-century actresses and directors might want to find pro-feminist arguments being made, such as Emilia's 'Let husbands know,/ Their wives have sense like them' (*Othello* IV.3). Against this, Kathryn Pogson, performing Ophelia in a nationally acclaimed production of *Hamlet*, and directed by a celebrated male director who only asked her to be 'beautiful' so that the Prince might fall in love with her, interprets the possibilities of the role differently. She argues that even in the silences of Ophelia's role the play creates the possibility for the actress to articulate the ways in which women attempted to survive in the early modern world. And that this speaks, even silently, to women in a contemporary audience. 'Shakespeare heard what women have to say in order to survive', she remarked, even though their strategies might not have been enough to survive to the end of the play.

Sarah Beckwith's 'The power of devils and the hearts of men' discusses *Macbeth* as a text involved with a new conception of masculine identity, a version of male personality and status that is predicated on the creation and persecution of 'witches'. As one conspicuous form of social text, the play in performance staged the fantasy of witchcraft and was complicit with the terrible realities of the actual witch trials – processes that were no less fictional and fantastic than the drama, but with actual and murderous consequences for the people, usually women, who were accused. *Macbeth* pandered to King James as Banquo's descendant, and perhaps also to him as the author of the *Daemonologie* (Edinburgh, 1597). An aggressive male politics was constructed at least in part employing the symbolic threat of demonic women as a scapegoat, and as a contrastive 'other' that menaced the social

13

order. This accounts for the disturbing, unlocated quality of the weird sisters in the play, beyond society as 'imperfect speakers' in the wilderness, yet simultaneously located at the centre of Macbeth's paranoid, male tyranny. In this way the tragedy demonstrates the dangerous insecurity of the novel version of subjectivity which the Elizabethan/Jacobean stage was so effectively 'personating', a new word in the 1590s for the new phenomenon of presented identity on the stages.

Sarah Beckwith's chapter is an example of one kind of feminist criticism which is concerned to locate literary texts very precisely within the dynamics of gendered politics in the early modern period, a kind of reading where text and context are highly complicit (and for this reason her chapter is very fully referenced). The theatre is defined as a particular kind of spectacle, able to articulate socially determined meanings of gender, and put them to question. From this kind of awareness of the construction of male and female identity in renaissance texts, classroom discussion can move to our own experiences of social conformation and the management of social insecurities. This critical practice is more genuinely social than that of a 'new historicist' reading of *Macbeth* such as Jonathan Goldberg's 'Speculations: *Macbeth* and source'; here the troubling status of female roles in the play is consigned to a murky psychologism – 'a further reflection of the disturbing questions raised about the sources of the Shakespearean imagination' (Goldberg 1987: 257).

In 1606 *Macbeth* drew on superstitions that were cultivated by a cynical administration in order to orchestrate the persecution of easily identified minorities; and this was done in the hope of imposing a false consensus on the majority whose perception of their own vulnerability is heightened by the scare tactic. At this point our critical practice becomes contemporary in very direct ways. The Local Government Act (1988) includes a Section 28 which states that local authorities should not 'intentionally promote homosexuality' or publish material with that intention; nor should any authority 'promote the teaching in any maintained school of the acceptability of homosexuality as a pretended family relationship'. This notorious legislation was framed following the 1987 general election during which an intensive smear campaign in the Tory tabloid press was directed against Labour local authorities such as Haringey which had begun to develop policies to promote positive images of lesbians and gays in schools (Stop the Clause Education Group 1989).

Section 28 was quickly denounced as legally meaningless, since no court could effectively prove such a nebulous charge as the 'intention to promote'. But the Section did its work in appealing to homophobic prejudice in the electorate, and strengthened the Conservatives' completely spurious posture as 'the Party of the Family', while the Opposition was demonized as an irresponsible 'loony left' (Shepherd 1990). Section 28 is sinister and ugly – and wrong; how dare a supposedly responsible government ridicule the choices of private citizens as to whom they live with, by describing anyone's loving association as 'a pretended family relationship'. Is pretence completely unknown within the conventionally heterosexual family unit? And the malignant prejudice represented by Section 28 clearly makes the discussion of adolescent sexual orientation much more difficult within any enlightened school's policy for sex education. Elaine Hobby's contribution in this collection responds vigorously to the coercion of Section 28, detailing the intimidation of specific teachers and groups, which the legislation has encouraged, and examining the more subtle effects of self-censorship that it can also promote: teachers may choose to avoid discussion of exactly those areas of sexuality and prejudice which most need to be addressed: 'Censorship creates an under-censorship', observes Vladimir Solodin of the situation in his own country, and he should know, occupying as he does the office of Soviet State Censor.

Elaine Hobby describes teaching *As You Like It* to an A-level group, where she declared her own lesbianism as a part of the class's work on conventional assumptions about sexuality and gender both in the Elizabethan period and in her pupils' own experience. An examination of the two households of *As You Like It* as they are elaborated in the conflicts of Act I will demonstrate the tangible meanings of patriarchy. For wives: 'thus doth St Peter preach to them, "Ye wives, be ye in subjection to obey your own husbands." . . . them they must obey, and cease from commanding, and perform subjection' ('The Sermon of the State of Matrimony', from the *Sermons or Homilies Appointed to be Read in Churches* 1562.) Celia and Rosalind refuse to 'perform subjection' within their motherless, pretended families, and their roles present a double threat to early modern assumptions about decorous gendered behaviour: first as 'women' who assert their independence by vanishing into Arden, and second, at another level of the game, by playing with the instability of the female/male distinction within the roles themselves. Here Elaine Hobby restores a number of jokes and ambiguities to our interpretation of the play which conventional scholarship ignores or glosses over. But this approach works at more fundamental levels than simply adding nuances of interpretation: by reading the play as an instance of early modern expectations about family, obedience, and what was thought to be legitimate in gendered behaviour, Elaine Hobby demonstrates the workings of convention in the social sphere and within the theatres, together with the ways in which those restricting expectations were challenged by the drama and can be contested in our own discussions.

The chapter which derives most directly from the introduction of theoretically developed readings of literature during the 1970s is Val Richards' contribution, ' "His majesty the baby": a psycho-analytic approach to *King Lear*'. Taking her title from Freud's view of the infant's voracious demands and desires, Val Richards outlines the way in which a particular description of language has been related to the Freudian account of the psyche's development. Through close attention to symptomatic patterns of imagery in *King Lear* she offers an explanation for the virulence and power of Lear's response to Cordelia, Goneril, and Regan. This speculative approach is fruitful in several ways: it introduces a new model for thinking about character in the early modern world, and it provides some of the terms for a psychological understanding of the various effects that performances have on us, both as audience and as actors (and see Cunliffe 1988).

Concern about apparent increases in difficulties with reading and writing among young people is common to 'developed' societies in the early 1990s. Varieties of explanation are offered, but film and television always figure prominently in analyses of the problem. Our final two chapters explore ways of using rec-orded versions of Shakespeare's plays, not as simple relief from the supposed drudgery of hacking through the written text with detailed attention, but as independent interpretations of the plays possessing particular virtues. Increasing critical attention is being given to the extensive range of film adaptations of Shakespeare, and Peter Reynolds describes how analysis of particular pro-ductions – *Hamlet* directed by Olivier (1948) and Kozintsev (1964) – develops awareness of the specific production values of each film and can encourage a closer knowledge of the written text through the kind of attention which film requires.

The systematic incorporation of television and videotape technology into our teaching should be used to reinforce verbal literacy, not as a substitution for, or distraction from, reading and writing skills. Nigel Wheale makes use of current work in audiovisual literacy studies to advocate the use of video-based approaches to Shakespeare which draw on the students' own familiarity with televisual conventions. The videotapes discussed share one fundamental aim: to heighten awareness of the conventions and values implicit in performance of the plays by contrasting assumptions from Shakespeare's early modern stage with our own electronic forms.

A LESSON PLAN FOR THE MILLENNIUM

O, change thy thought, that I may change my mind!
(*The Sonnets*, 10.9)

What kinds of argument about Shakespeare do these new approaches encourage? Imagine that we've been lucky enough to take our class to Stratford and see David Thacker's 1989 production of *Pericles*, not as a play on the syllabus, but because it's a good production, with fine acting and intelligent direction. We see it in the Swan theatre, a modern version of an indoor theatre from the early seventeenth century, where the audience sits on three sides of the projecting stage, and then in three tiers above it, and where at its best the relation between actors and spectators can be very direct. We are impressed by the beautiful woodwork, and have already learnt something about the renaissance acting space. Because the playing is located more within the audience, we're consistently aware of everyone's participation, and the acting itself has an edge. The fiction of the drama is heightened in some ways, lessened in others. This is very appropriate for one of the later plays by Shakespeare.

Yes, *Pericles* isn't a common choice, but we can demonstrate some central arguments by starting from this apparently tangential play. It's a ramshackle tale based on a medieval retelling of a late-classical romance. Beginning with Act III: at sea during a storm, Thaisa, Pericles' wife, is thought to die in childbirth, her body is given sea burial, and her surviving daughter is named

Marina. Pericles is heartbroken, and returns to Tyre, leaving his daughter to be brought up by Cleon, governor of Tarsus, and his wife Dionyza. Sixteen years pass, and Dionyza has become insanely jealous of Marina. She plots to have her murdered, but instead Marina is stolen by pirates who sell her into prostitution. Here we can follow specific aspects of David Thacker's production.

Act IV, Scene 2, the brothel at Mytilene, produced like a debauched scene in a Hogarth print, much business with buckets and slops: the Bawd's three poor creatures lie around exhausted and groaning, shockingly ill, make-up graphically picturing their description – 'The stuff we have, a strong wind will blow it to pieces, they are so pitifully sodden.' Their illness is vividly drawn and acted, and we can't help but think of Aids victims, and want to call in help. Boult (the pimp) introduces Marina as a 'piece' worth 'a thousand pieces'. Marina is now also a commodity, but stands as a pure figure among the literally fallen females on the stage around her. She is a saint about to be martyred, her actions are dignified and grave: Boult has sold her by description in the market place: 'I have cried her almost to the number of her hairs.' (He is less precise than God: 'the very hairs of your head are all numbered': Matthew 10:30, Luke 12:7). Like Cordelia, Marina is a kind of test-case who demonstrates what men will do – which are the cruellest lines in *King Lear*? Take the brief remark made by the Captain who replies to Edmund's sealed order for the execution of Lear and Cordelia:

> I cannot draw a cart,
> Nor eat dried oats. If it be man's work, I'll do't.

These lines are only found in *The History of King Lear*, Scene 23, line 38. The reply is not present in the Folio text, *The Tragedy of King Lear*, Act 5, Scene 3, line 34 (Wells and Taylor 1986). Is this a consequence of a deliberate process of revision which cut small moralizing, moralistic passages? (Warren 1983: 64). Marina's situation is tensioned in ways comparable to that of Cordelia: she is marked by providence, but finds herself in the hands of men. The Bawd says to her 'If it please the gods to defend you by men, then men must comfort you, men must feed you, men stir you up.'

Cordelia dies because the Captain is willing to do inhuman work. Within the insanely disordered priorities of the drama's society, he refuses to work like an animal – draw a cart, eat dried oats – and so he opts to perform the work of a man, which is worse than animal. Marina survives because the action of *Pericles* is structured around wild improbabilities, offering miracles and coincidences as in a pantomime (or a miracle play), though much of its material is disturbingly 'adult'. Marina is defended by her own virtue and the strength of her example as she preaches divinity to the customers at the brothel, converting them 'out of the road of rutting for ever'. We see how she does this when the governor Lysimachus is introduced to her as a potential client. She is saved by her eloquence:

> I did not think thou couldst have spoke so well,
> Ne'er dreamt thou couldst.
> Had I brought hither a corrupted mind,
> Thy speech had altered it.
>
> (*Pericles*, IV.6.99–102)

Marina's argument also persuades the disgusting Boult to place her in an honest household where she teaches polite female accomplishments – singing, dancing, sewing – to pupils of 'noble race'.

So we have watched this improbability, an emblem of virtue defended by its speaking power. The fifth act continues these miracles by bringing the dead back to life, restoring complete losses. Marina is reunited with her father who has not seen her since she was a babe; she revives him from his melancholy retreat from life. Marina appears as a vision of complete integrity to him: falseness cannot come from her, she looks modest as justice, she smiles like the figure of patience on a tomb. They discover each other as father and daughter. T. S. Eliot wrote his best poem out of this incident:

> What is this face, less clear and clearer
> The pulse in the arm, less strong and stronger –
> Given or lent? more distant than stars and nearer than the
>   eye
>
> ('Marina', 1930)

(A delicate exercise: 'Compare and contrast the portrayal of Pericles in Eliot's poem and in Act V, Scene 1 of Shakespeare's play.') In a dream vision Pericles is told by the goddess Diana to travel to Ephesus. There he is reunited with Thaisa, who had been miraculously revived from her watery grave and has been living a devout life in Diana's temple ever since. Marina is brusquely married to Lysimachus.

It was a great performance; most of our students were moved and impressed, not having had very high expectations of the evening. What could criticism add? The cultural-materialist teacher decides to organize discussion around a tableau: let's imagine that there was a Censor's Office in 1610, and that the position was occupied by a sophisticated reforming Puritan, someone able to appreciate the plays, and who was therefore suspicious of their appeal because he understood it so well. In fact the Master of the Revels was the official who had responsibilities something like this in the period; he read and authorized all play texts, ensuring that no material was included that was blasphemous or that appeared to be critical of authority (Mullaney 1987; Clare 1990). Our Censor is concerned about these issues, but he is also more aesthetically developed: he knows that the theatre is in competition with Christianity for people's attention, and that it is a potent arena for reviewing dangerous ideas: he would have a lot to discuss with Walter Benjamin or Bertolt Brecht (or Prince Charles). He has just attended our performance, and he decides to call in the author and management, as is his prerogative. Checking over the text from a recently printed paperback, he begins by congratulating the nervous group of entrepreneurs who are fiddling with their ruffs and shifting about, especially the balding, bearded one with the earring who is trying to look inconspicuous on the back row. Then our Censor, let's call him Reverend Sinmore, begins by detailing some of the production's successes; at this the management relax a little, but not before he has delivered judgment: 'We will have to close you down, tonight.' He gives his reasons, and they sound uncannily like some of the perspectives of late twentieth-century theory. First:

Marina and the sodden creatures. 'The emblem which your stage creates of this pure woman within the context of the brothel is troubling; it is theatrically exciting, and this worries me. We have as you know many reservations about the practice of youths personating women on stage, and this is a particularly clear example. There is something in the juxtaposition of great purity and extreme, involuntary degradation that is unsettling. I am concerned about the poor creatures who are *not* saved; it is almost as if Marina can only be exalted so long *as there are also* the fallen, and against whom she alone is defined.'

'I put it directly: her image of virtue is complicit with their unresolved misery. You offer her as a paragon of womanly decency, but she only shines so clearly because of the human darkness against which you place her, and for which you do nothing. Please do not mistake me: I have the greatest respect for the effects which your company creates with lights, music, and finery, and I take it seriously for exactly that reason. Your theatre is a scandalous place, it arouses our emotions and attaches them to specular images, individuals who personate ideals, or who dangerously offer versions of the great and powerful. But the degree of our irrational attachment to these ideals which your shadows embody does not allow us sufficiently to reflect upon them, to cultivate a decent perspective upon what we are shown. And so we receive these illusions in a state of diminished reason.' (The Reverend Sinmore has studied abroad at the most advanced continental universities – Wittenberg, Bologna – *not* Paris, then full of a meretricious clapped-out medieval sign theory, and his theology is at times very audacious, anticipating utopian secular ideals of much later date.) 'Second:'

Her golden speech. 'I notice that in the governor Lysimachus's attempt to buy Marina's virtue, what saves her, according to his account, is the power of her eloquence. (I am also troubled, in passing, by the rather inferior quality of the numbers in the dramatic verse, here and elsewhere in the play; but a formalistic concern with rhetorique is not my intention; we must concentrate upon the effects of the meaning within its auditors.) To say that the character Marina is saved only by her speech is itself an example of the power of speaking, but I put it to you, what if she had been only an *indifferent* speaker? Have you not deplorably confined the active exercise of virtue to the eloquent, the learned, in other words to the privileged? Here as in many other aspects I feel that your theatre is socially exclusive, addressed to the concerns and abilities of an elite – yes, yes, I know that in the recent past you have attracted a very wide spectrum of the citizenry, but this seems of late to be narrowing, and the middling sort of person is not sufficiently addressed in these fashionable romancing plays. Your *Pericles* is a great success, and I am concerned that it might start a trend in romantic puerilities on the stage. Which brings me to my final objection:'

In feathered briefness sails are filled,/ And wishes fall out as they're willed. 'Really! How can you equate wishes and the will so flippantly? This genre of romance is childish, it is full of absurdity, which you partly seem to admit by the use of the antique narrator, Gower. The action of the two final scenes restores daughter and wife to your hero. You give total conso- lation in a way which is not possible in this world. You use this old Greekish story, with strange echoes of the travels of the Apostles – Tarsus, Antioch, Tyre, Ephesus – to make the kind of happiness which only true religion can bring. I find the mixing of pagan materials together with an opportunistic use of Holy Writ to be again troubling: it seems to me that you are seeking ways to circumvent the legislation against blasphemy on stage, which we may need to enforce more strictly. By these magical stratagems in the final scenes you appear to be defeating death and human error in ways which mere players have no right to employ. You would seem to be creating a secular religion, you wish to cure sorrows and melancholy as if you were priests for the mind, but again you can only offer simulacra, illusions of the happiness of plenitude. Your audience is beguiled, they flock to you and you have given them false doctrine. . . . You will close tonight.'

It is a lively discussion; the students take the part of manage- ment, actors, backers, and that author, arguing desperately to keep their production on stage. Reverend Sinmore's criticisms sometimes contradict the students' own responses to the perform- ance, but sometimes they strike a sympathetic chord. What, in our own contemporary terms, was he saying?

Pericles is not very much taught or written about, and the obvious reason for this is the dubious status of the text; it was not reprinted in the First Folio. The new Oxford *Complete Works* is characteristically forthright and offers 'A reconstructed text' 'By William Shakespeare and George Wilkins' (Wells and Taylor 1988: 1037–64). Censor Sinmore was alert to metrical irregularity in the 1609 Quarto which he was using to refresh his memory of the performance, and this may also account for the reputed author having so little to say for himself, outside of his dramatic eloquence. *Pericles* is a collaborative piece of work, and the printed text is a poor version of the staged original, perhaps one of those reconstructed from the partial memories of actors. For their own production, David Thacker's company had to work hard to create a performable version, relying on Wells and Taylor's conjectural text as well as drawing on an early seventeenth-century 'novelization' of the story by George Wilkins, *The Painful Adventures of Pericles Prince of Tyre*. David Thacker described the process:

> *Pericles* was, for me, the paramount example of actor-participation. In the first two weeks of rehearsal, Pericles saw 15 other actors play Pericles – including women. Old men and young men played Marina. . . . The actors incorporate the work of other actors. In Stratford they worked with enormous generosity.
>
> (Chaud 1989: 19)

These textual problems illustrate our concern in this collection to relate current critical/theoretical and editorial work together with production values, because in combination they offer so many new options for reconsidering the plays and their processes of construction.

To think what an intelligent early seventeenth-century opposition to the plays might have been is to dramatize their period-specific features, make more difficult that total and uncritical appropriation of the plays and their implicit assumptions into our own period as a universalized achievement. So our sensitive Puritan friend was worried by the direct mapping of a complete virtuous purity on to a particular class only, because this might appear as tacit endorsement for social hierarchies that need to be questioned, and it had nothing to say to those lost within 'impurity' (Stallybrass and White 1986). Definitions of morality are always socially interested, and when they are offered with such conviction and affective power, then they become difficult to assess dispassionately. Perhaps the reverend gentleman would have been happier at a performance of John Milton's *A Masque presented at Ludlow Castle*, in the mid-1630s, with its much cooler, puritanic treatment of similar themes.

Sinmore was also concerned by the way in which female gender was represented in the performance of 1610, which was by youths; at the time moralists found this highly improper. Marina of course is a figure of absolute propriety, but 'she' articulates a problem for our own contemporary criticism in that the female roles are, as it were, doubly artificial within the plays, created for performance within an absolutely male institution, masculine expectations. Males personated males-as-characters, but young males personated women-who-were-also-characters: are the female roles compromised by this additional set of conventions, now obscure to us? The Censor objected to the way in which Marina was effectively saved by her class training, but himself bound by the social conventions of his time, he did not go on to question the limitation placed on Marina by the skills she does possess: only the decorative domestic arts appropriate to the education of females of her station. Late twentieth-century readings and productions need to understand the implicit limits to early modern roles, and then decide how to argue with those diminished parts (McLuskie 1985: 106). How much is our compassion for Lear given pause by his old-fashioned lament – 'Her voice was ever soft,/ Gentle and low, an excellent thing in women' (*The History of King Lear* scene 24, line 269), which is revised to the even more absolute 'woman' in the Folio text?

So for our historical reconstruction to have been authentic, we would have had to ignore the fine acting by women in the production, which was fortunately impossible. And here also is another question raised by the exercise. How much did the vivid and explicit Stratford staging add to the Censor's worries? A vulgar academic argument often made for not giving serious attention to plays-on-the-stage is that their texts are 'distorted' in production: so much better, the logic continues, to construct an ideal version from reading. Cultural materialist criticism accepts that all production is reinterpretation, and that is the inescapable condition of reproducing texts. The question then must focus on the kinds of meaning created by each particular production, and the institutional context for that interpretation (Sinfield 1985; Armstrong 1989; Collick 1989; Holderness 1989).

Renaissance literary theory focused on the ways in which texts worked their effects within readers and audiences (Evans 1989: 3–5). As a reforming Christian, Sinmore is acutely conscious of the power of individual interpretation of the Bible for readers, and of the effects of sermons upon listeners. The persuasion of an effective theatrical performance must have been perceived as extraordinarily potent competition by those groups concerned to have the ears, and so minds, of the people in early modern society. The nature of the sympathetic attention linking actors and audience was at the heart of opposition to the theatres as it was voiced by clerics and the magistracy. And the process of our enjoyment in theatres/cinemas/the TV lounge, remains a problem for cultural materialism. What repressive complacencies are endorsed in the audience, what ideological values are systematically reproduced within plays that have become national institutions?

It is at this point that we meet the major problem with cultural materialism: how does it articulate anyone's felt response to a text or production? Cultural materialist approaches are committed to the analysis of ideology, that is to the description of systematic structures of belief which articulate sectional interests within societies. This gives us much more critically adept descriptions of early modern society than the paradigm within English studies which cultural materialism largely displaced, that of the 'Elizabethan world picture' (Dollimore 1985, 1989). But as an analytic procedure, always turned upon external belief systems and the ways in which individuals are conformed by the social, how does cultural materialism deal with subjectivity itself? This is The Big One, and this is not the place to even begin to resolve it. It can seem as if thirty years of debate still have not answered Sartre's *Problem of Method*:

> It is precisely this expulsion of man, his exclusion from Marxist Knowledge, which resulted in the renascence of existentialist thought outside the historical totalization of Knowledge. Human science is frozen in the non-human, and human-reality seeks to understand itself outside of science.
>
> (Sartre 1963: 179)

(But now at least woman claims her right to join man in a shared expulsion.) Competing descriptions of the 'subject' and the 'social' have motivated the critical theoretical argument which this book draws on, and because the whole enterprise has been dedicated to moving beyond lazy assumptions about human nature and personality, there remains a central silence about the experience of persons. In order to describe the construction of the 'individual', materialist analysis sets aside subjectivism: 'Because informed by contradictory social and ideological processes, the subject is never an indivisible unity, never an autonomous, self-determining centre of consciousness' (Dollimore 1989: 269).

This perspective reveals determining constructions: but are

there no quasi-autonomous options left to the consciousness?
How does this critique allow for anyone's immediately apprehended perceptions, the claims of our subjectivity? Obviously, in
teaching this immediately presents itself as a difficulty: our pupils
will know what they think and feel, vociferously, even if Louis
Althusser would have it that they don't. There are two immediate
aspects to this problem. First, so much primary and secondary
learning is experientially based, depends on a process of the pupil
encountering proferred knowledge on her/his own terms in order
to become familiar with it, and this pedagogy based upon the
internalization of ideas conflicts directly with the cultural material
critique of 'interior experience' as such. Second, at an even more
general level, cultural material practice has throughout to incorporate anyone's subjectivity to its process, and of course without
lapsing into the comfortable old wing-chairs of good taste and
intuitionist criticism of yore. How is this to be done? The classroom activities and drama workshops described here may be a
part of that continuing research.

The appeal to canonical texts which will revive the nation through
the power of their language is an ignorant fundamentalism. While
competing nationalisms re-emerge in our period as a consequence
of the collapse of 'superpower' hegemonies, the British Isles must
also carefully define their identity, and the educational curriculum
plays a crucial role here. Shakespeare is not now just a quaint
icon of Englishness, but a world text, and we can make use of
this huge dissemination of the plays as a way of celebrating and
reflecting on diversity, dispersion, interdependence, in cultures
and in values. This is not a bland process: it should incorporate
active enquiry into reasons for conflict, subordination, and misrecognition as they are produced in cultural exchange. This is current
work:

> If *The Satanic Verses* is anything, it is a migrant's-eye view of
> the world . . . written from the very experience of uprooting,
> disjuncture and metamorphosis. . . . *The Satanic Verses* cele-
> brates hybridity, impurity, intermingling, the transform-
> ation that comes of new and unexpected combinations of
> human beings, cultures, ideas, movies, songs. It rejoices in
> mongrelisation and fears the absolutism of the Pure.
>
> (Rushdie 1990: 18)

Not a defensive, backward-looking nostalgia for a small island with a supposedly 'homogeneous' racial identity: the violent and coercive campaigns by which the margins were subjugated to the centre can be very effectively studied in Shakespeare (Holderness 1985). Rather, we propose a use of the plays and poems as bizarre and mongrel hybrids, which voraciously drew in diversities of material from the period of European expansion, and which don't belong just to ourselves any more:

> The fact is that we are mixed with each other in ways that most national systems of education have not dreamed of. How to match knowledge in both the arts and sciences with these integrative realities is, I believe, the issue of the moment as the decade closes.

(Said 1989: 38)

REFERENCES

Quotations at the start of each section are from Shakespeare's *Sonnets*, given by poem and line number from *The Complete Works*, general editors Stanley Wells and Gary Taylor, Oxford, Clarendon Press, 1986.

Armstrong, Isobel (1989) 'Thatcher's Shakespeare?' *Textual Practice* 3/1 (Spring): 1–14.

Baldick, Chris (1983) *The Social Mission of English Criticism*, Oxford: Oxford University Press.

Beehler, Sharon A. (1990) '"That's a certain text": problematizing Shakespeare instruction in American schools and colleges', *Shakespeare Quarterly* 41/2: 195–205.

Chaud, Paul (1989) 'Profile: David Thacker', *Drama. The Quarterly Theatre Review*, 4: 18–19.

Clare, Janet (1990) *'Art Made Tongue-tied by Authority': Elizabethan and Jacobean Dramatic Censorship*, Manchester and New York: Manchester University Press.

Cohen, Walter (1987) 'Political criticism of Shakespeare', in Jean E. Howard and Marion F. O'Connor (eds) *Shakespeare Reproduced. The Text in History and Ideology*, New York and London: Methuen.

Collick, John (1989) *Shakespeare, Cinema and Society*, Manchester: Manchester University Press.

Crowley, Tony (1989) *The Politics of Discourse: The Standard Language Question in British Cultural Debates*, London: Macmillan.

Cunliffe, Helen (1988) '"The story of the night told over": D. W. Winnicott's theory of play and *A Midsummer Night's Dream*', in Edward J. Esche (ed.) *Ideas and Production* 8: 'Drama in Theory and Performance'.

Dollimore, Jonathan (1985) 'Introduction: Shakespeare, cultural materialism and the new historicism', in Jonathan Dollimore and Alan Sinfield (eds) *Political Shakespeare. New Essays in Cultural Materialism*, Manchester: Manchester University Press.

—— (1989) *Radical Tragedy: Religion, Ideology and Power in the Drama of Shakespeare and His Contemporaries*, 2nd edn, Hemel Hempstead: Harvester Wheatsheaf.

Donald, James (1989) 'Beyond our Ken: English, Englishness, and the National Curriculum', in Peter Brooker and Peter Humm (eds) *Dialogue and Difference: English into the Nineties*, London and New York: Routledge.

Doyle, Brian (1989) *English and Englishness*, London: Routledge.

Evans, Malcolm (1989) *Signifying Nothing. Truth's True Contents in Shakespeare's Texts*, 2nd edn, Hemel Hempstead: Harvester Wheatsheaf.

Ezell, Margaret J. M. (1987) *The Patriarch's Wife: Literary Evidence and the History of the Family*, Chapel Hill and London: University of North Carolina Press.

Garber, Marjorie (1990) 'Shakespeare as fetish', *Shakespeare Quarterly* 41/2: 242–50.

Gerschel, Liz and Nasta, Susheila (1989) '"There's no such thing as 'only literature'": English teaching in an anti-racist and multicultural context', in Peter Brooker and Peter Humm (eds) *Dialogue and Difference. English into the Nineties*, London and New York: Routledge.

Goldberg, Jonathan (1987) 'Speculations: *Macbeth* and source', in Jean E. Howard and Marion F. O'Connor (eds) *Shakespeare Reproduced. The Text in History and Ideology*, New York and London: Methuen.

Greer, Germaine, Medoff, Jeslyn, Sansone, Melinda and Hastings, Susan (eds) (1988) *Kissing the Rod: An Anthology of Seventeenth-Century Women's Verse*, London: Virago.

Hawkins, Harriett (1990) 'From *King Lear* to *King Kong* and back: Shakespeare and popular modern genres', in *Classics and Trash. Traditions and Taboos in High Literature and Popular Modern Genres*, Hemel Hempstead: Harvester Wheatsheaf.

Hobby, Elaine (1988) *Virtue of Necessity: English Women's Writing 1649–1688*, London: Virago.

Holderness, Graham (1985) *Shakespeare's History*, Dublin: Gill & Macmillan. New York: St Martin's Press.

—— (ed.) (1988) *The Shakespeare Myth*, Manchester: Manchester University Press.

—— (1989) 'Are Shakespeare's tragic heroes "fatally flawed"? Discuss', *Critical Survey* 1/1: 53–62.

Howard, Jean E. (1988) 'Crossdressing, the theatre, and gender struggle in early modern England', *Shakespeare Quarterly* 39/4: 418–40.

Jardine, Lisa (1989) *Still Harping on Daughters: Women and Drama in the Age of Shakespeare*, 2nd edn, Hemel Hempstead: Harvester Wheatsheaf.

Light, Alison (1989) 'Two cheers for liberal education', in Peter Brooker and Peter Humm (eds) *Dialogue and Difference: English into the Nineties*, London and New York: Routledge.

McLuskie, Kathleen (1985) 'The patriarchal bard: feminist criticism and Shakespeare: *King Lear* and *Measure for Measure*', in Jonathan Dollimore

28

and Alan Sinfield (eds) *Political Shakespeare. New Essays in Cultural Materialism*, Manchester: Manchester University Press.

Mullaney, Steven (1987) *The Place of the Stage: License, Play, and Power in Renaissance England*, Chicago: University of Chicago Press.

Penley, Constance (1989) *The Future of an Illusion. Film, Feminism, and Psychoanalysis*, Minneapolis: University of Minnesota Press.

Rushdie, Salman (1990) 'In good faith', *The Independent* 4 February: 18–20.

Said, Edward (1989) 'Uprising', *The Guardian* 16–17 December: 36–8.

Samuel, Raphael (ed.) (1989) *Patriotism. The Making and Unmaking of British National Identity*, London: Routledge.

Sartre, Jean-Paul (1963) *The Problem of Method*, trans. Hazel E. Barnes, London: Methuen; first published 1960.

Shepherd, Simon (1990) 'Promotional Agencies: Section 28, Law and Education', *Text and Context* 4.

Sinfield, Alan (1985) 'Royal Shakespeare: theatre and the making of ideology', in Jonathan Dollimore and Alan Sinfield (eds) *Political Shakespeare. New Essays in Cultural Materialism*, Manchester: Manchester University Press.

Stallybrass, Peter and White, Allon (1986) *The Politics and Poetics of Transgression*, London: Methuen.

Stop the Clause Education Group in association with All London Teachers Against Racism and Fascism (1989) *Section 28. A Guide for Schools, Teachers, Governors*, £2.50 p&p from Room 216, 38 Mount Pleasant, London WC1X 0AP.

Taylor, Gary and Warren, Michael (eds) (1983) *The Division of the Kingdoms. Shakespeare's Two Versions of 'King Lear'*, Oxford: Clarendon Press.

Warren, Michael (1983) 'The diminution of Kent', in Gary Taylor and Michael Warren (eds) *The Division of the Kingdoms*, Oxford: Clarendon Press.

Wells, Stanley and Taylor, Gary (general eds) (1988) *William Shakespeare. The Complete Works,* compact edn, Oxford: Clarendon Press.

Werstien, Paul (1988) 'McKerrow's "Suggestion" and twentieth-century Shakespeare textual criticism' in Mary Beth Rose (ed.) *Renaissance Drama* new series 19, Evanston: Northwestern University Press and The Newberry Library Center for Renaissance Studies.

Williams, Raymond (n.d.) [1983] 'Crisis in English Studies' [1981], 'Beyond Cambridge English' [1983], in *Writing in Society*, London: Verso.

Wrightson, Keith (1982) *English Society 1580–1680*, London: Hutchinson.

1

Shakespeare in the National Curriculum

Lesley Aers

For those of us who have been in the classroom throughout the 1980s, the teaching of literature to 14–15 year-olds has undergone a sea change. At the beginning, it all seemed quite clear, and well compartmentalized. O level meant the teaching of three texts, more or less drawn from the 'Great Tradition of English Literature', including one Shakespeare, and they were taught as separate entities. In 1984, for example, I taught *1984* (a flash of humour from the examining board there), *Far from the Madding Crowd*, and *A Midsummer Night's Dream*. Rudimentary literary critical terminology was introduced, and some students coped very well with the minimum effort. I had one student who gained a Grade B after watching the film of *Far from the Madding Crowd* and reading most of *1984* and *A Midsummer Night's Dream*, though he had to be discouraged from making remarks like 'Helena is just a slag' in his essays. (This comment did lead to a successful discussion of words like 'slag', and sexual stereotyping in general.) Some examining boards enabled a more liberal-seeming approach by allowing texts in the examination room (notes had to be removed, making them 'Plain Texts'), and setting questions that required a close consideration of certain passages.

Candidates for CSE usually covered more texts, and these could have some relation to one another – for instance there might be two texts by the same author, or certain novels, plays, or poems would be chosen because they fitted in with a particular theme. This approach was never quite as flexible as it appeared, because the choice of texts was always limited by what happened to be in the stock cupboard at the time.

It was generally felt that, in terms of breadth of reading, the CSE candidates were better off than the O-level class. Gradually

30

the O-level exam boards began to venture beyond the 'Great Tradition' – though the requirement was still three texts, which would probably be taught in isolation. In 1987 one of the set texts on the Cambridge Board's list was the video of a television play, *Flying into the Wind* by David Leland. (It was important that the film was the text, not the script.) This introduced the idea of considering a visual medium as text, and unpacking the imagery on the screen in much the same way as verbal imagery in a written text. The other two works studied by the O-level candidate could be two novels, so the range was often very narrow; poetry did not have to be studied at all, and Shakespeare was certainly not compulsory. The O-level candidate and the CSE candidate who gained a Grade 1 were both likely to go into the sixth form without having read any Shakespeare, though the O-level candidate might be more used to attending to detail in language.

In 1986 the GCSE syllabuses began to come out, along with an agreed set of national criteria. These allowed the teacher a very free choice of the texts to be studied, as long as general aims such as these could be supported:

> The syllabus aims to give candidates the opportunity to engage with and respond to literary experience . . . develop a critical appreciation of the writer's craft through close textual study and through wider reading . . . explore literature as a means of emotional and intellectual growth.

Such aims leave it open to the teacher to establish her own priorities, and to choose texts which she finds relevant and important and which would suit a particular group. It is also stated that students should have different kinds of reading experience – 'both individually chosen and "shared" '. So the students should read some texts together, either in a small group or a whole-class setting, and they should also go to the library and choose other books for themselves which they would read alone. The course has to cover all three genres of poetry, prose, and drama, and there must be evidence of wider reading, as in the 'Open Study' set by one board: for this the students have to consider 'any aspects of literature of particular interest to them. The choice of material is left open.'

This particular syllabus gives an advisory book list which suggests most of the old favourites from CSE courses and the O-level syllabus, including Shakespeare. This advisory list is exactly what it says – there is nothing compulsory about any of the books mentioned, and the rubric states 'Where it is desired to use a text not in the advisory list care should be taken to ensure that it is of comparable quality and demand.' Comparable to which ones, we might wonder, for there is no way in which these texts are comparable with each other; the drama list, for example, contains *Twelfth Night* and Bill Forsyth's *Gregory's Girl*. No doubt an excellent course could be built around the fantasizing and romantic image-making that goes on in both texts, but there is, nevertheless, no way in which these plays could be called 'comparable' in terms of language and subtlety.

This is an area that GCSE left unresolved. One GCSE examiner was quoted as saying that to obtain a Grade A it is the quality of the response not the quality of the text that counts, which suggests he would award a Grade A for a study of Enid Blyton, so long as it was a study of amazing cultural penetration. Other examining boards try to give more guidelines:

> To provide opportunity for the awarding of the full range of grades, the texts studied should be comparable with those in the lists for the selected books examinations. Most of the texts traditionally used for the range of CSE and GCE assessment purposes are likely to be considered comparable for the purpose of GCSE assessment but some texts used in the past for CSE candidates may not make possible the discrimination of GCSE Grades A and B. Teachers, knowing their candidates, will need to ensure the use of texts and tasks which will permit appropriate grades to be awarded so that differentiation can arise from the texts chosen, the tasks set and from a combination of the two.
>
> (Midland Examining Group)

I would take this to mean that *Gregory's Girl* might not be acceptable for a Grade A or B; *Twelfth Night* would be safer. Some texts are, after all, more equal than others.

GCSE is still the dominant examination at 16+ although it will soon become subsumed into the assessment at the end of Key Stage 4 of the National Curriculum. Levels 7 and above of the Attainment Target for Reading – and it is here that we are likely to find a description of the skills to cover a study of literature – specify that the student must 'read a range of fiction, poetry, literary non-fiction and drama, including pre-20th century literature'. The programmes of study, which are statutory, actually name some individual writers:

Pupils should be introduced to:
- the richness of contemporary writing;
- pre-20th century literature;
- some of the works which have been most influential in shaping and refining the English language and its literature, e.g. the Authorized Version of the Bible, Wordsworth's poems, or the novels of Austen, the Brontës or Dickens;
- some of the works of Shakespeare.

(DES 1990: para.15)

These are the General Provisions for Key Stages 3 and 4, and they are saying that every pupil 'should be introduced to' some of the works of Shakespeare, and certainly versions of *Romeo and Juliet* (and the Zeffirelli film) can be presented very successfully to the lower echelons of the fifth year. The Detailed Provisions make it sound as though this range of writing, including Shakespeare, is not compulsory until the student wishes to attain Level 7 or above: 'In order to achieve level 7, pupils should read some texts written for adults, including pre-20th century fiction, poetry and drama, including Shakespeare,' (DES 1990: para. 24).

Wordsworth, Austen, the Brontës and Dickens, who only feature in an 'e.g.', are not statutory: Shakespeare is the only compulsory writer. No particular approach is statutory, however: it must not be thought that the National Curriculum is advocating a return to GCE-type essays. Indeed, the original document, *English for Ages 5–16* (DES 1989), goes out of its way to let teachers focus on the plays in whatever way they like; so, although Shakespeare is no longer chosen just because the teacher *wants* to do a certain play with her class (or just because there are masses of unused copies in the stock cupboard), there is complete freedom to adopt any approach:

In particular, every pupil should be given at least some experience of the plays or poetry of Shakespeare. Whether this is through the study, viewing or performance of whole plays or of selected poems or scenes should be entirely at the discretion of the teacher.

(DES 1989: Ch.7, para.7.15)

Apart from a general adulation of Shakespeare, which appears to be statutory here, no particular interpretation is given higher status than any other:

> Many teachers believe that Shakespeare's work conveys universal values, and that his language expresses rich and subtle meanings beyond that of any other English writer. Other teachers point out that evaluations of Shakespeare have varied from one historical period to the next, and they argue that pupils should be encouraged to think critically about his status in the canon. But almost everyone agrees that his work should be represented in a National Curriculum. Shakespeare's plays are so rich that in every age they can produce fresh meanings and even those who deny his universality agree on his cultural importance.
>
> (DES 1989: Ch.7, para. 7.16)

In the 'Programmes of Study for Reading' there are some general guidelines about approaches to literature – 'Pupils should discuss the themes, settings and characters of the texts they read in order to make a personal response to them' (DES 1989: para. 20) – but there are some more specific instructions on knowledge about language change, and Shakespeare will probably be used as a favourite source here (as well as supplying 'universal values' and so on):

> From their reading of pre-20th century literature, pupils should be encouraged to identify some of the major changes in English grammar over the centuries, eg the loss – except in some dialects and in religious uses – of 'thee' and 'thou'; the simplification of the verb system, eg. from 'have', 'hast', 'hath' to 'have' and 'has'; the change in structure of negatives, eg. from 'I know not' to 'I don't know'.
>
> (DES 1989: Ch.7, para. 26)

It would seem that there is plenty of scope for teachers to devise their own courses, as long as they include Shakespeare in some form. The context in which he is to be set is a far cry from the traditional O-level syllabus. Reading for Attainment Target 2 does not just refer to literature; it is specified that 'Pupils should be introduced to a range of media texts, and be encouraged to consider their purpose, effect and intended audience.' To be literate in the National Curriculum requires (quite rightly) that pupils should be able to view television and film in a sophisticated way. For all their reading, of whatever type of text, pupils 'should be taught how to compare surface meaning in a text with an implied sub-text'. With Shakespeare, the teacher will construct the sub-text according to her own perceptions and set of associations. But there still remains the problem of how actually to present the play to her pupils.

As Shakespeare has to form part of the programmes of study, the element of choice for the teacher – whether to teach Shakespeare or not – is removed. The plays she then chooses, and the approaches she adopts, are still open. Shakespeare must be sold to the class. I have used the word 'sold' quite deliberately: the imagery of consumerism is unavoidable in talking about education. Schools now have to market themselves, and are in competition with other schools: notions of collaboration, of 'consortia', are becoming largely irrelevant. The students, the consumers of education, are now demanding. They know how efficiently goods are packaged and sold in the world outside; they are accustomed to responding to the persuasion of advertising media, and are becoming skilful at rejecting spurious claims that are poorly presented. They know that they are being encouraged by careers teachers, teachers of PSE and teachers involved in the pre-vocational programme to present themselves as goods on the job market. There is no way that they are going to be sympathetic with tentative claims that Shakespeare offers them a vital human experience. If Shakespeare is going to be sold to the class, he has to be sold with vigour. I am reminded of Edward Dorn's description of how to sell Pyramid Lake to the tourists:

> Six hundred and fifty thousand 150-foot trees of pure epoxy can be stuck on the mountains. Paint the pyramids decorator colors. Rout the injuns out every morning with 'The Star-spangled Banner' so the whole thing will look REAL for the kids – who have been to Disneyland and aren't going to settle for any sleepy valley.
>
> (Dorn 1966: 49)

Teachers are already working out, very successfully, strategies to show that Shakespeare is 'relevant', to make the situations Shakespeare depicts closer to the ones in the students' own experience or fantasies. The approaches make use of drama as an active learning technique, and the students are acting right from the start. So the opening scenes of *Romeo and Juliet* can be used to find contemporary parallels – rival gangs of football supporters, clashes between black and white groups, or Catholics and Protestants. *Midsummer Night's Dream* is about the father who disapproves of his daughter's boyfriend, and the pain that is caused by the boy who suddenly finds he no longer wants to be with his girlfriend and goes after someone else. These situations can be acted out directly. Scenes from *Macbeth* can be improvised: the wife who is manipulating her husband to do something he really doesn't want to – 'You're just a wimp . . .'. The problem lies in deciding how far these are free-standing activities, and how much they actually enhance the study of Shakespeare. An extreme is reached when an activity is described as 'a non-textual approach to *King Lear* . . .'. But these approaches are validated by the National Curriculum English Working Group because of the interest, and inspiration to find out more about Shakespeare, that might be generated: 'Pupils exposed to this type of participatory, exploratory approach to literature can acquire a firm foundation to proceed to more formal literary responses should they subsequently choose to do so' (DES 1989: Ch.7, para. 7.16).

Nevertheless, I think teachers must be as clear-sighted as possible about the objectives of a particular activity. I have seen a group of fourth-formers using lines from *Macbeth* in scenes about boarding the wrong train, or trying to get the drinks machine to work; what is meant to be going on must be conveyed by the tone in which the line is said (the line might be, perhaps, 'It is a tale told by an idiot'). *This* activity was justified by the teachers who used it because, they said, the students were actually using Shakespeare's words, maybe even internalizing the language. If this is one way of 'selling' Shakespeare to a GCSE class, then is it really Shakespeare we are selling, or some entirely different product altogether? It is a delicate balance that teachers have to achieve. In teaching Shakespeare, they have to make it appeal to the students, otherwise the students will, quite simply, reject it; but they still need to be able to say, without fudging, that they are 'teaching Shakespeare'. The crucial point must be the language. If we can get the students to engage with the language, with its structure and imagery, and to relate it to the situations and emotions of the character without losing the sense of immediacy and relevance to themselves, then we are succeeding.

A favourite activity with A-level students, who have already studied the text, is the 'five-minute version' in which the play must be distilled to an essence which is not allowed to last more than five minutes. One group of students gave a hilarious version of *Measure for Measure* which showed a devastating ability to send the whole thing up. Claudio, on being informed (necessarily briefly) that the law requires him to die for his involvement with Juliet, responded with a squeal 'You cannot be *serious.*' This is not quite the same as:

> Thus can the demi-god Authority
> Make us pay down for our offence by weight.
> The words of heaven; on whom it will, it will;
> On whom it will not, so: yet still 'tis just.
>
> (I.2.112–14)

So what was this activity really achieving? Enabling the sixth-formers to show their own wit and creativity? For that purpose, it was highly successful, but was it really engaging with the text? It gave the group an experience they would remember, and I am not saying that such activities should not happen; I am saying, however, that we must be very clear why a particular activity has been set up, and what the students will get out of it.

Even though Shakespeare is compulsory, teachers should feel liberated in the way they teach him. They can experiment; they may not feel that every activity is successful, but they can try out different ideas in the drama hall or classroom. They can use film versions, and compare the effect and meaning of visual with verbal imagery. Different film versions show the effect of interpretation and demonstrate how the text is recreated each time it is produced by a different director. Stage productions can be seen, and made. New questions can be considered about the plays that would never have appeared on the old-style examination papers: questions of gender, class, politics. Students can discuss politicians' image-building, with Claudius as an example – and is Prince Hal's strategy for self-presentation so different to the media creation of modern politicians? The secret in politics is to achieve the maximum impact at precisely the right moment. (Macbeth, of course, blows it.)

In treating the plays in a new style and considering questions that are not just the traditional ones, issues that are important to the students can be brought to bear, and still keep the text in view. The teacher's role is similar to that of a director:

These different 'interpretations' are not, however, competing equals in the struggle for meaning. They each involve
re-ordering the terms in which the text is produced, which
of its conflicting positions are foregrounded, and how the
audience response is controlled. In Jonathan Miller's production of the play, for example, Isabella literally refused
the Duke's offer of marriage and walked off stage in the
opposite direction. Miller has been a powerful advocate for
the right of a director to reconstruct Shakespeare's plays in
the light of modern preoccupations, creating for them an
afterlife which is not determined by their original productions.

(McLuskie 1985: 95)

GCSE can accommodate a variety of written work on Shakespeare: reviews of plays or films, a diary account of putting a
production on, the old favourite newspaper accounts (*Verona
Times* or *Dunsinane Express*) as well as the discussion essay. There
is also the opportunity offered by the extended essay or open
study in which Shakespeare could be discussed alongside other
plays, or novels, perhaps linked by a theme, as in one open
study that I saw entitled 'Disastrous Relationships'. Quite a few
Shakespearean liaisons fit in here.

There are clear implications for the study of Shakespeare
beyond Key Stage 4 – that is, what is still A level. Students will
enter the sixth form accustomed to looking at Shakespeare in a
variety of ways, reordering and reinterpreting the text. They will
not want to switch to a traditional A-level mode, but will want
the same freshness, using film and drama and experimenting with
different kinds of written response. This can only sit easily in an
A-level syllabus that the members of a department choose for
themselves, using texts which complement each other, and
making the links they wish to make. The old academic-style essay
at this level will become a thing of the past, and universities will
have to take account of this. They will, however, take in students
who have to deal with a variety of text and are accustomed to
analysing different media. Such students will be knowledgeable
about contemporary culture and will make connections with the
literature and societies of the past with ease and confidence.

REFERENCES

Dorn, Edward (1966) *The Shoshoneans. The People of the Basin-Plateau*, text by Edward Dorn, photographs by Leroy Lucas, New York: William Morrow.

Lever, J. W. (1965) *Measure for Measure*, The Arden Edition of the Works of William Shakespeare, London: Methuen.

McLuskie, Kathleen (1985) 'The patriarchal bard: feminist criticism and Shakespeare: *King Lear* and *Measure for Measure*', in Jonathan Dollimore and Alan Sinfield (eds) *Political Shakespeare: New Essays in Cultural Materialism*, Manchester: Manchester University Press.

Department of Education and Science (DES) and the Welsh Office (1989) *English for Ages 5–16*, London: HMSO (June).

—— (1990) *English in the National Curriculum* (No. 2), London: HMSO (March).

2

A school perspective on Shakespeare teaching

Bob Allen

The following quotations are taken from a survey of ideas about Shakespeare, written down by third-year pupils (13+) in a mixed comprehensive school serving a prosperous middle-class catchment area in the east of England. Some pupils are already well read and articulate; others still struggle to read and write.

> Shakespeare was a man who conducted or composed classical music and he made up the play Romeo & Juliet . . . I've never read any of his plays. They sound boring. . . . He was born in Stratford-upon-Avon. . . . He wrote plays which are very heavy going. You need a degree in English and tonnes of A levels to be able to understand them . . . Hamlet, Midsummer Night's Dream, Macbeth, Romeo and Juliet. . . . He wrote many plays in the late eighteenth century. . . . Nearly all his plays have been turned into books which have been translated into most languages . . . he use to be a playwrighter some of play were 'to be or not to be' . . . Shakespeare wrote really good plays . . . 'Romeo Romeo where for art thou Romeo?' . . . 'Romeo Romeo were four ought though Romeo' . . . 'rome oh rome wher for they romeo'. . . . His plays were shown at the Rose theathe in London. . . . He was born before Guy Fawkes. The most famous theartre that is associated with him is the globe theartre and the rufe shape is a circle and the roof goes into a slight point. He wrote the twelth night . . . I think Shakespear is a great Poet as well as a play wrighter. This is some of his work just parts of plays, Alass pour Yorik I new him so well. Bouble Bouble boil trouble. I have not seen any of his plays . . . I don't know who he

40

is. I think it will be boring. I think he is a painter. . . .
Carling black label advert . . . Shakepeare wrote the BiBle.

The survey is not printed in full, but the sample indicates the
range of knowledge, identifies the known titles, and records the
most familiar quotations. Perhaps the most disturbing comment
– often repeated – was that although they knew nothing else,
about Shakespeare, they knew he was boring!

The written comments were followed up by informal discussion. The authorship of the Bible was quickly reconsidered,
but the pupils were less certain about classical music and painting.
Clearly Shakespeare was linked to the notion of the great arts,
even if these were only dimly perceived. In addition to *Desert
Island Discs* (the Bible and Shakespeare) we can perhaps identify
the influence of advertisements, and the recent media coverage of
the site of the Rose playhouse. The stress on language through
quotation or 'sayings', as one pupil put it, testifies to Shakespeare's currency outside the text, even though many believed that
Juliet was enquiring where Romeo was hiding. The compulsive
rhythms of the witches' chants, too, had a mysterious life of their
own.

It emerged that few pupils had attended a live performance of
Shakespeare; several had seen parts of the plays on TV, but no
one could remember working on the plays or poems in school.

If this class is fairly typical then we have cogent reasons to
think hard about the teaching of Shakespeare, especially in the
light of the National Curriculum English document:

> Many teachers believe that Shakespeare's work conveys uni-
> versal values, and that his language expresses rich and subtle
> meanings beyond that of any other English writer. Other
> teachers point out that evaluations of Shakespeare have
> varied from one historical period to the next, and they argue
> that pupils should be encouraged to think critically about
> his status in the canon. But almost everyone agrees that
> his work should be represented in a National Curriculum.
> Shakespeare's plays are so rich that in every age they can
> produce fresh meanings and even those who deny his uni-
> versality agree on his cultural importance.
>
> (DES 1989: Section 7.6)

I suspect that the 'canon' may be a somewhat arcane notion to the average adolescent, never mind the five-year-old, but the intention of the passage is clearly to reassert the importance of Shakespeare in the English curriculum. We can probably agree that most teachers accept the 'cultural importance' of Shakespeare, in the sense of being of value to contemporary cultures as well as those of the past, but there the agreement stops. Very few teachers in schools have time to consider recent criticism or literary theory: simply keeping up with the accelerating pressures of a crazy system precludes that; and many have little opportunity to reflect deeply on the strengths and weaknesses of their own teaching styles. In these circumstances it is vital that the debate should be lively and accessible, and the issues clear. In recent years significant influences have modified the traditional consensus view of Shakespeare studies; they include new critical perspectives; the changing values of society relating to gender, morality, and class; and political agitation from both right and left, anxious to appropriate Shakespeare for themselves.

WHAT'S WRONG WITH TEACHING SHAKESPEARE?

It is probably worth pausing to consider the challenges in more detail. For convenience, I have summarized some of the more familiar ones here:

1 It is argued that Shakespeare's plays appear to promote values at odds with those of modern society, particularly in the presentation of women, and that the plays are constructed within conventions which essentially promote a hierarchical view of class relationships. Seen from this perspective, Shakespeare's values seem to be largely those of the 'right', politically speaking.

2 The examinations system, and inevitably the teaching that supports it, tends not to encourage fundamental critical evaluation of the economic, social, and political cultures embodied in the plays. It is suggested that examination questions tend to favour students with cautious and deferential approaches.

3 Some teachers and examiners tend to present the plays as if they were self-contained, coherent entities, embodying universal values, rather than works read, performed, and watched in an evolving historical and social context. The idea of 'charac-

ter', too, is often accepted without an awareness that the term is itself unstable and problematical.

4 Many teachers have welcomed the developments in the last twenty years which have emphasized 'response' in pupils. The Cambridge Board 'Plain Texts' O-level paper in particular sought to promote teaching and learning where the pupil's knowledge and organizational skills served to bring out a considered personal viewpoint. Clearly this approach was a reaction against the knowledge-based rote learning of traditional O-level. GCSE courses have followed the same trend. Marxist critics tend to be wary of an approach that celebrates 'individual' response, on the grounds that it may underplay the historical and social context and that it reinforces notions of apparently unchangeable and timeless values, which Marxists and cultural materialists might view as manifestations of an undesirable dominant ideology. A further challenge to 'response' comes from those who observe that it can be reduced to a formula – a system of clever tricks – and taught. In short, it need not be essentially different from the worst aspects of examination teaching which it was designed to replace.

5 The Shakespeare 'industry' can be regarded as providing an initiation into a minority higher culture, valuable only because it is part of a system providing access to social and economic rewards. It sets the touchstone for 'great literature'; pupils' own culture is relegated to 'popular' status. Hypocrisy and double standards are claimed to be the realities of Shakespeare in education.

6 Most urgently, however, the challenge to teaching comes from those pupils and students who still emerge from school, college, and even university, bored and mystified, unlikely ever voluntarily to attend a performance of a Shakespeare play, let alone read one, and who have never been moved or enthralled by Shakespeare's poetry because they have not begun to understand it.

I would not claim to have all the answers to the difficulties of teaching Shakespeare in the 1990s, but I do believe that each English department and each teacher of Shakespeare needs to address these and other relevant issues which may emerge. The National Curriculum gives our deliberations additional urgency.

WHY SHOULD WE TEACH SHAKESPEARE?

After consultation with many colleagues, students, and pupils, I would argue the case on the following grounds.

His works are a central part of the heritage of English literature: we have a moral obligation to teach Shakespeare. The critical approach which constructed a narrow, elitist hierarchy of texts with Shakespeare at the apex as a touchstone of excellence against which to match inferior productions seems to us now a remote view, unresponsive to the great variety and richness of human experience in the arts. Nevertheless it is necessary to have some personal sense of works which have the capacity to communicate deeply with many people: not as the key to the ivory tower, but rather as a shared celebration, worthwhile in itself, and giving us access to a tradition of communal dramatic experience, of infinite variety.

Shakespeare's language not only belongs to a specific historical and cultural context, but has inspired and informed all kinds of subsequent linguistic development. It opens ways of seeing and thinking. Enrichment of our own language, concepts, and perceptions can arise from contact – however fleeting – with Shakespeare's language.

If we believe that poetry is essential in education, then Shakespeare provides us with dramatic and lyric poetry which speaks powerfully and directly. Further reading and reflecting evokes new responses: we can return to the poetry again and again without exhausting its potential. Textual analysis sometimes seems to promote the idea that good poetry is deep, rich, obscure, and complex. Ideally it should tend towards the tragic mode. For those who wish to read in that way Shakespeare can provide ample material; but there is also depth in simplicity, and wisdom in direct and unrestrained laughter: readers of Shakespeare's poetry will find both in abundance.

Dr Johnson saw Shakespeare as 'a poet of Nature' whose universal sympathies filled the plays with 'practical axioms and domestic wisdom' (Preface to *The Plays of William Shakespeare,* 1765). We may be less certain today about the notion of a character encompassing a universally valid 'species' to guide moral action, but we do find in Shakespeare's treatment of his characters in action a depth and variety of insight which can sharpen both our self-knowledge and our knowledge of the human condition. This

44

knowledge does not necessarily promote happiness or shape our moral actions, but it provides a context within which we can test out our potential for good or ill in private reflection or in discussion with others.

In relation to drama and the theatre, Shakespeare provides scripts which can be used for the full range of practical activity, from workshop improvisation and mime based on specific moments or themes to full-scale public performance. Through their formal and narrative structures as well as their language and poetry, the plays create experiences which can be rewarding for children from primary school onwards. These practical processes at each level can bring us back to deeper understanding of the text.

In spite of the economic and social conditions of the sixteenth and early seventeenth centuries, and the constraints of form and convention, there is no consistent single ideological position adopted in Shakespeare's plays: in their critique of values they are neither uniformly radical nor reactionary. They are 'open' texts, and one of the particular joys of teaching them is to explore the way in which apparently settled notions of kingship, order, harmony, nobility, and social class and gender are threatened by unresolved forces which cannot be neatly pigeonholed and so which have the potential to disturb us all. As Prospero says of Caliban, 'This thing of darkness I acknowledge mine.' He claims ownership of his (Black?) slave at the same time as articulating a self-knowledge of the potential for chaos which we have seen demonstrated at each level of the drama. The 'mechanicals' in *A Midsummer Night's Dream* may be coarse and ignorant according to one scale of values, but they can also be the group with which we most closely sympathize. Theseus may have been Titania's lover in another time, but of the mortals it is only Bottom who is allowed to experience her 'female ivy' enringing his 'barky fingers' in this play. Only a very simplistic reading of the *Dream* could finally consider it to be about the exploitation of working people by a patronizing and narrow-minded aristocracy. Like all great art, the play continually challenges us to reassess our perceptions.

Many of the challenges we face in teaching Shakespeare are, inevitably, opportunities. Any hostile views expressed sharpen the debate; they put the teacher in the 'hot seat', unable to retreat into dictated notes and reach-me-down opinions, and it is my belief that a vigorous informed awareness of the issues is the best preparation for essay writing and examination success. I am quite sure that deskbound approaches will fail to interest many pupils, but I am convinced that other pathways can and must be found if (as the National Curriculum requires) we are to give an experience of Shakespeare to all our pupils.

HOW HAS RECENT SHAKESPEARE TEACHING IN SCHOOLS EVOLVED?

During the last twenty-five years teaching and learning in schools in general has been radically transformed. The process has inevitably been patchy and inconsistent, but pupils today work in a variety of ways which were largely unknown to their parents. There is an emphasis on the process of learning within different contexts; oral as well as written outcomes are valued, and active modes of learning (such as role-play, group discussion, and independent learning) stand side by side with more traditional didactic approaches. The HMI *Curriculum Matters* series highlighted the balanced entitlement curriculum, a 5–19 continuum for all pupils in which the work could be differentiated according to need. That balance is increasingly under threat as the emerging National Curriculum enshrines a hierarchy of subjects, marginalizes the arts, and is likely to accelerate the demise of English literature at GCSE level.

Time for English used to be quite generously allocated in comprehensive schools. In recent years, however, English departments have seen their time cut as new subjects have emerged (information technology, business studies, and so on) and this process is accelerating as the notion of a 'core' entitlement to languages, combined science, technology, the humanities, and the arts squeezes English time. Media studies and the influence of popular culture have extended the range of linguistic and visual experiences which might be explored within English time. Literature is no longer perceived as the central study in English; it is rather one of a range of possibilities which might also include increased emphasis on language work in response to the Kingman Report (DES 1988), or on keyboard skills for information technology and word processing. Shakespeare not only competes for time with other literature, but increasingly with the role of English as a support subject across the curriculum.

In school Shakespeare studies there have been many fruitful developments, two of which have been significantly formative and require special mention: the growth of practical drama work through workshop and Theatre-in-Education, and 'plain text' examinations. Henry Caldwell Cook's pioneering work and the establishment of the 'mummery' at the Perse School, Cambridge, were seminal influences on teaching through drama (Caldwell Cook 1917; Beacock 1943). Many of the elements of 'active learning' have their roots in the ideals and methods of progressive Victorian and Edwardian educationalists, but it was not until the growth of educational drama in the late 1960s that these were widely introduced into the teaching of Shakespeare in state schools.

Before turning to consider 'plain text' examinations, it may be helpful to summarize some aspects of the 'mummery' approach, which can be adapted for a wide range of literature as well as drama. Ideally the room is equipped as a studio, with simple stage lighting, blackout, and sound facilities, a 'tiring house' cupboard for costumes and props, rudimentary blocks for settings, and versatile seating for the audience. One possible way of working is to group the pupils into resident companies of four or five, each named after an Elizabethan theatre company, and to divide up the text being explored so that each 'company' is responsible for a particular part or 'movement'. After discussion and improvisation in groups, the class works towards a final performance and evaluation. The essential processes of the model are now familiar and in widespread use, but they seemed like a breath of fresh air when I first saw them practised by Keith Crook at the Perse School in 1968: the 'mummery' provided a clear way forward.

The second key development was of 'plain text' examinations, particularly at O level. By providing the text in the examination room the focus shifted distinctively towards the response of the pupil to the words themselves. Inevitably this innovation embodied the assumption that the importance of reading literature lies in the process of considering and responding to text – a response often articulated primarily through feelings and empathy – and that the process is capable of being quantified and recorded. This raises questions which cannot be considered here, but the general approach of 'plain texts' was welcomed by many teachers as profoundly liberating at the time.

A vital element in the early stages of such schemes was the regional conference for teachers and examiners which enabled a real partnership to develop. Teachers felt involved and valued in curriculum development; many were recruited as examiners, and there was a shared delight in the achievements of pupils of all abilities as we discussed sample scripts. The best writing was breathtakingly good: pupils often showed original insights, and even candidates who would never have been entered for traditional O-level papers were rewarded when their responses were clear and justified from the text. One Chief Examiner once drew a model describing the kind of writing we were seeking: she drew an unstable triangle poised on its apex, representing 'response'. Two supporting triangles, set firmly on their bases, labelled 'organization' and 'knowledge', supported the 'response' triangle. It was a telling image. From their earliest pre-school reading and listening to stories children's personal emotional involvement with character and narrative is central; for many readers this remains the core of their experience. Others become more sophisticated as they absorb academic culture: at A level and beyond empathy is only one among many possible reactions to reading, as the conventions of psychologically plausible 'character' are challenged. It remains true, however, that some measure of personal engagement and commitment lies at the heart of all English studies, including Shakespeare, in a process which draws from and in turn enriches the culture.

SOME RECENT USEFUL PUBLICATIONS

Both of these key developments – practical drama work, and the focus on informed personal response – can open the experience of Shakespeare by placing the pupil at the centre of the process. The most significant recent initiative drawing these and other strands together has been the 'Shakespeare and Schools Project', directed by Rex Gibson of the Cambridge Institute of Education. The Cox Report drew attention to the project, noting that 'secondary pupils of a wide range of abilities can find Shakespeare accessible, meaningful, and enjoyable' and recommended 'exciting, enjoyable approaches that are social, imaginative and physical' (DES 1989: para. 7.16). A lively and stimulating collection of papers arising from the project written by secondary teachers has been published by the Cambridge Institute under the title

Secondary School Shakespeare (Gibson 1990). Rex Gibson's introduction sets the tone: 'Each teacher's contribution speaks for itself,
and the relationships between the articles are open invitations to
innovative thought, discussion, and action.' The recommenda-
tions provide sensible guidance, especially for those embarking
on their careers, and the case studies (conveniently arranged
according to age group, and thoughtfully subheaded) offer a cor-
nucopia of detailed experiences, incorporating the perceptions of
the consumers as well as the teachers. Just a quick browse opens
up all kinds of bright possibilities. It is the sense of a shared
enterprise, backed by expertise, INSET, and time to compare
notes with colleagues which gives this collection such sparkle.

There may be pitfalls for the unwary in such a collection: the
invitations to cut and paste the text, and the infinite possibilities
of drama activities and parallel sub-texts can illuminate Shakespeare in fresh, incisive ways, but they can also conceal real muddle,
and lead to a free-for-all in which the potential richness of Shakespeare *as* Shakespeare somehow is missed – and this is not to argue
for a restricted, elitist interpretation; rather it is to call attention
to the nature of the experience we want our pupils to have. This
is where the support of a team of colleagues is invaluable in
shaping teachers' understanding and perceptions. Again, time for
preparation, reflection, and evaluation of the work is crucial.

There are vast publishing enterprises supporting Shakespeare
studies. Many of the revision files and booklets purport to be
written for GCSE students and pay lip service to the notion of
response: often they consist largely of dreary old summaries and
received opinions about character. One publication which
attempts to provide lively and relevant materials for use in class
is the *Shakespeare File* (Wilcock et al.: 1987). Much of the file is
designed to be duplicated and used as appropriate within the
teaching scheme; its great strengths are its openness and the range
of stimulus materials provided for pupils of all abilities. Many of
the sheets provide the framework for simple but enjoyable activities which may later contribute to more formal writing. A chart
identifying 'order' and 'disorder' in *Romeo and Juliet* can be filled
in and then transformed into a graph showing moments of tension
and conflict in the play: the process enables pupils to handle
complex ideas in an ordered visual way. The artwork has a
curious bland quality which pupils seem to find stimulating: tiny
fragments of notes, views, maps, and incomplete lines can

become the focus for investigation of the text; and key moments are illustrated without captions for the pupils to identify. One pupil wrote about a picture of a warrior facing the viewer with sword upraised:

> I think this picture is near the end of the play when Macbeth is fighting to keep his kingship. This is threatened by the Scottish contingent and the English forces – ten thousand soldiers who join up together to fight Macbeth. Macbeth meets Macduff in the battle who he has feared since he went back to the witches to find out more of what will happen to him. This is an important part in the play as it shows that after the witches telling Macbeth what will happen it all became true. Also showing that after all the killings Macbeth had committed it all backfired on him. In the end Macbeth had no one on his side and his wife had committed suicide, he went out to fight the army by hiself.

The writing is plain and straightforward, and the pupil has grasped the broad significance of that confrontation; the final comments show her attempting to articulate what the audience may feel for Macbeth as he faces the inevitable. The materials in the *Shakespeare File* are just what a teacher might have prepared, given sufficient time. One copy of the file for the department can add significantly to its bank of stimulus material. It demystifies the language and critical apparatus, and much of it can fruitfully be used by independent learners and small groups.

SHAKESPEARE AND THE ARTS

Recent developments in the arts in schools have encouraged teachers of art, music, dance, and drama to work more closely together in collaborative schemes, based on particular arts skills or concepts, agreed themes, or narrative/dramatic texts. This work is often linked with curriculum development, especially in preparation for a wider arts entitlement through the National Curriculum. Although some teachers and educationalists express reservations about the depth and quality achieved, the best of these schemes are genuinely productive of new and exciting relationships for pupils and teachers. The high level of staff motivation and the generous resources of time, materials, and equipment allocated to such schemes create ideal conditions for innovative

work. Teams of pupils are now becoming skilled in video production and editing, and many schools are beginning to grasp the
creative possibilities of allowing pupils to work loosely supervised
outside the classroom within the guidance of the arts faculty. It
would be good to see more English faculties and departments
linking with the arts to explore Shakespeare. At the same time
they might well be meeting Attainment Targets in a range of
National Curriculum subjects such as technology and history,
in addition to the drama, speaking and listening, and literature
components of English. The publications of the NCC 'Arts in
Schools Project' (now the National Foundation for the Arts at
Warwick University) provide interesting case studies.

INTRODUCING *MACBETH* – A CASE STUDY

Finally I want to examine a little more closely some introductory
sessions on *Macbeth* with a GCSE class of twenty-six mixed pupils
in a comprehensive school. A banding system creams off most
of the pupils who would be likely to attain grades A, B, or C
at GCSE level, so the group in question included the full range
below that level.

I wanted to introduce them to Shakespeare with the very practical aim of gathering some written work for their GCSE folders,
but the first objective was to make the play accessible and enjoyable. The Polanski film on video seemed to offer a way in: we
could examine the story, revise, replay, and freeze the action; the
visual impact of Polanski's version has long been recognized as a
strength in working with this age group and relates directly to
their experience of video and TV at home; and differentiation for
the mixed-ability group was helped by the many different ways
in which the experience could be approached. After we had fin-
ished our initial viewing, I asked the pupils to record their first
impressions in a brief written note, before any substantial discussion had taken place. The results were as follows:

> At the beginning of the film I couldn't really understand
> what they were saying . . . the further on I watched the
> more I understood.

> Polanski made it easy to understand. I have always associ-
> ated Shakespeare's play's boring and hard to understand.

but he showed it in such a way that you were able to see what was going on . . . I especially liked the witches. I thought they gave the play its scarey touch.

I saw a production of the play *Macbeth* and I found it hard to understand and I did begin to lose interest. After seeing the film and looking at the outline of the story I found it very interesting. During the film I could relate some of the scenes to those in the play . . . I was glued to the set.

I think the idea of the witches and their prophey's is good they give the film play a very weird supernatural feeling.

The opening scenes were too dull and dark there should have been some more bright scenes with blue skies to show happier times like after the battle.

The family killing was very well done and it said to me how cruel Macbeth can really be. I don't blame all his so called friends leaving him.

I wish I knew how they did Macbeth's death that was particually rememorable. I find the death of the family sad but I would of liked to see more of the family it would of given a larger scale of the massacre.

The killing of the family was very disturbing . . . the young boy was being pushed around and he was pushed into one of the murderers and he put a knife in the child's back . . . and the child ran to his mother saying he has killed me.

I feel sorry for Macbeth all the way through and I also feel sorry for his wife at the end although to start with she began the murders.

Later on Macbeth goes down to lower levels just cold blooded murder then hiring thugs to do the murders for him.

The music had a mystical tone and made me feel uneasy and nervous.

The thing which was of most interest to me was the scene when Lady Macbeth was convinced that water washing away Duncan's blood would clear them of their deed. You knew because she was so calm that eventually it would catch up with her.

The one thing I didn't like was the language as it was difficult to follow.

It poses questions and options for people . . . I found myself trying to think what I would do in the same situation.

Their comments largely speak for themselves: the range of response is reflected both in depth of insight and linguistic sophistication (or the lack of it), but each quotation shows some insight worth following up, and there is a refreshing open quality which provides the context for the work that followed. The interest in the Macduff massacre was echoed in several other written comments and frequent requests for action replays. Their notes provided me with material for further discussion: we gathered ideas and a framework of the action on the board (using cartoons, flow charts, and other visual devices) which the pupils copied down for reference. An important principle in my approach at this stage was to acknowledge as many reactions as possible, and to try to act as an amanuensis for the whole group, suppressing the urge to shape or direct their responses. Often it was necessary to act as arbiter, but I directed the decision-making back to the class.

Our final film-based session included a more focused discussion of Malcolm's description: 'this dead butcher and his fiend-like Queen' (V.11.35). Working first in small groups and then reporting back, the pupils gathered material from the film to support or challenge Malcolm's assertion. Although the pupils had no access to the text, they were able to specify quite detailed evidence of both words and visuals; and their comments revealed considerable insight. Even the pupils who struggle to read and write were able to articulate some views, as this comment from a later piece of writing shows:

Macbeth how he become a butcher is hes wife make him butcher she said to him you are not a man. That's way he became killing people like butcher

The next stage was to introduce the text, and to open up some of the ways in which Polanski's film was itself a version of *Macbeth* including quite radical changes and additional scenes. I put together a shortened version, containing almost the whole text up to the murder of Duncan, and extracts from the rest of the play, and duplicated one for each pupil to keep in their files. I deliberately excluded all notes and critical apparatus, but made sure that the typeface was large and attractive. I was determined to see whether I could help these pupils to engage with the words that many found so difficult. We spent the following sessions in a drama area, containing rostra, seating, and the open-plan rehearsal stage set for the school production of *Animal Farm*. The atmosphere broke the mould of the classroom. It was informal, active, participatory, and related directly to earlier experiences of practical group drama. The pupils worked mainly in groups on specific tasks, but the whole class came together to share their ideas at appropriate moments. The range and content of these workshop activities was established by negotiation with the pupils. Some worked on dramatizations of scenes or moments, using 'hot seating' (characters in role responding to questions from other characters or from an audience), role-play, and forum theatre as necessary; others made tape recordings of discussion or dramatized readings. Parallel activities examining the psychology of prophecy were useful in highlighting just why Macbeth's reaction to the witches is so different from Banquo's.

I selected a number of scenes and speeches for detailed attention. At first I asked the pupils to work alone, and to find words or phrases that they liked, or that puzzled them. Then, working with their group, they compared their reactions. At a later stage I asked the groups to try to sort out what was being said in specific speeches. As they continued their discussions, I went round to listen and observe, participating when it seemed useful to explain some difficulty of vocabulary or syntax. It was astonishing to see how much they could understand from their own group resources. It is difficult within the scope and form of this chapter to convey the diversity and complexity of the total experience for the pupils. Some extracts from their tape-recorded spontaneous discussions of specific moments will perhaps provide a flavour. Each group consists of three or four pupils. I have not identified individuals, but each break indicates a change of speaker:

I.5 (Lady Macbeth reads Macbeth's letter)

She doesn't think he has the stomach to go through with it
. . . he's too kind . . . a bit of a coward . . . she considers
herself a nice person . . . she appeals to somebody . . . she
knows she's got feelings and she goes take my – . . . she
thinks of herself as a right bitch really . . . she's appealing
. . . – and she goes take my milk for gall . . . her feminine
feeling's taken away . . . a completely evil person . . . and
gall is that stomach acid you cough up . . . pure acid . . .
he's too kind to get what he wants . . . he's got the ambition
but he doesn't want to be ruthless . . . he really really wants
it, but he won't do it. . . . She thinks he can become king
and she's overcome by greed . . . but thinks he's too weak
to become king . . . but the guilt finally gets to her in Act
V sc. 1 where she can't get the blood of Duncan off her
hands . . . the letter made her greed start up . . .

V.1 (Lady Macbeth sleepwalking, watched by the Doctor of
Physic and the Waiting-Gentlewoman)

She rises from her bed every night and she walks in her
sleep . . . and she washes her hand but she can't get rid of
the blood . . . all the day she's tortured by it and all the
night too . . . she smells all the blood . . . she says who
would have thought the old man to have had so much blood
in him so she's obviously been washing her hands for ages
. . . the doctor says this disease is beyond my practice, so
it's all in the image in her mind, she can't get it out . . .
she's cracking up . . . hell is murky . . . she thinks she's in
hell . . . there's knocking at the gate . . . maybe she's knocking on the doors of hell. . . . Yes . . . but there was knocking on the gate after she killed the king, wasn't there? . . .
Yes . . . Banquo's buried . . . obviously she's tortured by
everybody's death that he's done . . . she can't get rid of
the feeling . . . she deserves to go to hell doesn't she, she
was the one who started it all off . . .

The doctor says unnatural deeds do breed unnatural
troubles . . . she's been dabbling in the devil, and of course
she goes mad . . . she's got rid of all her good . . . the
doctor can't cure her . . . you feel sorry for her when she's
sleepwalking, don't you . . . she didn't know what she was

doing when she wanted to be unsexed . . . she thought she could get away with murder . . . at the beginning she didn't think it was going to affect her . . . she's a very greedy woman . . . she wants sort of power . . . she couldn't just live with him being Thane of Cawdor . . . she blackmails Macbeth into killing Duncan by saying he's not a man . . . you've got to feel sorry for her . . . why should you when she kills people? . . . it's like feeling sorry for a murderer . . . she deserves to go mad . . . she deserves it in some ways . . . she shouldn't be dabbling in the devil . . .

These transcripts will be very familiar in content to GCSE English teachers; there is nothing particularly unusual about what the pupils are saying; but what is perhaps striking is that they have come to these kinds of opinion through active participation: they are not my opinions or the opinions of critics or commentators, they have arisen from a genuine struggle with visual images, words, actions, and ideas. This kind of introduction can provide a stimulus for more considered further writing and GCSE coursework, but, more significantly, it can give pupils the confidence to go on enjoying Shakespeare throughout their adult lives. One of my Open University students remarked recently 'School killed my interest completely, with awful readings by children ploughing through texts.' In adult life she came back to Shakespeare studies. She went on to say 'There are certain passages which I find myself coming back to again and again – encapsulating my own thoughts – he covers all the great basic emotions of life in common problems across all ages and classes. He has something relevant to say about nearly every aspect of life. You can find you own level within Shakespeare.' I want school Shakespeare to open up that kind of experience for all pupils.

REFERENCES

Beacock, D. A. (1943) *Play Way English for Today*, London: Thomas Nelson.

Caldwell Cook, Henry (1917) *The Play Way*, London: Heinemann.

Department of Education and Science [DES] (1988) *The Report of the Committee of Inquiry into the Teaching of English Language*, London: HMSO (The Kingman Report).

—— (1989) *English for Ages 5 to 16*, London: HMSO (The Cox Report).

Dollimore, Jonathan and Sinfield, Alan (eds) (1985) *Political Shakespeare*.

New Essays in Cultural Materialism, Manchester: Manchester University Press.

Gibson, Rex (ed.) (1990) *Secondary School Shakespeare: Classroom Practice,* Cambridge: Cambridge Institute of Education.

Robinson, Ken (ed.) (1989) *Arts in Schools Packs,* NCC. Further information from the National Foundation for Arts in Education, Department of Arts Education, University of Warwick, Westwood, Kirby Corner Road, Coventry CV4 7AL.

Taylor, Gary (1990) *Reinventing Shakespeare: A Cultural History from the Restoration to the Present,* London: Weidenfeld & Nicolson.

Wells, Stanley and Taylor, Gary (general eds) (1986) *William Shakespeare. The Complete Works,* Oxford: Clarendon Press.

Wilcock, Eric, Redsell, Patrick and Little, Robin (1987) *Shakespeare File,* London: Heinemann Educational.

3

Recovering Shakespeare: innocence and materialism

Fred Inglis

I

Shakespeare criticism and the background noise which accompanies it in the intellectual corners of common-rooms are nowadays remorselessly *knowing*. In those decidedly specialized as well as conscientiously dissenting coteries, it's hard to speak straight out any old truisms about Shakespeare's being amazing art or Shakespeare himself being the greatest poet of the language. Art; literature; greatness; the old categories are down, and the old poet must make his own way as best he can through the riotous Cheapside of late consumer capitalism and the jammed stalls of the culture market.

The terrific knowingness I name is, of course, a minor sympton of cultural competition. The loopy excesses of postmodernism and literary theory, the logorrhoea which characterizes the Lacanian madness and so leads astray some of the best minds looking for the truth in feminism are all and each new voices crying their wares in the cultural market place. For it is the necessary, urgent business of each new generation in its thought, its production, and its love to defeat in competition and therefore to supersede its predecessor generation. This perpetual motion is enfolded in the vaster tides of market competition and given much more ruthless drowning power. The generations abbreviate; you're past it at forty.

The political economy of culture works to the same rhythms and structures,[1] but of course must do so in negation. Pierre Bourdieu proposes an austere axiom with which to grasp this inversion. 'Intellectuals . . . will always struggle to maximize the autonomy of the cultural field and to raise the social value of specific competences . . . by raising the scarcity of those competences' (Bourdieu 1984).

More compactly, we may say that the intelligentsia keeps its distinctiveness by making its subject difficult to do. Amongst the employees of the meaning industry (or as Bourdieu sometimes mouth-fillingly has it, within the dominated fraction of the dominant class whose concern is with the exercise of symbolic power), there are different groups struggling for dominance within their corner of the division of labour, the allotments in the fields of their subject. Thus new structuralism came to subvert old humanism, and in a trice even newer poststructuralism (after which, like after postmodernism, there can be nowhere to go), subverted structuralism. Such and such are the competitions between the lines of which thinkers must try to tell their particular truths.

At the same time an equivalent class fraction joined the battle of the books on the side of the Ancients. The historical moment of the 1960s unseated a certain kind of genteel liberal humanism from the chairs of Shakespeare, and the fight was on to win authority over the commanding heights of the cultural economy. The new New Left spoke the unspeakable jargon of theoreticism, the argot of its site in the social structure. The new Old Fogeys called up spirits of the vasty deep in order to quote groanings which cannot be uttered but which audit Shakespeare's timelessness, his storehouse of recorded values, his capital of words. Then the most fashionable of producers pick and mix like good consumers their selections from both camps in the sightlines and programme notes of national and school theatres. The timeless struggle between traditionalists and avant-garde parallels that between universities and polytechnics, between men and women, between old and young.

The momentum of the mechanism demands an equivalent ruthlessness in the ambitious individual. In all intellectual fields, the battle is on between those who have made their name and those who can only do so by supplanting (and therefore relegating to the past) the established figures, whose establishment is founded upon a frozen present. The radical, by definition, always wants to melt the foundations. The political struggle, in the culture as in society, is between continuity, similarity, reproduction on the one hand, as against rupture, difference, revolution on the other.

The radical and the avant-gardiste must alike 'produce time' (in Bourdieu's powerful phrase) by innovation and 'originality'

59

FRED INGLIS

(a key cultural value). To innovate is to date what is established, and shift it into the past, together with all those who remain defined by it. Thus the radical's support and audience is all in the future; the conservative of the present must find coevals in the past. In market terms, the ascription of genius by both radicals and conservatives will only be made when the artist balances regulated innovation (for which the cultural value is 'creativity') against product reliability (for which the symbol is 'mastery').

Naturally, the line between creativity and mastery, or originality and authority, or simply between novelty and familiarity, is lambent, mobile, and in high tension. Different groups of custodians (teachers and critics) keep the gates marked avant-garde (radical) or traditionalist (conservative), disputing which terrain shall be considered legitimate, trying to hold down novelty or eject familiarity in the name of their camp. In this dispute, the innovatory, where judgement is risky and criteria unstable, dominates the ephemeral media such as newspapers and television, whose position in the cultural discourse is largely defined by their function as producers of that reliably changeable commodity, news (which has to be new). Stable and safe texts, which have been accorded access to the timeless realm of culture, are the literal stock in trade of the academics and educationalists whose function it is to organize the official classification of culture and to regulate formal aesthetic diction, teaching the new generation (or the new class) how to say the right thing and to talk properly.

This is the systemic nature of the cultural competition and the economy of symbolic goods. If this last section of my argument is not to lapse into the unattractive and moralizing exhortation which characterizes the concluding chapter of liberal pedagogy, it is important to reiterate that there is no way to avoid competing. The (Shakespearean) poetics I want to propose, with its strongly moral and political flavour, must make its way, like everyone else's, by appealing truthfully to the intrinsic values of culture, as against these others who have thwarted those values and distorted true aesthetics. No one can avoid the operations of the cultural economy; I can only achieve the limited freedom (to be offered to those who follow me) which comes from pointing out what is happening while it happens. If such a poetics of popular culture then were to become popular, it would provoke in response a competitive specializing of new areas of cultural capital, certainly.

But it would also have done its bit for human freedom and virtue by opening up some of the closed parks of culture, and giving back some of their own capital to the people who produced it. It just can't be helped when the political economy of culture produces new surpluses elsewhere. One can't do everything.

II

In our present contested circumstances, all one's intuitions and allegiances of a political sort pull every decent teacher leftwards. But anybody whose cultural vows have been taken before such grand old totems as a man speaking to men, unacknowledged legislators of the world, and tales which hold children from play and old men from chimney corners, can only recoil from the gibberings of theoreticism. To appeal for calm, and restate the case for an ecumenical Shakespeare, apprehended straight, without misprision and as both historical and immediate voice (however heteroglossed) is to come out as a naif with a vengeance. I remember gratefully a little meditation by Michael Frayn upon the transience of worldly wisdom.

Frayn reached *his* peak of worldly wisdom round about the age of seventeen (Shakespeare critics reach theirs a bit after thirty).

> You'd have had to get up very early in the morning to pull the wool over my eyes in those days. I knew that nothing was what it appeared to be in this world, that it was really all fixed behind the scenes by the Great Conspiracy – Krupp, the United Fruit Company, Vickers Armstrong, and the rest of them. I knew that the newspapers, the Government, and everything else was just a facade. A fellow I met in a Youth Hostel told me . . .
>
> And yet, as the years went by, all that bright plating of worldly wisdom began to wear off. In some cases, I came to see, one was pretty well forced to the conclusion that to a certain limited extent things were more or less what they appeared to be – up to a point, with reservations.
>
> I only realise quite how naive and credulous I've become these days when I meet young people who have the bloom of worldly wisdom still upon them. They're not fooled – they're not fooled by *me* for a start.

(Frayn 1983: 128)

Well, this essay is fond and foolish, no doubt; but it isn't intended to fool or fool about. I only jest, poison in jest, no offence in the world. My small plea to

> Those who are not bad at heart
> Who remember Shakespeare with a start

and even, it may be, to the editor of *The Faber Book of Historical Verse*, is to take instructions in the National Curriculum, and claims about Shakespeare's greatness and timelessness at absolutely face value. The small stratagem I commend to my comrades in this book and in classrooms elsewhere is simply to aim, hope, and pray for the shock of recognition which James Baldwin spoke of so movingly in a little essay called 'Why I stopped hating Shakespeare'.

I still remember my shock when I finally *heard* these lines from the murder scene in *Julius Caesar*. The assassins are washing their hands in Caesar's blood. Cassius says:

> 'Stoop then, and wash. – How many ages hence
> Shall this our lofty scene be acted o'er,
> In states unborn and accents yet unknown.'

What I suddenly heard, for the first time, was manifold. It was the voice of lonely, dedicated, deluded Cassius, whose life had never been real for me before – I suddenly seemed to know what this moment meant to him. But beneath and beyond that voice I also heard a note yet more rigorous and impersonal – and contemporary: that 'lofty scene', in all its blood and necessary folly, its blind and necessary pain, was thrown into a perspective which has never left my mind. Just so, indeed, is the heedless State overthrown by men, who, in order to overthrow it, have had to achieve a desperate single-mindedness. And this single-mindedness which we think of (why?) as ennobling, also operates, and much more surely, to distort and diminish a man – to distort and diminish us all, even, or perhaps especially, those whose needs and whose energy made the overthrow of the State inevitable, necessary and just. . . .

My relationship, then, to the language of Shakespeare revealed itself as nothing less than my relationship to myself and my past. Under this light, this revelation, both myself and my past began slowly to open, perhaps the way a flower opens at morning, but, more probably, the way an atrophied muscle begins to function, or frozen fingers to thaw.

(Baldwin 1964)

Listening to Baldwin's fluent honesty would, I'm afraid, be easier for a member of HMI or the Federal Curriculum Authority than for somebody who had just followed Gary Taylor breathlessly through to page 461 of *Reinventing Shakespeare* (Taylor 1989). Taylor is after all *the* sign of the times, and after him and his host, we now know that the cultural history of Shakespeare paraphrases as the stupefying agglomeration of context. It is 'the history of the theatre, of publishing, censorship, journalism, education, sex', and so on until that history has been reviewed so embracingly that it takes in 'the complete entirety of . . . society, its economics, politics, ideology, its total social and material structure'.

After such knowledge (as produced by Taylor), what forgiveness? His book, as once was immortally said, owes more to the history of publicity than to that of literature, and indeed will sell copiously to any syllabus more concerned with the formalist semiotics of *approaches* than with content and, indeed, art. The moral of the whole business, such an important tributary of the cultural industries, is that Shakespeare, as playwright perhaps but as text-function certainly, has always been the tool of cultural conservatism, nationalism, and imperialism. This anachronistic silliness has given a wonderful fillip to the sales of Shakespeare criticism (to which no doubt this collection bears witness – an example of sawing off one's own branch which sorts happily with the delirium of postmodernism).

III

The ideologues of the left have responded from the only power base they have (and a modest one it is) to the politicizing of culture which has been so marked a feature of public life in Europe and the USA since the early 1970s. One may speculate that such ideologizing arose as part of an effort to push vertiginous economic crisis out of the political realm, where governments could not control it, into the cultural one where it could be readily contained (Habermas 1975). Thus the legislation on the part of rulers as various as François Mitterand, Kenneth Baker, and William Barrett intended to tie education to national cultural glory and teachers down with it, signified this surely unsuccessful dislocation.

The trouble is that to join issues directly by declaring a class struggle over art and the art of living is to sentence oneself to ineffectuality and derision. The self-styled cultural materialists, having taken the term from Raymond Williams, declare that 'cultural materialism . . . sees texts as inseparable from the conditions of their production and reception in history; and as involved necessarily in the making of cultural meanings which are always, finally, political meanings' (Holderness 1989: introduction). Well, even if solecistic, this is merely truistic. For while texts clearly *can* be separated from their production – I can simply sit down and read the *Sonnets* – they must be received *somewhere*. But our authors go on to declare their pieties, 'cultural materialism registers its commitment to the transformation of a social order that exploits people on grounds of race, gender, sexuality and class' (Holderness 1989: Foreword by Jonathan Dollimore and Alan Sinfield).

Does it, indeed? Of course, Marxism has always offered itself as both scientific method and mode of redemption, but I doubt if that great man Raymond Williams saw his oxymoron as capable of carrying such a burden. I even wonder if the slogan can carry anything at all. At this date, nearly forty years after Wittgenstein's *Philosophical Investigations* came out and, moreover, after so much work on indeterminacy from Derrida, Davidson, and Quine has been taken to heart, the old fight between idealism and materialism should surely be stopped. Let us more roundly say that an utterance cannot be understood without a context being either taken or ascribed, and that this is as true of literary art as it is of speech, but that art as a form of speech further compounds our difficulties by being of the character it is.

In other words, what Richard Wollheim designates the institutionalist and externalist accounts of art, which purport to explain the significance of art by sociological or historicist accounts of its strictly social construction, fall by virtue of their failure to take account of art's special character (Wollheim 1987: 16–19). Thus, although Sinfield, for example, can tell us so much of interest about the ideological loadings of the dialogue in *Henry*

VI, he cannot say anything about its artistic force; his theory forbids him to (Sinfield 1985: 160–1). This blank leaves him treating Shakespeare much as he would Richard Hooker and this, in turn, leaves so much out as to make his method seem at key conjunctures too feeble to do anything much except raise a leisurely clap from the family.

IV

Capital, it is plain, has invaded Shakespeare as part of the huge, uncolonized domain of leisure awaiting its belated domination. Culture became political at the moment at which it became radically overhauled as an underexploited market.

This being so, the cultural materialists have much to tell us about the connections between the old Shakespeare firm and the cultural industries. In so far as they overuse ideology as an explanatory concept, their work has the thinness of all ideology critique; but there are still things to say in the idiom. In so far as they essay economic analysis, they are just embarrassing, since so few intellectuals on the left know any respectable economic theory. There is a good book to be written by somebody on the editorial board of *Media, Culture & Society* on the political economy of the Shakespeare industry, but its author would need to understand Kalecki rather than *Marx for Beginners*.

If some such inquiry were to be the proper study of the pious materialist-Shakespearean, where does that leave those of us who believe, certainly, that culture should be held and renewed in common, that poets are indeed men and women speaking as directly as they can to other men and women, and that the greatest literature may somehow so free minds and open spirits that they are no longer held in thrall to states and principalities and powers?

To speak so of literature is not to ratify that old class enemy, the set book and all its mystifications. It is to appeal to certain master symbols of both socialism and its far longer-lived ancestor, humanism. It is to endorse Georg Lukács's aphorism when he wrote in *Goethe and His Age* that 'all great literature contains within itself the seeds of its own criticism.' Those master symbols cannot be laid consecutively along the linear axis from power to exploitation. To do so in the language of cultural materialism is to shrivel and enfeeble a long moral tradition and its highly argumentative vocabulary. It is to cut out such values as 'love, joy, peace, long-suffering, goodness, faith . . .' (and I had better add to that quotation (Galatians 5.22), in order to avoid misunderstanding, that I write as a convinced atheist). This arid tongue entirely prevents that open meeting of honest men and good women which the Romantic poets so stirringly believed was made possible by imaginative literature. Leavis's 'third realm' of the poem offered the freehold space upon which an equal encounter with something *else* and something precious could be enacted. In the best traditions of working-class education – the Mechanics Institutes, let us say, or one or two of the more freethinking Dissenting Academies – the eponym of such a freehold was always Shakespeare.

This is not a vision to be lost. Even at this date, it is a vision still to be found shyly invoked by a few secondary school teachers and adult educators in the outreaches of the University. If we think again of Lukács's aphorism, we may be cheered up enough to reflect that the insistence in the National Curriculum of Britain or the State Anthology in New Jersey on teaching Shakespeare to the toughest eggs of the eighth grade may still be an activity capable of restoring freedom to the status of a virtue. At a more buoyant moment for Marxism than 1990, Trotsky wrote:

> What the worker will take from Shakespeare, Goethe, Pushkin or Dostoievsky, will be a more complex idea of human personality, of its passions and feelings, a deeper and profounder understanding of its psychic forces and of the role of the subconscious, etc. . . . [His] class cannot begin the construction of a new culture without absorbing and assimilating the elements of the old cultures . . . a new class cannot move forward without regard to the most important landmarks of the past.
>
> (Trotsky 1960: 226)

Trotsky sings an old humanist song; and so do I.

V

The ancient, argumentative way of auto-didacticism and popular culture was not, it should be noted, necessarily a grave and admonitory form of life. The rum thing about the dealings of the left with culture has been that, since Orwell, Caudwell, and

W. H. Auden, that same left has dealt with these matters in so remorselessly formalist a way. Doubtless this particular misprision was and is the causal product of the class provenance of those who knew best what was best for the working class, but reading the esays of cultural materialism shows the contention still to hold.

Another tradition, however, would drive the wrong way up the road to Vitebsk. Against the formalists of then and now, it would seek out, say, radical Schiller translating Shakespeare into *Sturm und Drang;* Verdi turning Shakespeare into opera for the Risorgimento; Kozintsev taking Pasternak's translation of *King Lear* and turning it into his incomparable work in the bleak, ice-cold hills of the Ukraine.

Each man had a drastically non-formalist version of Shakespeare to tell to his people. In a primary, intuitive motion of mind they had a work of art – among the greatest works of their continental civilization, to be ranked with Handel (for Schiller), Michelangelo (for Verdi), Pushkin (for Kozintsev) – to match with an historical moment. Their intense concern was to fit the story to the history of their side of the historical divide. They sought, in other, more technical words, to hold a balance between art object and local experience without giving the prize to either.

That is the balancing act which ought to be the real foundation of a socialist pedagogy, in school or in the extra-mural class or among the local Thespians. In my rather scholarship-saturated judgement, the essays of the Shakespeare industry won't be much help, though Shakespeare-in-the-Park and the National Theatre of Brent may well be. Trotsky's and Lukács's samplers are to hand. Without making Caliban hero-victim of *The Tempest* (the creature is an aspiring rapist, after all) there are anti-capitalist sermons to be read in *Timon of Athens* which haven't been much heeded in twelfth grade and sixth form, and – though it doesn't do to say so too loudly these days – there are non-sexist fragrances to be drunk in from the courtship of Florizel and Perdita.

I suppose what is most to be looked out for is this kind of mischievousness as well as this historically contradictory reverence – the product of collaboration between a White Russian, bridge-playing Jew and a Sephardic balletomane Jewess, writing together at the height of the Blitz in 1941 and in between their duties as ARP wardens.

Master Pyk sat down. 'Oh dear,' he said. 'I do not think you really want me in the company. You are only keeping me here to please Master Polonius.'

Shakespeare inclined his head. 'We did at first, boy,' he agreed. 'But we are all beginning to like you very much. We enjoy your high spirits when you are not crying.' Master Pyk blinked hard. 'And,' said Shakespeare, suddenly serious, 'you can speak a line. By God – you can speak a line.'

Master Pyk leant back and laid his cheek upon his hands. 'Can I?' he asked roguishly.

Shakespeare blinked. What were boys coming to? Still, he must work now. He crossed to the table.

'See,' he said, 'the speech that I have written specially for you.'

He began to declaim:

> 'If I did love you in my master's flame
> With such a suffering, such a deadly life,
> In your denial I would find no sense;
> I would not understand it.'

Master Will was no actor. He spoke his lines badly, he wrenched the accents out of place, and he kept stopping to peer at his own writing. But Viola sat very still and spoke the words to herself after him.

> 'Make me a willow cabin at your gate,
> And call upon my soul within the house;
> Write loyal cantons of condemned love,
> And sing them loud even in the dead of night;
> Holla your name to the reverbrate hills,
> And make the babbling gossip of the air
> Cry out, "Olivia." O, you should not rest
> Between the elements of air and earth,
> But you should pity me.'

Shakespeare stopped. He saw the awed little face looking at him. He beamed.

'A good speech,' he said.

A candle flickered and went out.

'And you wrote these lines for me,' said Lady Viola Compton.

(Brahms and Simon 1941: 193–4)

What Brahms and Simon found for the moment of 1941 was a rare combination of playfulness on the part of two people who loved the works, and a new context for the quotation of those incomparable lines which, comical in itself, rediscovered their power to move, their unstoppable eloquence.

VI

Eloquence, of course, hasn't had much of a press for a while, except from Tony Harrison. Empson once wrote that 'Gross misuses of Eng. Lit. for political and sectarian purposes are bound to crop up, and might destroy it; but with periodic sanitary efforts it can probably be got to continue in a sturdy, placid way, as is needed' (Empson: 1967–8). Gross misuses surround us on Left and Right hands; is it possible to persuade a few of our pupils to those conversive moments after which, having truly heard Shakespeare, they can never be the same again?

I realize that, a bit combatively, I am now trying to call up rather elderly spirits. Once again, perhaps quotation can be made to do the job for me. There is no space here to suggest *how* such 'conversive moments' may come about for this or that student. Simon Shepherd's or Nigel Wheale's chapters in this book are admirably to this point. In any case, other teachers are more experienced that I am as well as plain better at finding them. But it seems probable that all teaching in the arts counts on some such falling in love as happens to the central figure in the following passage from an American novel. It describes a young man of twenty or so, son of desperately poor Midwest dirt farmers, and is itself written in 1963 by a man much of Stoner's formation, son of a very poor Mississippi family, educated after a fashion by the USAF in Burma in 1944.

The young man, William Stoner, is at the university to study agriculture in order to return home to his father's grim, dry farm and squeeze from it another drop or two of sap in the grain. He is obliged to do a survey course of English literature as well. The teacher, a strong, reticent, disdainful man in middle age, is called Archer Sloane.

> He found that he could not handle the survey as he did his other courses. Though he remembered the authors and their works and their dates and their influences, he nearly failed

his first examination; and he did little better on his second. He read and reread his literature assignments so frequently that his work in other courses began to suffer; and still the words he read were words on pages, and he could not see the use of what he did.

And he pondered the words that Archer Sloane spoke in class, as if beneath their flat, dry meaning he might discover a clue that would lead him where he was intended to go; he hunched forward over the desk-top of a chair too small to hold him comfortably, grasping the edges of the desk-top so tightly that his knuckles showed white against his brown hard skin; he frowned intently and gnawed at his underlip. But as Stoner's and his classmates' attention grew more desperate, Archer Sloane's contempt grew more compelling. And once that contempt erupted into anger and was directed at William Stoner alone.

The class had read two plays by Shakespeare and was ending the week with a study of the sonnets. The students were edgy and puzzled, half frightened at the tension growing between themselves and the slouching figure that regarded them from behind the lectern. Sloane had read aloud to them the seventy-third sonnet; his eyes roved about the room and his lips tightened in a humorless smile.

'What does the sonnet mean?' he asked abruptly, and paused, his eyes searching the room with a grim and almost pleased hopelessness. 'Mr. Wilbur?' There was no answer. 'Mr. Schmidt?' Someone coughed. Sloane turned his dark bright eyes upon Stoner. 'Mr. Stoner, what does the sonnet mean?'

Stoner swallowed and tried to open his mouth.

'It is a sonnet, Mr. Stoner,' Sloane said dryly, 'a poetical composition of fourteen lines, with a certain pattern I am sure you have memorized. It is written in the English language, which I believe you have been speaking for some years. Its author is William Shakespeare, a poet who is dead, but who nevertheless occupies a position of some importance in the minds of a few.' He looked at Stoner for a moment more, and then his eyes went blank as they fixed unseeingly beyond the class. Without looking at his book he spoke the poem again; and his voice deepened and soft-

ened, as if the words and sounds and rhythms had for a
moment become himself:

'That time of year thou mayst in me behold
When yellow leaves, or none, or few, do hang
Upon those boughs which shake against the cold,
Bare ruin'd choirs where late the sweet birds sang.
In me thou see'st the twilight of such day
As after sunset fadeth in the west;
Which by and by black night doth take away,
Death's second self, that seals up all in rest.
In me thou see'st the glowing of such fire,
That on the ashes of his youth doth lie,
As the death-bed whereon it must expire,
Consumed with that which it was nourisht by.
   This thou perceiv'st, which makes thy love more
      strong,
   To love that well which thou must leave ere long.'

In a moment of silence, someone cleared his throat. Sloane
repeated the lines, his voice becoming flat, his own again.

   'This thou perceiv'st, which makes thy love more
      strong,
   To love that well which thou must leave ere long.'

Sloane's eyes came back to William Stoner, and he said
dryly, 'Mr. Shakespeare speaks to you across three hundred
years, Mr. Stoner; do you hear him?'

William Stoner realized that for several moments he had
been holding his breath. He expelled it gently, minutely
aware of his clothing moving upon his body as his breath
went out of his lungs. He looked away from Sloane about
the room. Light slanted from the windows and settled upon
the faces of his fellow students, so that the illumination
seemed to come from within them and go out against a
dimness; a student blinked, and a thin shadow fell upon a
cheek whose down had caught the sunlight. Stoner became
aware that his fingers were unclenching their hard grip on
his desk-top. He turned his hands about under his gaze,
marveling at their brownness, at the intricate way the nails
fit into his blunt finger-ends; he thought he could feel the
blood flowing invisibly through the tiny veins and arteries,

throbbing delicately and precariously from his fingertips through his body.

Sloane was speaking again. 'What does he say to you, Mr. Stoner? What does his sonnet mean?'

Stoner's eyes lifted slowly and reluctantly. 'It means,' he said, and with a small movement raised his hands up toward the air; he felt his eyes glaze over as they sought the figure of Archer Sloane. 'It means,' he said again, and could not finish what he had begun to say.

Sloane looked at him curiously. Then he nodded abruptly and said, 'Class is dismissed.' Without looking at anyone he turned and walked out of the room.

(Williams 1965: 11–13)

NOTE

1 I develop this analysis more fully in my *Popular Culture and Political Power*, Hemel Hempstead, Harvester/Wheatsheaf, 1988.

REFERENCES

Baldwin, James (1964) 'Why I stopped hating Shakespeare', *London Observer*, 19 April.

Bourdieu, Pierre (1984) *Distinction: a Social Critique of the Judgement of Taste*, London: Routledge.

Brahms, Caryl and Simon, S. J. (1941) *No Bed for Bacon*, London: Michael Joseph.

Empson, William (1967–8) 'Letter to the Editor', *The Hudson Review* 20(4): 534–8, replying to Roger Sale (1966–7) 'The achievement of William Empson', *The Hudson Review* 19(3): 369–90.

Frayn, Michael (1983) *The Original Michael Frayn*, ed. James Fenton, Edinburgh: Salamander Press.

Habermas, Jürgen (1975) *Legitimation Crisis*, London: Heinemann.

Holderness, Graham (ed.) (1989) *The Shakespeare Myth*, Manchester: Manchester University Press.

Lukács, Georg (1968) *Goethe and His Age*, trans. Robert Anchor, London: Merlin Press.

Sinfield, Alan (1985) 'Royal Shakespeare: theatre and the making of ideology', in Jonathan Dollimore and Alan Sinfield (eds) *Political Shakespeare. New Essays in Cultural Materialism*, Manchester: Manchester University Press.

Taylor, Gary (1989) *Reinventing Shakespeare: a Cultural History from the Restoration to the Present*, London: Weidenfeld & Nicolson.

Trotsky, Leon (1960) *Literature and Revolution*, Michigan: University of Michigan Press; first published 1924.

Williams, John (1965) *Stoner*, New York: Viking.
Wollheim, Richard (1987) *Painting as an Art*, Princeton, NJ: Princeton University Press.

4

Does it matter which edition you use?

Ann Thompson

Outside theological tradition, no body of writings has been
subjected to more in the way of interpretative comment and
textual scholarship than the works of Shakespeare. Yet the
upshot of this activity . . . is to cast increasing doubt on
the power of criticism to distinguish between the two. . . .
Even textual scholarship, with its self-denying ordinances,
finds itself repeatedly *crossing over* from a strictly ancillary
to a kind of rival-imaginative role.

(Norris 1985: 56–7)

Editing, especially editing Shakespeare (because he's the
national dramatist) is worth political analysis because it
affirms all sorts of values, even while it claims to be dispassionate, almost a science.

(Shepherd 1986: xix)

WHY EDIT SHAKESPEARE?

What, to begin with, does it mean to 'edit' Shakespeare? Why is
it necessary to do it at all, and why do people keep doing it over
and over again? When I edited *The Taming of the Shrew* for the
New Cambridge Shakespeare (1984), I studied over a hundred
previous editions of the play ranging from the earliest text published in 1623 to ones published as recently as 1981 and 1982.
The work took me four years (allowing of course for a full-time
job and various other commitments). How can I justify that
expenditure of time and effort, apparently repeating what over a
hundred people had done before? What exactly was I doing all
that time? How could I claim that my edition was different from

any of the others? Without, I hope, mounting a direct apology for my own work, I shall draw on my (first) experience of editing to address some of these fundamental questions.

The business of editing Shakespeare can be divided into two main tasks. Firstly, the editor must establish, in all its details, the actual text of the play that is to be printed. Secondly, she or he must explain or communicate that text to the readers – by adding an introduction, notes, glossary and so forth. The first activity falls broadly into the area of scholarship, the second into the area of criticism. Both are complex and require the editor to make many decisions, large and small.

What is so difficult about establishing the text? Why not simply reprint the earliest original? For a start, there is no authorial manuscript of *The Taming of the Shrew* (nor indeed of any Shakespeare play) so early printed versions are our only sources. These are available in photographic facsimiles which naturally preserve the typeface, spelling and punctuation of the originals – deterrents, though not insuperable ones, to the modern reader. Moreover, these early texts were more often than not rather carelessly printed by modern standards and are liberally sprinkled with misprints and other errors. They are frequently inconsistent about the names of characters and places and erratic in their stage directions. Sometimes we have two or more early printed texts of the same play which are significantly different from each other.

In the case of *The Taming of the Shrew* there is really only one authoritative early text, the version printed in what has come to be called the First Folio, the large volume containing most of Shakespeare's plays which was put together and published by his friends and colleagues in the theatre, John Heminge and Henry Condell, in 1623. But two problems immediately arise from this circumstance: firstly, Shakespeare had died in 1616 so obviously had no opportunity to approve the text of his work that was published. (Even when plays were published in the smaller Quarto volumes during his lifetime they usually seem to have appeared without his knowledge or permission.) Secondly, we have evidence that *The Taming of the Shrew* was performed as early as 1594, some thirty years before the text was published. Questions arise over what happened to the text during that time: What was the source of Heminge and Condell's copy? Was the text printed the same as that performed thirty years earlier or had it been cut, added to, revised, or otherwise altered? Had the author himself made any changes to the play during that period or had someone else intervened, perhaps to adapt it for a different company of actors or a different theatre? Was the First Folio text itself printed from Shakespeare's own manuscript or from a copy made by someone else? If from a copy, when, why, and by whom was that copy made? And what about the number of variations between extant copies of the First Folio itself?

Over the years, editors and textual scholars have devised ways of attempting to answer some of these questions. This scholarship is cumulative over time so the most recent edition of any particular text will (in theory at least) incorporate the latest research. For example, evidence external to the text itself continues to build up: we now know much more than we did twenty or even ten years ago about the circumstances in which Shakespeare's plays were originally performed. We know more about the theatres and the acting companies; we even know more about the actors' pronunciation. We also know more about the circumstances in which they were printed: as well as undertaking general research on the handwriting, spelling, and punctuation of the period, scholars have studied particular printing houses and even the habits of individual print-workers. From this, and from research identifying the work of particular scribes who were employed to copy texts, editors can be more confident about ascribing certain kinds of error to the copyist or printer rather than to the author. They can often detect what sort of manuscript lies behind a printed text and what is the relationship between two or more texts.

Having answered these preliminary questions as far as possible, or at least summarized the relevant evidence lucidly, an editor could stop there and print an old-spelling text of the play with the most obvious mistakes corrected, inconsistencies regularized and so on. The result would be something like the Original-Spelling Edition of the *Complete Works* recently published by Oxford University Press (1987) and described in their publicity as 'an "ideal" text of Shakespeare's works as they would have appeared in his own time'. Because no such ideal edition actually did appear, the Oxford editors have been driven to some curious shifts: they have, for example, supplied the frequent deficiencies in stage directions by making them up in pastiche Elizabethan/Jacobean English. The text is somewhat more accessible to the modern reader than a straight facsimile of the First Folio, but at £75 this volume is clearly not intended for the mass market.

Most editors are in fact encouraged by their publishers to take a more active, interventionist role in relation to their text by adding various forms of interpretive material – an introduction, commentary, and so forth. This is a more subjective area and one more open to changing times and fashions. Each age reads Shakespeare for its own purposes and, perhaps, in its own image. Some editorial assumptions do go out of date. Modern readers would be surprised by the emphasis on sheer philology in the notes to earlier editions of Shakespeare: that is, information about the history and meaning of individual words. This pedagogic role, along with the more general 'history of ideas' function, is now performed by the *Oxford English Dictionary* and other standard reference works, leaving the editor free to pursue different concerns.

Most editors today are much more concerned than their predecessors to present their plays as texts intended for performance. While older editors often informed their readers that scenes took place 'on the heath', 'in the forest', 'in a walled garden' and so on, modern editors tend to insist that everything takes place on a stage. Readers of course change too: earlier editions, including many still widely available, assume a homogeneous white middle- or even upper-class readership with a thorough knowledge of the British landscape, British culture and customs. This is no longer realistic, even for editions aimed primarily at the British market, let alone for those which will be read in the rest of the English-speaking world. And apart from the neutral-seeming business of simply informing readers about unfamiliar words, allusions, and figurative expressions, editors inevitably participate in the political/theoretical/critical climate of their own time.

WHAT'S NEW IN SHAKESPEARE EDITING?

Editors in the late twentieth century are continuing to build on and refine the work of their predecessors, but at the same time they find themselves in the midst of a fundamental revolution in attitudes to some of the basic assumptions of editing and textual scholarship taken for granted in the past. Although there is not much apparent consciousness amongst editors of recent developments in literary criticism, there may at some level be a link between deconstructionist views of texts and a greater willingness on the part of editors to challenge the notion of a precise, stable text and entertain ideas of a more fluid text or a multiplicity of texts.

This is perhaps most obvious, and certainly most widely publicized, in changing notions about how to deal with a play in a case where the editor is faced with two or more early texts. Since *King Lear* has attracted the most attention as well as the most radical solution of the problem, it will serve to exemplify the current debate, though it should be remembered that it is an extreme case. No fewer than four books (and a number of articles) have been published since 1980 which challenge traditional assumptions about the text of this play and cast doubt on the validity of all previous editions. So what exactly is going on?

There are two important early texts of *King Lear*, the Quarto published in 1608 and the First Folio published in 1623. The Quarto is a badly printed (and presumably unauthorized) text, whereas the Folio is more carefully produced and contains fuller stage directions as well as act and scene numbers. The Folio contains a number of short passages amounting to more than a hundred lines which are not in the Quarto, but it omits some three hundred lines of text which *are* in the Quarto. It is generally agreed that the Folio text is based on the Quarto text altered by reference to the promptbook used in performance; this would account both for the greater care taken over stage directions and for the cuts which in the past were assumed to have originated in the theatre: either the play was simply too long or some passages were thought not to have been effective on stage. All existing editions of *King Lear* (with the exception of the new Oxford *Complete Works* – of which more later) conflate the two texts so as to produce the longest possible version of the play.

Those who challenge this traditional editorial orthodoxy argue that the two texts represent two distinct stages in Shakespeare's own development of the play: that the Quarto represents his first version and that the Folio represents his own revision, undertaken in order to improve the play on stage. Hence the traditional conflation of the two texts is perceived as a muddle which was never performed in Shakespeare's time and which fails to present either version clearly. In particular, specific changes made by Shakespeare to the roles of Albany, Edgar, Kent, and the Fool are obscured by conflating the two texts, as is Shakespeare's attempt to refocus the ending of the play. The implication of this line of argument for the editor is to print not one but two separate texts of *King Lear*, and the Oxford *Complete Works* (edited by Stanley Wells and Gary Taylor, 1986) is the first edition to do that. While on the one hand not all textual scholars are convinced by the new theory about *King Lear*, on the other hand very similar theories involving authorial revision are beginning to come forward in relation to *Hamlet* and *Othello*.

While one might look to the New Cambridge *Hamlet* (Philip Edwards, 1985) or to the forthcoming Arden *Othello* (E. A. J. Honigmann) for the latest views on those texts, the Oxford Shakespeare project has been most prominently in the forefront of the editorial revolution. Stanley Wells and Gary Taylor have already published the *Complete Works* in two versions, modern spelling and original spelling, as well as the 576-page *Textual Companion* which aims (according to the Press's publicity) to be 'the most comprehensive reference work on Shakespearian textual problems ever assembled in a single volume', and will undoubtedly have a major influence on all editions in the foreseeable future. They have also argued their general editorial policies and explained their reasons for rejecting some kinds of traditional thinking in *Modernizing Shakespeare's Spelling, with Three Studies in the Text of 'Henry V'* (Wells and Taylor, 1979) and in *Re-Editing Shakespeare for the Modern Reader* (Wells, 1984). Unfortunately, there are problems over the publication of the commentary for the *Complete Works* (the general commentary that is, as opposed to the textual commentary), so the usefulness of these volumes may be severely restricted.

The two plays called *King Lear* (actually, the Quarto text is called *The History of 'King Lear'* in the running titles while the Folio text is called *The Tragedy of 'King Lear'*) constitute the most obvious novelty in the Oxford *Complete Works*, but there are some equally startling changes in the naming of characters and indeed whole plays. There is no Falstaff in *1 Henry IV*, the character being presented under his original name of Oldcastle, which both explains the various quibbles on the word 'castle' and (through reference to the historical Oldcastle) the ominous predictions of an ignoble death. The heroine of *Cymbeline* is at last called Innogen rather than Imogen, as indeed she was on stage in the National Theatre's 1988 production – a very belated correction of a misprint. There is no play called *Henry VIII*, a title which appears merely as a subtitle to *All is True*, setting up incidentally an arbitrary but eerie link between this late Shakespeare collaboration and Orson Welles's unfinished film *It's All True*. The plays formerly known as *2 Henry VI* and *3 Henry VI* appear under the titles of their Quarto editions as *The First Part of the Contention of the Two Famous Houses of York and Lancaster* and *The True Tragedy of Richard Duke of York and the Good King Henry the Sixth* respectively. New arguments about the chronology of the entire canon lead to these two plays appearing earlier in the *Complete Works* (which is chronologically arranged without genre divisions) than *1 Henry VI*, to *All's Well That Ends Well* appearing after *Othello* and to *Cymbeline* appearing after rather than before *The Winter's Tale*. Finally, to complete this very superficial indication of the thoroughly radical nature of the whole enterprise, Thomas Middleton is named as the reviser of both *Measure for Measure* and *Macbeth* and as Shakespeare's collaborator on *Timon of Athens*.

In addition to the *Complete Works* in a single volume (available in the two different spelling formats), the Oxford Shakespeare also involves the production of one-play-per-volume editions of all the individual plays which are (a little confusingly) quasi-independent of general editorial policy. In that series, for example, *1 Henry IV* (David Bevington, 1987) does include a character called Falstaff. These volumes, which are very competitively priced in paperback, are clearly intended as rivals in the large sixth-form and undergraduate market for the established Arden (now published by Routledge) and the New Cambridge Shakespeare. In fact both Oxford and Cambridge University Presses launched their new editions at the same time, with the first volumes appearing in 1982 (Oxford) and 1984 (Cambridge). To date (March 1991), Oxford have published twelve plays in their series while Cambridge have published eighteen.

A piquant rumour at the time of the launch of these new editions claimed that both Presses had decided to go into Shakespeare publishing in a big way as the logical solution to the world-wide decline in bible sales, formerly an important source of their profits, but even without that comparison it is clear that the publishing of editions of Shakespeare is a major commercial activity. Routledge is fighting back with new editions of the older and more eccentric volumes of the Arden, Penguin deservedly dominates the mass market in Britain with its combination of low price, attractive layout and accessible scholarship, while in North America Signet is advertising newly revised editions of the most popular plays and Bantam has leapt dramatically into the field by publishing the entire canon in twenty-nine volumes (the less popular plays being consigned to anthologies) all at once in January 1988. The Riverside Shakespeare continues to be seen as the standard edition of the *Complete Works* on the other side of the Atlantic, even though its text is considered eccentric by many scholars. Meanwhile there is also a market for ventures like the Contemporary Shakespeare series from the University Press of America and the Shakespeare Made Easy series from Hutchinson, both of which provide modernized versions, the latter by means of a parallel-text prose paraphrase, the former by the more dubious procedure of, as their publicity puts it, 'removing difficulties – archaic grammar, difficult abbreviations, unintelligible words and the like –' from the text itself.

EDITORS VERSUS CRITICS?

While all this activity has been going on amongst editors, the last decade has also of course seen much ferment and innovation in criticism with the rise of what are loosely termed 'theoretical' approaches: structuralism, deconstructionism, feminism, new historicism, cultural materialism, and so forth. Unfortunately, there does not seem to be a great deal of contact between the two groups: editors often ignore recent developments in criticism while 'theoretical' critics sometimes write on *King Lear* in complete ignorance of the textual debate and use the soon-to-be-replaced Arden edition of *Othello* (Ridley, 1958) apparently unaware that its choice of text is unusual, indeed unique.

It seems in fact surprising that 'theoretical' critics have not involved themselves in the textual debates. Books like *Political Shakespeare* (Dollimore and Sinfield 1985) and *The Shakespeare Myth* (Holderness 1988) set out quite explicitly to study the reproduction of Shakespeare in our contemporary culture and contain essays on Shakespeare in the education system, Shakespeare on television, the Royal Shakespeare Company, even the Shakespeare tourist industry, but nothing on the editions we all use when we act, read, teach, or write about Shakespeare, which might seem to be an equally significant topic. Terence Hawkes in *That Shakespeherian Rag* (1986) has investigated the interaction of literary interpretation and political/social issues in the careers of Shakespearean scholars like A. C. Bradley, Walter Raleigh, W. W. Greg, and John Dover Wilson who had such a strong influence on the construction of 'English' as an academic subject as well as on the construction of Shakespeare as its central pillar, but he does not pursue the argument into the issue of editing, which is in fact an important part of our heritage from both Greg and Dover Wilson. And while, in the passages quoted at the beginning of this chapter, both Christopher Norris and Simon Shepherd have pointed to the need to examine the accepted distinction between supposedly dispassionate scholarship (editing) and subjective interpretation (criticism), neither has yet followed this up.

More efforts have been made by textual scholars. Margreta de Grazia's essay, 'The essential Shakespeare and the material book', published, significantly, in the 'theoretical' journal, *Textual Practice* (1988), discusses the relationship between the New Bibliography of the early twentieth century and the New Criticism, and goes on to speculate on the similarities between editorial and interpretive approaches in our own time. And D. C. Greetham, in a recent essay published in the more traditional journal, *Studies in Bibliography* (1989), argues that textual scholars need to be aware of the theoretical assumptions that lie behind their editions, and that some of the conceptual and methodological premises of literary and textual theory could benefit from a simultaneous investigation.

This is obviously a large and important topic, beyond the scope of this chapter, but to illustrate the ways in which editors do indeed, as Simon Shepherd puts it, 'affirm all sorts of values', especially political ones, I shall take a couple of examples from one of the most widely read and taught plays.

THE CASE OF *JULIUS CAESAR*

On stage, *Julius Caesar* has been a politically contentious play. During the Restoration and the eighteenth century it was interpreted as an attack on tyranny and a rousing celebration of republicanism: Caesar was the villain and Brutus the noble defender of the liberties of Rome. This tradition continued into later times, with the representation of Caesar as a totally unsympathetic dictator reinforced by overt allusions to Fascism in productions from the 1930s to the 1950s. In more recent times, however, an increasing cynicism about politics and politicians in general has led to less partisan productions which still see Caesar as an unacceptable tyrant but fail to glorify Brutus as a credible alternative, stressing instead the apparent futility of both revolution and counter-revolution.

A parallel tendency in literary criticism up to 1950 is perceived by T. S. Dorsch who, in his Arden edition of the play (1955), consciously sets out to reverse the traditional view of Caesar as a tyrant and Brutus as a hero. He argues that if Shakespeare had 'really wished to denigrate Caesar' he could have found plenty of material in his sources (p. xxviii), defends Caesar against the charge of arrogance by remarking that 'we have good-humouredly accepted arrogance of this kind in recent English leaders who have served us conspicuously' (p. xxxi), and against the charge of susceptibility to flattery on the grounds that this weakness is 'not uncommon in great men' (p. xxxiii). He stresses constantly throughout his Introduction that Caesar was 'the one undoubted genius of his age' (p. xxxix), 'a great national leader' (p. xlv), 'the greatest man of his age' (p. l), minimizes his faults ('Caesar's shortcomings give him concrete reality as a fallible human being like ourselves', p. xxxviii), and asks rhetorically 'Can it be doubted that Shakespeare wishes us to admire his Caesar?' (p. xxxviii). The murder is referred to as Brutus' 'treachery' (p. xxxvi), his 'crime' (p. xliv), and as 'this almost incredible piece of criminal folly' (p. xxxix). Consistently minimizing the play's politics and presenting its conflicts in personal terms, Dorsch naturally denigrates Brutus as 'pompous, opinionated and self-righteous', and, worst of all, 'an ineffectual idealist' (p. xxxix).

Subsequent editors of *Julius Caesar* have been less partisan in their approach to the play, often stressing Shakespeare's apparent ambivalence both towards the characters and towards their politics rather than taking sides, but one of the most recent, Arthur Humphreys (in the Oxford edition of 1984), while conceding that 'Whatever the political rights and wrongs of the situation, it is for most readers the republican cause that moves the heart' (p. 36), nevertheless calls the murder of Caesar 'sacrilege' (p. 35) and comments that 'Caesar's authority and popularity are in fact Rome's safeguards, and the generosity his will reveals does more for the common good than does republican idealism' (p. 36). This fundamentally pro-Caesar attitude also creeps into his commentary, as for example on the first mention of Decius Brutus at I.3.148 when he comments quite gratuitously that, as one especially favoured by Caesar (a fact not of course mentioned by

Shakespeare), 'his participation in the conspiracy is gross treachery, and carried through most unscrupulously' (p. 127).

Bias of this kind in the commentary or notes is perhaps more of a problem, because less easy to identify and challenge, than bias in an introduction where, as quite explicitly in the case of Dorsch in the Arden *Julius Caesar*, the editor is engaging in critical debate. Bias in the notes, however, can masquerade as neutral glossary (the editor simply explaining what the words mean) or scholarly reference to sources. An example of this occurs towards the end of I.2 of *Julius Caesar* when Casca reports to Brutus and Cassius that 'Marullus and Flavius, for pulling scarfs off Caesar's images, are put to silence.' What exactly does this mean? The parallel-text translation in the Shakespeare Made Easy edition (Alan Durband, 1984) reads 'For pulling the decorations off Caesar's statues, Marullus and Flavius have been executed.' This is arguably how most people in an audience would understand 'put to silence' since the interpretation is supported both by the general context of anxiety about Caesar's potentially tyrannical ambitions and by the linguistic fact that 'put to' formulations are often sinister, as in 'put to the sword', 'put to torment', or 'put to execution'. Editors steer readers away from this interpretation. In the Signet edition (edited by William and Barbara Rosen, 1963), the note on 'put to silence' reads 'silenced (by being stripped of their tribuneships, and perhaps exiled or executed)'. The Bantam edition (edited by David Bevington *et al.*, 1988) has 'dismissed from office (so reported in Plutarch)', while the Penguin (edited by Norman Sanders, 1967) actually quotes the passage from Plutarch to support this reading. Finally, Arthur Humphreys in the Oxford edition (1984) acknowledges the sinister implication, saying 'This looks like a euphemism for "put to death", but reference to Plutarch makes it less odious – "deprived of their Tribuneships".' What seems to have happened here is that Shakespeare has been in effect rewritten by editors anxious to apologize for Caesar. (In their haste to excuse him from the 'odious' charge of executing the tribunes, they seem to overlook the fact that to dismiss elected representatives from their offices might also constitute an act of tyranny.)

SO DOES IT MATTER WHICH EDITION YOU USE?

It will probably be apparent that I would answer this question in the affirmative: yes, it does. I have not had space to deal with considerations such as cost and durability which are obviously important, nor with issues such as whether the notes are at the foot of the page of text, on the facing page or at the back of the book. These choices will be a matter of personal preference, or they may be determined by the kind of use envisaged for the edition. I have, though, tried to indicate the most significant *kinds* of difference between available editions in two crucial areas: the choice and handling of the text itself and the question of editorial input into the introduction and commentary.

As far as the text is concerned, it is unlikely that all readers will acquire the expertise to become textual scholars, but we can all be aware of the general nature of the debates that are going on. This is an area in which it is very important that an edition should be as up to date as possible. (Publishers are sometimes rather coy about this: the publicity for the 1988 Bantam Shakespeare, for example, relies heavily on the modernity claim – 'the only absolutely current and complete mass-market Shakespeare series available (Competing editions are at least twenty years old)' – and you have to read the small print in the copyright acknowledgements to discover that the copyright for the text goes back to at least 1951.) It is also important that the textual information should be as accessible as possible. The material *is* complicated, but it ought to be possible for an editor to describe what procedures have been followed and why, in language that an interested but non–specialist reader can understand.

While there are some aspects of textual editing that genuinely are quite like a dispassionate science, where truths can be established (and disputed), the introduction and commentary to an edition, though they may acquire authority from the generally formidable expertise of an editor who has spent a long time working intensively on the play, remain subjective and open to bias. There is nothing wrong with this so long as it is openly acknowledged and understood by both editor and readers: attempts by editors who aim for 'balance' are likely to result in dullness as well as dishonesty. But by all means let us have the republican *Julius Caesar* as well as the fascist *Julius Caesar*, the feminist *Taming of the Shrew* as well as the archly apologetic male chauvinist *Taming of the Shrew:* there is room in the market for variety and it would be refreshing for editors not to have to pretend to be above the critical fray. Meanwhile, it is up to buyers and users of editions to be alert to the ways in which editors can influence what text they read and how they read it. Teachers in particular might consider ways in which students can be made aware of these issues – perhaps by comparing a passage of an edited text with a facsimile of the original to see how many changes have been made and why; or by comparing passages from the Folio and Quarto texts of plays like *King Lear* or *Othello* where substantial differences exist; or by comparing the commentaries provided by different editors on particular passages as I have done with the *Julius Caesar* passages here. In my experience students who are bored with the standard 'lit. crit.' approaches to Shakespeare often enjoy doing the sort of detective work involved in such exercises, when resources (including time) allow.

NOTE

I have written on the texts of *King Lear* in my book on the play in Macmillan's 'Critics' Debate' series (1988) and have drawn here upon a brief passage from that book. Currently, I am editing a book called *Which Shakespeare?* to be published by the Open University Press in 1991, which will be a comprehensive guide to editions of Shakespeare available at that time.

REFERENCES AND READING LIST

General references on editing:

Hinman, Charles (1963) *The Printing and Proof-Reading of the First Folio of Shakespeare*, 2 vols, Oxford: Clarendon Press. (The classic, monumental study of this subject.)

Jackson, MacD. P. (1986) 'The transmission of Shakespeare's text', in Stanley Wells (ed.) *The Cambridge Companion to Shakespeare Studies*, Cambridge: Cambridge University Press, pp. 163–85. (An up-to-date introductory essay on general issues.)

Wells, Stanley (1984) *Re-Editing Shakespeare for the Modern Reader*, Oxford: Clarendon Press.

Wells, Stanley and Gary Taylor, (1979) *Modernizing Shakespeare's Spelling, with Three Studies in the Text of 'Henry V'*, Oxford: Clarendon Press.

Wells, Stanley and Gary Taylor, with John Jowett and William Montgomery (1987) *William Shakespeare: A Textual Companion*, Oxford: Clarendon Press. (Published to accompany the Oxford Shakespeare

Complete Works (1986), a comprehensive reference work on textual editing.)

On the texts of *King Lear:*

Blayney, Peter W. M. (1982) *The Texts of 'King Lear' and their Origins: Vol. 1 Nicholas Okes and the First Quarto*, Cambridge: Cambridge University Press. (The most detailed study to date of an Elizabethan/Jacobean printing house.)

Stone, P. W. K. (1980) *The Textual History of 'King Lear'*, London: Scolar Press.

Taylor, Gary and Michael Warren (eds) (1983) *The Division of the Kingdoms*, Oxford: Clarendon Press.

Urkowitz, Steven (1980) *Shakespeare's Revision of 'King Lear'*, Princeton, NJ: Princeton University Press.

'Theoretical' approaches

Dollimore, Jonathan and Alan Sinfield (eds) (1985) *Political Shakespeare* Manchester: Manchester University Press.

de Grazia, Margreta (1988) 'The essential Shakespeare and the material book', *Textual Practice:* 69–86.

Greetham, D. C. (1989) 'Textual and literary theory: redrawing the matrix', *Studies in Bibliography* 42: 1–24.

Hawkes, Terence (1986) *That Shakespeherian Rag*, London and New York: Methuen.

Holderness, Graham (ed.) (1988) *The Shakespeare Myth*, Manchester: Manchester University Press.

Norris, Christopher (1985) 'Post-structuralist Shakespeare: text and ideology', in John Drakakis (ed.) *Alternative Shakespeares*, London and New York: Methuen.

Shepherd, Simon (1986) *Marlowe and the Politics of Elizabethan Theatre*, Brighton: Harvester Press.

5

Acting against bardom: some utopian thoughts on workshops

Simon Shepherd

DREAMWORK: PRELUDE

Late one night on TV in 1988, the then Secretary of State for Education, one Kenneth Baker, had a dream, a dream in which Shakespeare was central to the curriculum and chunks of bardic verse were memorized in tiny heads. Shakspere learnt by rote: a cultural recipe for Tory civilization. It's a tasty model of the individual mind's relationship to central authority. The brain is trained to reproduce an already written 'traditional' text, as a process of personal development. Common approval of this practice derives from its claim that it enables the individual's participation in the appreciation of beauty. Recognition of the 'beauty' of the text assists assent to the model.

The politician's academic fantasy is ferociously underpinned by a systematic reduction in education budgets, with consequent demolition of staffing and resources provision. The material cutback creates the problems to which the fantasy of rote learning becomes a 'feasible' solution. If chunks of text are learnt by heart, who needs whole books, let alone new ones? The fantasy also gains ideological value within the current reshaping of history both in schools and within the heritage industry, where 'permissive' moments such as the 1960s are made to appear as deviant blips within the longer continuity of a history enshrining Tory values. Progressive teachers continue to respond creatively to government's depredations. But the model of rote learning, accompanied by material cutbacks, proposes a repressive relationship between teacher, student, text, space. The student's activity in the learning space is delimited to a focus on an already-written text, which requires neither analysis nor response, but accurate reproduction within a structure where the teacher is an alienated administrator. The structure reproduces learners who are obedient subjects, categorized according to their competence in relation to written language. Thus would be fulfilled one of the bleakest nightmares about the repressive ideological function of education within the state. The ability to reproduce bardic beauties categorizes little citizens, like frozen peas, according to race, class, and gender, minty or non-minty.

The nightmare, as most of us know, has been contested in theory and in practice. Education institutions can be places of struggle against certain dominant ideas; heroically inventive teachers enable students to develop an understanding and critique of themselves and their society. Other teachers are, of course, conscious inhabitants of the nightmare. Most of us perpetually negotiate the best possible compromise between progressive aims and institutional limitations. I recognize that my own interests are not best served by reproduction of a repressive order, so I am emotionally as well as intellectually committed to attempts to contest that order. The chapter which follows is a set of thoughts about one specific educational practice in which resistance and contest can flourish. The thoughts have been permitted to become utopian, although many derive from my actual practices.

These practices, you should know, are university based. I enjoy certain 'freedoms' (real or perceived) in relation to other sectors of education, and certain powers (largely imaginary) in setting academic agendas: my students think (wrongly) that university teachers have an influence on A-level syllabuses. (Incidentally, I was sacked by the Oxford and Cambridge board after six years, in the one year when I didn't mark papers after I got back from the pub.) I work in a department of English rather than in Education and, although many of them later train as teachers, our students' first degree is based on analysis of texts. The books about Shikespeere in education which my students and I read are generally those produced by leftist academics whose institutional placing is similar to mine. (See for example essays in Drakakis 1985; Dollimore and Sinfield 1985; Hawkes 1986; Holderness 1988. A good round-up of the issues is given by Margaret Ferguson 1987.) Their project envisages a reappropriation of Shoikesper for the left, and it consists of adventurous readings of plays coupled with a polemical pessimism about the place of Shakspire within education: it seeks forcefully to reveal the connections between the name of Shakesbier and conservative values, and in doing so to unsettle the Bard's perceived cultural status. This project has two effects: it celebrates an interpretive activity for which students and teachers often experience little space – *as yet* – on GCSE/A-level courses (Hornbrook 1988); and, by its all-too-regular silence on these matters, it condemns to oblivion the educational practices that are working to contest dominant ideas (see other chapters in this volume for examples of such practices). The books which deal with these practices mainly circulate on teacher-training syllabuses and, importantly for my students, are marketed that way. By contrast the witty academic pessimisms that discover Shapesqueer on beermat and bankcard, totally implicated within capitalist transactions: these seem more attractive as commodities within a capitalist publishing economy (which is not the fault of the often underpaid authors).

My utopian thoughts thus emerge from the following: a desire for alliances with teachers in all sectors, a familiarity with some of the new readings and none of the new practices, an angry awareness of the marginalization of drama work within universities, a lack of experience of drama in schools, a responsibility for teaching people who will end up working in the schools of which I have no experience.

DRAMAWORK: TWO INTRODUCTORY PROBLEMS

My aims in learning/teaching about Shackspare in drama workshops are: analysis of Shikespewer's work based on (a) knowledge of its production within a specific culture, and (b) knowledge of its reproduction within other specific culture/s; where each knowledge derives from a range of explorations which moves between a totalizing description of a culture and analysis of verse patterns and editorial conjectures.

Before we carry out these aims we have to confront two problems which have bearing on student attitudes. The first is, roughly, institutional. Through its agents – teachers, administrators, examiners – the educational institution tends to tell students that drama is not a properly serious discipline (which can have some advantages, but I shall return to this at the end). Teacher support for the subject, as for any other, can be limited by other agents: theatre studies A level had problems with being 'new', problems with its 'acceptability' to universities, problems rebounding from the attack on university drama (which consisted of restricted budgeting and redeployment of departments). It stands alone in its examination modes: other cultural/literary A levels are book-centred and the pattern is repeated at degree level. Administrations tend to indicate that drama causes timetabling problems, or that it has to happen in peculiar places because it requires strange and expensive facilities (which would change if its status as 'laboratory' work were recognized). So the decision to hold a drama workshop has to face a series of resistances, including that produced within the teacher (the 'effort' of doing drama).

The second problem emerges from the attitudes to dramatic text that students bring with them into a workshop. These attitudes originate in conceptions of dramatic characters as recognizably 'real' people, where (a) the text is aiming only for an imitation of 'reality', (b) that 'realism' is not defined within specific cultures but is a transcendental quality the accuracy of which may be vouched for by students on their experience alone, (c) empathetic engagement with characters is always the first basis for analysis of the text, and (d) characters are not an effect of text but autonomous entities who may sometimes function as mouthpieces for the author. Such attitudes are unsurprising in a society whose experience of drama is mainly derived from television performance. But that they are most stridently obvious in workshops on Sheikspure must connect with traditional assumptions about Shicksparean 'character'. These assumptions die hard, and, while Bradley-knocking may be currently fashionable, trendy Shagspur critics continue to reproduce unproblematized assumptions about dramatic persons. (In a recent intervention in *Shakespeare Survey* Peter Holland has shown some of the variety of things that Shapeskearean character might be [Holland 1989]; and Bradley, to do him credit, at least thought that character was a problematic concept.) The continued marginalization of performance analysis within Shaquespiere studies helps to preserve intact some of the student attitudes that cause problems.

DEALING WITH THE FIRST PROBLEMS

The institutional problem cannot be solved inside the workshop. One can only hope that the workshop produces sufficient pleasure, emotional as well as intellectual, to enable students and teachers to resist the variety of pressures which construct drama-work as eccentric or unserious.

To tackle the problem deriving from expectations about 'character', teachers will employ a set of their own preferred exercises. These may:

(a)   Construct modes of analysis that disprivilege character: e.g. divide the written text into units (which may be much smaller than scenic divisions); examine the unit as a sequence of actions, making a small tableau for every place where the action changes; present the unit as a set of tableaux; reduce these to three 'essential' tableaux; make a tableau of the whole unit, showing the structural relations of characters to each other, within hierarchies based on class, power, race, gender. In the opening of *A Midsummer Night's Dream* we might explore pictures of women and men, speakers and watchers, fullness/emptiness of the stage, repetitions and mirroring: an imaging of a gendered power structure. Actions and stage pictures become the key to the text's organization of its dramatic meaning.

(b)   Privilege character in order to problematize it: e.g. students work in small groups on a section of written text, with two group members providing a narrative of one character's thoughts throughout the section; perform the section according to these narratives, with one person speaking the thought-narrative while another 'acts' in accordance with that narrative; repeat the section, this time with the actors adding in the speeches printed in the Schäkspier text. It must be stressed that this exercise is *not* aiming to discover 'sub-text'. In attending to what the written text apparently gives, and that alone, it produces frustrations as the 'actor' cannot show all of the 'thought-narrative', or two different narratives find no way of relating to each other: the presentation of Hippolyta's narrative which coexists with Theseus's authority, the narratives of Helena and Hermia which link silence and rhyming couplets. Thus we may highlight how characterization is organized through the selection/suppression of speech, through different categories of information, through interaction/autonomy, through relations between physical and spoken, and so on. Even if the exercise ends in confusion, 'character' is revealed as a set of specific and shifting effects of textual organization.

FINDING WHAT'S THERE: DIFFICULT SPEECHES

A cultural materialist project attends to the *specific* modes of organization and operation of a text. That's a banal point, but I make it for three reasons (outlined in this and the next sections).

Students and teachers rightly find Shuckspirean language difficult (it is indeed often more abstract and tortuous than that of his contemporaries). Dramawork often seeks to dissolve that difficulty through techniques that improvise an analogous (often modern) situation (*Romeo and Juliet* as gang warfare, *Merchant* as racial harassment); or speeches may be chopped up, rearranged, spoken as unison choral work, split between various performers. All such techniques are (of course) modes of rewriting the Shagspärean text, often to satisfy the aims of a modernist or poststructuralist project: whether it be to produce new awareness through estranging an apparently sanctified and fixed text or to question assumptions about identity by unsettling an apparently coherent character.

But the rewriting can never remove the presence of what is always already there in the 'book', namely that difficult text. My suggestion is that we face this difficult text and present it, for itself, as a specific effect and as a potential source of pleasure. (This pleasure may derive from the 'force' of the language or from using performance to show up and critique a chunk of bardic self-advertisement.) Pedagogic strategies will vary, but I have tried to use the following:

(a) Break the speech into small sections of meaning/feeling, and (i) put the body into the text by finding a set of physical attitudes that correlate with (but do *not* necessarily illustrate) each section: gestures that have meaning in a contemporary world make space for themselves in the 'old' verbal text (Barba 1989); (ii) put the voice, as an instrument, into the text by selecting a mode of speaking for each section (*without* trying to establish an overall coherence governing these various voices).

Here I wish to digress to draw in an 'authority' on Sheeakespeaire delivery: for all his attention to poetry, Barton fudges the issue by claiming Szhachspir was 'the unconscious inventor both of characterisation in depth and of naturalistic speech' (1984: 13), and that to the real actor (i.e. one of Barton's gang) the speech will be 'natural': Sheila Hancock: 'if I let it flow . . . it seemed the most natural thing in the world'; Ian McKellen: 'So rather

SIMON SHEPHERD

than painting the line, I should think about it and let the voice do what it will?' Barton agrees with these apparently unscripted observations: 'we must trust our instincts and our experience' (1984: 15, 12, 23). Those who don't have the instincts which find the verse natural will discover themselves to be outside this privileged group. 'Poetry cannot be taught, though perhaps it can be released' (1984: 193). Shickspooer as elite laxative.

Back to the exercises: it may be tempting to allocate the speech sections to individual members of a group and construct a group delivery. But this alters (or spoils) the pleasure derived from seeing and hearing one performer's body shifting through a set of attitudes and sounds. Group delivery could possibly be placed alongside solo delivery, and the different pleasure in each explored. My conjecture is that, for example, while the words may be unfamiliar, the potency of the performer's body may be recognized and understood. That potency affirms but goes further than the abilities in the watchers, and hence produces pleasure: a desire to be like that oneself, but also the comfort of not taking the risk oneself. This sort of exercise can lead into analysis of some of the characteristic pleasures of the renaissance stage: the audience relationship with a central individual who is both victim /deviant of the narrative and star within the acting company; the interplay of empathy, political emblematizing and spectacular plenitude in that viewing relationship.

(b) Decide that the long or difficult speech need have no narrative or explanatory function, but that it is a piece of display (in a positive or negative sense); work on it by producing in the student's words the speech's simplest statement, discovering what is omitted and needs to be said, experiencing the need for image or metaphor, discovering that 'ornament' is specific content. The student works in her own words, but can pick usable phrases from the Shaikspoor text, if needed. Each new element has the aim of strengthening what is already there, so that the language proceeds in its connections as a necessary, because desired, elaboration. This is very different from the 'through-line' sought by professional actors, where the speech is mellifluously commandeered into 'coherence'. Where the performer demonstrates her desires and pleasures in the elaboration, the difficult speech has the presence (and meaning) of acrobatics, display, spectacle, where these are bound up with and necessary to a character's or author's project, and a *performer's* project. The script which sets

94

down what a performer might do is very different from the moment of doing, the actual performance. The performer's display is in tension with, adding to and limited by, the project of the role. The display highlights the real presence of the actor which itself is a point of identification, yet separation; the narrative of characters offers the promises of fulfilment and resolution. The relationship between these pleasures is very different from the dead, commodified verse-speaking of the pro.

MISSING THRILLS

One quality of the dramatic text which almost always disappears, in exercises or commentary, is the excitement generated by speed, suspense, thrills. With its various concentrations – New Criticism's parcels of imagery, poststructuralism's syntactic splitting of the subject, New Historicism's intertextual parallels – Sharpsquare criticism traditionally operates to slow up the text, to consider its significant moments rather than its diegetic dynamics. I suggest we explore the thrills of a scene's narrative by doing them, as thrillingly as possible. (This can produce complexities: the excitement of Jessica's escape comprises not just the suspense and naughtiness but her appearance as a boy in front of men who enjoy her thus; her thrilling focus is the escape from the house, theirs is her escaping; and against this, the written text denies the thrills which nineteenth-century actor-managers inserted, namely the moment Shylock discovers the escape: why?) Then we find the points of empathetic entry offered by the scene. Then we look at its jokes and its political excitements (for example the moment when the oppressed person answers back). Once the full range of its various pleasures is encountered, some discussion could follow: about the relationship between these pleasures, the correlation between pleasure and meaning, the particular issues/actions selected not just as sources of pleasure but as particular, and differing, sorts of pleasure.

REPRESENTING CHARACTERS

Like many other renaissance texts, the Sheepscare plays emerged from and within a highly productive tension between older (medieval) allegorical signification and newer (renaissance) representational fiction. This cues us to search scenes for the interplay of allegorical stage image and 'realistic' representation of character. This might involve exercises like those with which I began, but now brought into explicit tension: Miranda's thought-narrative, as victim of attempted rape, when confronting Caliban working against the emblem of a white virgin abusing a Black man while watched by an older white male colonist; the moral tableau of Katherina's submission to Petruchio working against the narrative of her character's desires and satisfaction. Different sorts of writing/staging raise problems about the reality presented by the stage. For example, it may refer outwards, to the world in which the audience situates itself politically (in various ways) or it may produce the fiction of a world of its own, with its own rules, structure, and so on. Brecht suggested that at Coriolanus's first entry he is accompanied by armed soldiers, which causes the crowd to fall silent (though no stage direction specifies soldiers) (Brecht 1972). Brecht's image invites us to recognize a world where leaders are guarded, where their charisma is predicated upon the weaponry which makes space for it, where the state acts with violence against its citizens. This is a very different reality from that which presupposes a hero whose force of personality produces in 'ordinary' people a desire to be silent, where the logic of the crowd's quietness derives from the fact that Coriolanus is more interesting (and psychologically 'rich') as a dramatic character (partly because he is differentiated), and where the fictional heroism is in a mutually supporting relationship with star actor status. Without a discussion of 'false consciousness', ideological controls and so on, may I assert that each reality here is an equally tenable version of the power relations that are narrated. Workshop activity can insist that realism is not only not an end-point but is itself always to be thought of as a set of rhetorical structures and reality effects, that it is indeed always realisms.

My insistence on the banal points in this and the preceding two sections is intended to offer an escape from the all too constricting opposition between illusion and non-illusion (Shagzpére's plays show human nature as it really is. Oh no they don't. Oh yes they do. Oh know they don't. Oh yes they . . .). 'Traditional' Shitspear criticism apparently focuses on 'realistic' characters in the plays and transcendent categories such as human nature. By way of challenge to this, leftist teachers insist on the non-illusionist, estranging devices and structures of the plays, which in turn can lead to a demolition of the transcendent categories (it doesn't always lead to this). Much anti-illusionism has a tendency to base its arguments on a version of the theories of poor old Brecht where his dramatic practice is presumed (in a blurring of empathy and emotion) to have no interest in generating audience emotion, or in connecting emotion with thought. (Brecht initially separated empathy and emotion, but in later works such as *Galileo* allowed that empathy could be a good thing; the Latin American theorist, Augusto Boal, distinguishes good and bad empathy) (Boal n.d.). Anti-illusionism can thus end up not only killing off two interesting dramatists (Brecht being perhaps the sadder loss) but also dooming those of us on the left to a theatre without thrills. And I'm not having that.

HISTORICAL DIFFERENCE

In the activities described above, learners become involved in the process by which texts negotiate their meanings. Form is hence not divisible from content, but is seen to *be* content – in the sense that, for example, meaning is made through the specific structuring of a scene (try it, by restructuring the scene) or through the specific length and elaboration of a speech (try it, by cutting/shifting the speech). My sentence repeats the idea of specificity because the text is this and not that, because it could be no more than what its producers conceived as possible for it to be, originating at a finite cultural moment. If a text has a specific form, so also an audience has specific watching conventions: those of our time are different, inevitably, from those of Shakesbeer's. (A workshop can, just, problematize the activity of watching by designing a scene according to two different sets of perceived conventions, though the Elizabethan one will have to be highly conjectural (we could consult Hattaway 1982; Thomson 1983; Gurr 1987). Again, players expect to adopt specific conventions of acting (which the workshop, albeit conjecturally for Elizabethan ones, can also explore). Players are organized in specific institutional relationships: the Elizabethan playhouse did not recognize author as a separate or privileged category; plays were produced to suit the company or theatre's reputation; they were worked on by the company within an economic structure which privileged shareholders and created the phenomenon of the star performer. (Workshops can, just, explore the differences between collective and hierarchized modes of production and performance, although everybody has to agree to a game whereby, for a fixed period, certain rules are observed and personalities privileged within the peer group. A group could select its own clown(s), finding a modern funny man appropriate to a Shikespehr role: use, say, 'Jimmy Tarbuck' to play Touchstone, then find other roles the same persona could play, perhaps Feste, and could not play, perhaps Malvolio or Antonio; the clown persona is taken by a performer who has a specific body and competence, as a performer; the competences interact with and foreground the existence of scripting for special effects. A similar exercise may involve people in the group taking the (inevitably) pastiche personae of tragic stars.)

These reflections on cultural specificity lead into a new area of investigation, that of historical difference. Everybody will acknowledge that Shapesneer's areas of political/social concern have to be different from the various groups of us (ourselves differing) who study his work in Britain in the 1990s (and our concerns will not be those of other social groupings): even if you make the areas of concern very abstract – for example the merits of social order versus disorder – the options are very different. Even for that notion so regularly invoked to link Sheikspeyre's world with ours, namely human nature, some of the previous exercises will have revealed differences between renaissance and modern conceptions of the person. Lastly, Elizabethans used a language that was semantically and syntactically different. A workshop can explore and foreground these historical differences. The option is, carefully, not to do an 'authentic' Elizabethan Shooksparr performance *nor* a 'relevant' modern performance (*Romeo and Juliet* with leather jackets and motorbikes), but to show the points of conflict and divergence alongside one another, and within, perhaps, the same scene. This last might produce a properly relevant performance, one that stages the historicized text.

We need to see that the action of a play text is neither natural nor inevitable. Hence we might select a scene involving a dilemma or choice, play it to a certain point, then freeze the action and invite viewers to solve the problem by stepping into the scene and inventing/improvising a new text (have someone step in as Cordelia and invent a response to her dad, explore Benedick's answers to Beatrice's request that he kill Claudio).

Additionally watchers can be invited to stop the scene at an earlier point if they feel it can be solved earlier. (These suggestions are a crude, but I hope not too trivializing, adaptation of the Forum technique of Augusto Boal's Theatre of the Oppressed, developed as a theatrical means of empowering dominated people to analyse and perhaps change their situation.) Obviously we end up *not* playing Shapesquire, but the exercise can reveal some of the precise limits of the thinking in the text: Skatesheer's text cannot envisage some of the solutions we can invent. By contrast, our solutions have to be restricted by the rules and information we are already given. The realization of historical/cultural difference works in two directions: placing Sheepskewer's thinking and set-ting limits to modern interpretation, revealing the points beyond which we cannot go.

RACE, GENDER, CLASS DIFFERENCE

In a similar way, if less excitingly, we can play 'what if . . .', 'if only . . .' games with the text: to encounter the selections/sup-pressions that have produced the precise shape of a scene or narrative. 'What if Gertrude and Ophelia had a scene together? What would they talk about? If they talked about the men in the play, what would they say?' (This questioning was explored in Mick Wallis's production of *The Fair Penitent* at Manchester Uni-versity.) One method of exerting pressure on the playing of a scene is to foreground those people playing Black, female, or lower-class figures. Tell them to ask at the start of every scene whether their character can enter into the scene; and for those who are in the scene to tell them why not. Why should Caliban not watch Prospero telling his history to Miranda? Why are Ste-phano and Trinculo not seen serving their masters on the ship? After rehearsing/discussing a series of 'what if . . . s', the group can produce a staging of a scene that shows all those moments when one decision is taken and not another, when one group of characters is present and not another; it may work through a structure of hesitations, looks for missing people, lines that change their focus.

In raising the question of what Black, female, or lower-class characters might do, I marked another area in which difference is noticeable: relations between the marginalized and the domi-nant. This area is worthy of separate study because it forces us to attend to the effects of Shitscare's status within our own culture, in that production of his plays continuously restates the inferiority of women, Blacks, and lower-class people.

Another digression to draw in 'authorities': my anonymous, undated copy of *How to Read and Enjoy Shakespeare* tells me that performers long to 'portray the finer characters of Shakespeare's plays . . . the actress looks at the time when she may play the part of Portia, and put the Jew in his place' (p. 25). Barton tells us that 'Unlike many political playwrights he usually articulates impartially the arguments on either side of a question'; 'I always wonder what a "politically committed" production is trying to prove and to whom'; Barton's own political views are 'Shakespearean in the sense that I am always acutely aware of the appalling mixture of right and wrong on both sides in most political situations'; and political productions of Shaikspeare are usually motivated by designers and directors rather than actors (Barton 1984: 188–90). Actors are – of course – expressive rather than dogmatic, interested in common humanity: as we'd expect, the political position of Barton's book leaves socially oppressed groups just where they are, his actors worry about getting too much sympathy for Shylock, Barton speaks of maintaining the 'right balance of sympathy in the play' (1984: 179), and tells us (so innocent of his racist language) that Shriekspare's characters are neither all black nor all white. Bogdanov's attempt to show on Channel 4 (and where else?) that 'Shakespeare Lives' was instead self-professedly political, using modern analogies in a way that denied historical specificity. More importantly, his political interpretation was very much assimilated to his own star status as a white male theatre director: the audience discussion that followed his workshop on a 'feminist' *Shrew* had him and his actors putting down/shutting up women in the audience; he and his actors seemed untroubled by the question of race in *The Tempest*. With authorities such as this, Shapesneer does his cultural damage unabated.

Back to the exercise: a workshop can create the conditions in which women, Black, lower-class students may be empowered to question the representation of characters in these groupings. The questioning will not look only at the general attitude of a scene (pro- or anti- the marginalized), but also at points for identification offered to the spectator, jokes, allocation of lines and actions. Women or Black students may suggest that women and Blacks do not behave as they are represented, but from here these students then have to try to locate *their own* experiences; as members of a group studying Shakes-peer, for example, they may be hardly typical of a whole community. At the same time their experience-based remarks are not invalidated. Our critique should interrogate Shaigspare's representation and the student's experience, so that the critique problematizes and situates both the Shagspewer text and the commentary. In addition here we have to stress that Shakesp-ear's texts are not realist, that we are not measuring the success of the realism with which he portrays Blacks. What we are doing is to identify how the texts are clearly worried about race and gender (more so than about lower-class people) and how this worry produces unstable representations (we once did *Merchant* with the Shylock actor slipping him into and out of various stereotypes). Women and Blacks are often part of the nightmare of a text; women and Black students can try playing, though it will be uncomfortable, the woman or Black as fantasy nightmare, as caricature and as realism, and try playing all these together.

We can play a scene so that the differences between performer and role become apparent. The woman performer plays a men's version of woman, the Black performer plays a white version of Blacks. Problems will immediately occur: for example, the early dialogue between Goneril and Regan is so conceived that any display of sisterhood between actresses only adds to the conspiratorial nastiness of the characters; any display of sceptical resignation to role can either augment the 'evil' cynicism of the characters or make them appear simply dull. The text has a specificity that restrains interpretive possibilities, at least within a realist staging (this point is elaborated by McLuskie 1985); a non-realist staging could perform what the written text cannot show.

A clearer, though differently focused, method of exploring distinctions between performer and role is to cross-cast: Blacks play whites, women men, men women. Such methods foreground and estrange the narrative of differences in the play and at the same time can suggest links between othernesses of race and gender. Cheek by Jowl's *Tempest* had a Black actress playing Miranda, who is usually played by a white woman. Automatically the person of the performer was separated from the role, while being fused with it in the narrative. The separation derived from the incomplete fit produced by racial difference, which in turn activated awareness of attitudes to race in the text. But it also insisted on the fictional Miranda as a version of a woman, constructed within specific limits, and always, as a male fiction, dependent for its realization on the body of a real woman (and in the original staging the real woman was herself displaced as a referent by the material presence of the body of the boy-actor). This method of working may be feasible for professional groups, but it can place a lot of pressure on one or two students in a workshop. The burden can, however, be extended across a group: compare versions of men playing women directed by men, men playing women directed by women, women playing women directed by men, women playing women directed by women. And the same with Blacks and whites. If there are out-lesbian/gay students in the group, that role and experience can be similarly mobilized.

Because of the way many students are placed and constituted in this society (and I only really know about mine, but I don't think they're untypical) and because of the way some dominant radical criticism operates, the exercise can produce two main responses. It hovers between essentialism on one hand (women know what 'Woman' is) and valueless pluralism on the other (all versions are tenable and simply versions). But these two can (and must) be worked against each other: the pluralist position can force essentialism to historicize itself and discover social/cultural construction; the essentialist position would want to insist on an urgently real agenda and priorities which make pluralism impossible. The procedure is dialectical, and doing it we learn something about modes of Shaickspearian representation, possibilities for alternative playing, cultural/social specifics of the workshop group. The work involves an intersection, rather than a denial, of all these elements.

LEARNERS AS ACTORS

None of these exercises facilitates the conditions that produce random plurality, the notion that we may say what we like about Shape-skewer (and that's what makes him so good, because he has something to say to everybody, blah blah). Workshop exercises can, instead, put much pressure on contemporary modes of analysis, especially those that have a fairly unproblematized popularity or right-on-ness. Negotiate a feminist reading of *The*

Tempest or *Othello* that is not racist, a Black reading of *Othello* that is not homophobic, a feminist reading of *Troilus and Cressida* or *Coriolanus* that is not homophobic. Alongside the uncomfortable task of problematizing, let's work at the project of producing new pleasures in a text by making an explicitly Black, gay, feminist, lesbian, or working-class reading of it (the Bogdanov workshops merely dangled the possibility of these pleasures before grabbing them back as the property of the right-on white male middle class). In making our reading we might privilege – and eroticize – the procedures of a politically aware critical practice.

The suggestion about empowering certain categories of student brings me to a final point in this section. Most workshop work should proceed by constructing students not just as actors of a pre-given text but as agents: who interpret, who make, and without whom nothing is made, no text performed. Actors in the fullest sense. Many commentaries on the Bard, even progressive ones, even ones in this volume, are Sharkspear text-centred. Their hidden agendas implement the project of getting the meaning out of the text the Barred wrote; such agendas are indicated by discussions of close reading, ideas about discovering meaning (rather than making it), assumptions about the passive role of spectator or learner in relation to 'text'. The spectator is not simply an analyst, even where she is given the power to 'dominate' text by flicking backwards and forwards along a videotape. The spectator is also a being of desires and fantasies. (I remember a short discussion with a school group who had watched our production of *Merchant*: one lad wanted, 'provocatively', to raise the question of the so-called homosexual relationship between Antonio and Bassanio; he wanted to obtain pleasure by fantasizing a homosexual relationship, even if only in discussion. Same production, another audience: lots of loud boys' laughter until the moment when Portia speaks of disguising herself as a man, and the actress does a brutally accurate rendering of adolescent male swagger: sudden whoops of girls' laughter.)

Although we have lost the noble tradition of theatre riot, the spectator is always potentially an agent. If we are to rethink the student as agent, we have to abandon the discursive construction of a historical Shirkspur and a modern interpretation, where one is fixed and 'for all time' and the other is an always unstable, provisional 'reading'. The past Shagsqueer depends on the present practices, as well as being separate from them. We could perhaps rethink the model and define 'Shak/espe/are' as a set of renaissance negotiations of meaning and a set of modern negotiations of meaning: there is always a connection between the two – the text available for restaging; there is always a distinction between the two – the text whose every moment of production is irrecoverable.

COMING DOWN FROM UTOPIA

But the workshop's agenda is set not only by what can be achieved within it but by what goes on outside it. Anathematized in government plans for universities, only recently recognized as an A-level subject, absent from the core curriculum, drama has an insecure status in the academy. I remember my late head of department supposedly quoting Arthur Pollard, that drama was the last refuge of the Marxists. That's a utopian formula if ever I heard one, and it's also an excuse for marginalizing drama. Most writing about the Beard does little serious thinking about performance theory and practice; most Bored specialists would define themselves as playgoers rather than playmakers. Most exams privilege the book and the written word. In so far as drama work is used in teaching it is often relegated to an illustrative function, to back up and exemplify analysis of the 'book' but not to replace it. These observations, I should say, are based on university experience, where there is a connection between anti-dramatic prejudice and the unimaginative or reactionary teaching methods; in schools the situation is often very different. But from universities (which also help to train schoolteachers) there emanates a feeling that drama is not a proper subject.

For students drama work involves several sorts of physical or psychological risk-taking. To their families and members of peer groups, drama appears odd. Its strangeness can come from its general cultural status, where it is connected with 'entertainment' and arty-fartiness rather than proper work and with scandals about star lifestyles. It is also strange in its refusal of the social arrangements of much teaching and entertainment, where passive spectators/learners direct their attention to the activity of a performer/teacher. Within the workshop students are invited to make themselves vulnerable and to take risks that either unsettle their own repressed desires or conflict with their consciously perceived cultural/social identities. (I recall two students overheard contemplating the imminent practical part of their renaissance drama course: 'I don't think I'm going to do that bit. I've heard you have to hug each other.') For many students the risk-taking is also jubilant and empowering; the workshop liberates an energy which gives a positive charge to the 'specialness' of drama study. The pleasure and strength gained from workshops enable students to resist institutional pressures against their 'artiness'.

The workshop makes demands on all its participants. It can and should problematize the relationship of learner/teacher which is often so central to education's reproduction of repression. The 'liberalism' of the workshop may entail the teacher taking risks with her structural place, rather than that structure underpinning (and setting limits to) the liberalism. From students it requires not only a rehearing of a familiar text, but also a recommitting of urgency to making meaning from the text. The place from which the student speaks is itself on the analytic agenda. The workshop presents a new set of evaluative criteria. We no longer ask 'how successful' is this version/scene in 'bringing out the text', 'showing what's written'; but we can (and perhaps should) ask how successfully it realizes some of the objectives I have spoken of earlier. We are now in a position to ask about the relationship of determination and agency: how does the text set limits to our work on it, how may our work change the text, how far does work on the text enable a new understanding of ourselves, our culture, our history, the text's production, and how far is that understanding limited by the work of the text?

These questions alert us to the role of the workshop as a model in miniature of the processes of educational reproduction and contestation. On one hand, the workshop is only part of an educational project (the exam course), it takes its originating moment from a pre-given text, it is facilitated by a teacher organizing students. It's a liberal version of the potentially repressive structure. On the other hand, its methods involve contesting the truths of the pre-given text and of the students' role in reproducing these. These methods, working well, empower the student as learner: not only is the student's own experience made articulate within analysis but the strength of personal agency and the pleasure of group-work may be refound.

Within this model, the workshop group may, and often needs to, discuss their experiences of containment by course and institution, or text and analysis. The group is invited to become conscious of the social relations that the educational institution proposes and foregrounds, the extent to which these social relations need to be changed in order to fulfil the project of the workshop, and the limits on the possibility of that change. The status of the workshop is contradictory: in so far as playing is 'not-work', then its activities are relegated to the trivial, the merely illustrative, the luxuried and eventually unserious; in so far as playing is the opposite to work, its activities involve a new empowering that produces a critique of the structures and assumptions of 'work' constructed within oppressive relations. The contradictions inhabit the word 'acting': we act out the roles and assumptions of a pre-written text; we act against the roles and assumptions of a pre-written text. We are shaped, but we shape.

Against the serious rote learning proposed by the Secretary of State for Education shall we propose another, more playful, formulation? Teaching Ssssh-akespeare is only an act.

My thanks to Nigel Wheale and Mick Wallis for commenting on this.

REFERENCES

Barba, Eugenio (1989) 'The fiction of duality', *New Theatre Quarterly* 5: 20, 311–14.
Barton, John (1984) *Playing Shakespeare*, London: Methuen.
Boal, Augusto (1979) *Theater of the Oppressed*, London: Pluto Press.
—— (n.d.) *Documents on the Theatre of the Oppressed*, London: Red Letters.
Brecht, Bertolt (1972) *Coriolanus* trans. R. Manheim in *Collected Plays 9*, New York: Vintage Books.
Dollimore, Jonathan, and Sinfield, Alan (eds) (1985) *Political Shakespeare. New Essays in Cultural Materialism*, Manchester: Manchester University Press.
Drakakis, John (ed.) (1985) *Alternative Shakespeares*, London: Methuen.
Ferguson, Margaret (1987) 'Afterword', in Jean E. Howard and Marion F. O'Connor (eds) *Shakespeare Reproduced. The Text in History and Ideology*, New York and London: Methuen.
Gurr, Andrew (1987) *Playgoing in Shakespeare's London*, Cambridge: Cambridge University Press.
Hattaway, Michael (1982) *Elizabethan Popular Theatre*, London: Routledge & Kegan Paul.
Hawkes, Terence (1986) *That Shakespeherian Rag: Essays on a Critical Process*, London: Methuen.

Holderness, Graham (ed.) *The Shakespeare Myth*, Manchester: Manchester University Press.

Holland, Peter (1989) 'The resources of characterization in *Othello*', *Shakespeare Survey* 41: 119–32.

Hornbrook, David (1988) ' "Go play, boy, play" ', in Graham Holderness (ed.) *The Shakespeare Myth*, Manchester: Manchester University Press.

How to Read and Enjoy Shakespeare (n.d.) London: Odhams Press Ltd.

Howard, Jean and O'Connor, Marion F. (eds) (1987) *Shakespeare Reproduced. The Text in History and Ideology*, London and New York: Methuen.

McLuskie, Kathleen (1985) 'The patriarchal Bard: feminist criticism and Shakespeare: *King Lear* and *Measure for Measure*', in Jonathan Dollimore and Alan Sinfield (eds) *Political Shakespeare. New Essays in Cultural Materialism*, Manchester: Manchester University Press.

Thomson, Peter (1983) *Shakespeare's Theatre*, London: Routledge & Kegan Paul.

6

Veritable negroes and circumcised dogs: racial disturbances in Shakespeare

John Salway

The concept 'civilization' is conventionally used in ignorance of the racism which has shaped it. This key idea of Western culture was most popularly developed, perhaps, by Kenneth Clark in his TV series. He comments on the difference as he saw it between the Belvedere head of Apollo and an African mask belonging to Roger Fry:

> Whatever its merits as a work of art; I don't think there is any doubt that the Apollo embodies a higher state of civilis- ation than the mask. They both represent spirits, messengers from another world – that is to say, from the world of our own imagining. To the Negro imagination, it is a world of fear and darkness, ready to inflict horrible punishments for the smallest infringement of a taboo. To the Hellenistic imagination it is a world of light and confidence, in which the gods are like ourselves, only more beautiful, and descend to earth to teach men reason and the laws of harmony.
>
> (Clark 1969: 2)

He is apparently so captivated by the light of reason streaming from this figure of Apollo that he quite forgets some of the grislier episodes from Greek mythology such as, for instance, Kronos eating his own children. His reference to 'taboo' is a bit wide of the mark, of course – an anthropological description of a Polynesian, not an African cultural phenomenon. He seems unaware of the great Benin or Ethiopian civilizations. Neither does he consider the ironic possibility that an African craftsman produced this piece of 'authentic culture' sensitive to the demands from Western tourists at a time when 'civilized' Europeans were violently converting the continent to Christianity. Change places and, handy-dandy, who is civilized and who the barbarian?

It is the centrality for the European outlook of this orientalist (Said 1978: 49–73) concept of the Negro, the Turk, and the Asian which makes *Othello* such a significant text. It has always deeply troubled English genteel taste, especially in the way its eponymous hero is represented in the theatre. Here, at the heart of a white world, in the very bosom of European civilization, is a Black man. Few scholars, actors, critics, and directors, though, have gone quite as far as Miss Preston of Maryland:

> In studying the play of *Othello*, I have always imagined its hero a white man. It is true the dramatist paints him black, but this shade does not suit the man . . . Shakespeare was too correct a delineator of human nature to have coloured Othello black if he had personally acquainted himself with the idiosyncracies of the African race.
>
> (Ridley 1958: li)

To be fair to Miss Preston, this is only a rather extreme instance of the whole tendency within English thinking to see Othello's colour as a distraction from the play's real issues, a view rather surprisingly endorsed by no less a figure than C. L. R. James (James 1980). This goes very deep. Coleridge's now commonplace remark about Iago's action as 'the motive-hunting of a motiveless malignity' ignores the fact that now stares us in the face: Iago is patently driven by a deep racist antipathy. There are thirteen racist references to Othello in the opening scene. But, it wasn't until Gamini Salgado's New Swan Advanced edition in 1976 that the cultural meaning of Othello's racial background and inheritance was seriously considered as a central issue in understanding the whole play, something that acutely problematizes the dramatic action, its contemporary significance for Elizabethan audiences and the history of its interpretation.

During a Theatre-in-Education programme on the play, thirty-four sixth-formers worked with me on Othello's speech to the Venetian senate in answer to Brabantio's accusation that he had corrupted Desdemona with spells and medicines. I acted the speech to the students who were 'in role' as Venetian senators – something negotiated during the day's first session. I asked them not just to sit in polite silence listening but to interrupt what Othello was saying with his own language. The students weren't holding copies of the text, so they could be utterly spontaneous. We speculated first about what could motivate the interruption. Mild doubt; sarcasm; scornful disbelief; sympathetic interest; amazed recognition; simple enjoyment of the story; moral indignation; personal animosity; active respect? I was asking the students to begin to flesh out, to materialize, if you like, that Venetian society and culture (we'd done some preparatory work with pieces of historical 'evidence') which, I'd argue, doesn't just provide a flamboyant backdrop to the action, but is part of its very substance.

The first interruption came on the third word of the speech, 'Her father loved me, . . .' Several voices shared the same tone of incredulity. 'Loved?!' In the debriefing of the activity we discussed what love might mean here. In what way could a Venetian aristocrat 'love' a black mercenary soldier? 'Like a father', suggested one. 'Patronizing him' was another offer. 'He felt sorry for him.' 'Othello was famous and Brabantio was bathing in his reflected glory.' The initial surprise of the word provoked some important recognitions about Brabantio's possible motives for inviting Othello into his house.

I asked the students to identify which aspects of Othello's life and his 'story' would be of particular interest to Brabantio and Desdemona respectively. They answered in the form of two sequences of theatre images. Working on them, they realized there were two quite distinct stories – that of the 'battles, sieges, fortunes' told to Brabantio, and the sufferings of his youth which were what Desdemona especially wanted to hear. They also thought that Desdemona, in wishing that 'heaven had made her such a man', wasn't making a bold pass but hankering after the experience Othello had had. It is this desire for active participation in Othello's life which distinguishes her from her father, for whom Othello's adventures are simply a traveller's tale. The image this group produced of Desdemona (a 'bit of fantasy', they explained) staring defiantly ahead as she stood next to Othello in the slave market, seemed to visualize this well.

On another occasion, working on the same scene with a different group, I asked the students to improvise the pre-conference exchanges (again, 'in role' as Venetian senators) between various 'factions', supposing that rumours about Desdemona's covert marriage with Othello had already reached them. Preparations for this included careful attention to everything said about Othello

in the first two scenes. I also fed in information about the cosmo-
politan nature of seventeenth-century Venice. I didn't, though,
mention 'racism'. But, in both these cases, questions about racial
identity are to the point. The students, each time, found it more
difficult to imagine that Othello could be a highly distinguished
and influential military leader in a European state than that he
could be married to a white woman, even given that she was an
aristocrat. But I think that the Elizabethans perceived this dichot-
omy between public and private roles in quite the contrary way.
Brabantio, in particular, seems to see the political threat issuing
from the bedroom rather than the boardroom.

With a third group I planned an initial session which did focus
on the question of racism. I compiled a collage of utterances from
the play, spoken by Iago, Roderigo, Brabantio, the Duke, and
Desdemona which draw attention in various ways to Othello's
cultural identity. These were pictorially reproduced on a poster-
sized sheet as a swirl of language fragments round a blank centre.
I asked the group, in pairs, to try to sketch the character being
referred to here. I then filled the centre with some utterances of
Othello himself and asked the pairs to amend and expand their
'image'. We had worked with these fragments in the drama studio
earlier in the morning. Each student had had a single utterance.
Have conversations with your pieces of language, I had told
them. Meet each other spontaneously. Developing this phase of
practical drama work, I framed the 'free exchange' with a number
of speech contexts; tell each other a joke; exchange coded mess-
ages; raise the alarm at midnight; insult each other so no one else
can tell; accuse each other as if in court. Finally, each student had
to 'run the gauntlet' of the language with their eyes closed. The
fragments weren't shouted but whispered. My objective was to
make the racist implications fully visible and audible. It isn't too
difficult to slide into a lazy acceptance of the 'normality' of certain
utterances, even to enjoy them.

Given Iago's position in the play in relation to the audience,
this process of 'normalization' can be dangerously facilitated – as
I discovered myself when I acted Iago in a fifth-year secondary
classroom some time ago. My Iago was a bright spark, a cockney
(a bit inspired by Bob Hoskins), a beneficiary of the Venetian
Big Bang. As soon as I opened my mouth, four lads who had
theatrically sat behind the half-circle of the 'audience' grinned and
nudged each other. When I bellowed up to an imaginary Braban-

tio that an old black ram was tupping his white ewe, they exploded into paroxysms of stifled giggling. One of them had suggested in a small group 'discussion' I overheard earlier in the lesson that Othello ought to return to the rainforest. The four had then broken into a spontaneous (*sotto voce*) chorus of 'Jungle Bells'. Rarely does *Othello* connect with such demotic political energies in the professional theatre. I discovered a great deal about Iago from that particular audience.

Shakespeare doesn't directly paint Caliban black but it's difficult to escape the associations there with what Homi Bhabha calls 'those terrifying stereotypes of savagery, cannibalism, lust and anarchy which are the signal points of identification, scenes of fear and desire' (Bhabha 1986: 159).

It is, to be sure, by now common practice to recognize the dubious morality of Prospero's annexation of the island, to find his subjection of Ariel and Caliban distasteful. These features are, after all, there in the words on the page. But these acts are generally attributed to defects in Prospero's personality, his anger, his intolerance, his jealous guardianship of Miranda's virginity. And, in his defence, it's pointed out that he did release Ariel from the cloven pine and had to rescue Miranda from Caliban's attempted rape. But the whole play seems to problematize the stories people tell. The narrative surface of *The Tempest* is very compelling. Particularly notable is the extent to which Prospero's voice and language determine the history and identity of all on (and, for that matter, off) the island. He defines Miranda's past for her, tells Ariel about Sycorax and Caliban (since Ariel evidently 'forgets' his own history) and then frames the entrance of Caliban with a series of sneers and insults. The one 'alternative' history we hear is, of course, that of Caliban himself. It is apparent from this that Prospero's annexation of the island has followed a familiar colonialist pattern. First, gifts for the indigenous population ('water with berries in it' according to Caliban); next, a thorough survey of the territory (during which it's clear that Caliban was prepared to share his own knowledge and expertise); finally, the assertion of power. In Prospero's own account of his arrival – told to Ariel – he comes as the liberator. It is Sycorax who was the expropriated tyrant. Who has the 'natural rights' to the island? This question is never properly answered. It certainly doesn't interest Prospero, who has his own historical project to promote and who shapes the whole island and all its resources (particularly the considerable metaphysical ones) in pursuance of it. Prospero's desire for total control and his perpetual expectation of disorder and rebellion are fixated completely on Caliban. There appear to be far more dangerous forces at large (not least his brother Antonio, who successfully usurped him) but when Prospero dissolves the harmonious vision of the betrothal masque, it is his 'sudden recollection' of Caliban's plot which has woken him from this reverie. However much Caliban is cut down to comic size, represented as childish, credulous, incapable of grasping the scope of Prospero's 'Art', his presence as the 'other', the dispossessed, the violently subjugated, is too powerful a complex to be controlled without constant vigilance. Here, starkly, is the spectacle of the Black man as figment of white, paranoid imagination, defined by a colonialist discourse which, as Edward Said puts it, shapes a whole 'imaginative geography' in the 'timeless eternal' tense (Said 1978: 62). The claims for absolute knowledge of the colonial subject's needs and interests are always being threatened by the subject's potential autonomy. Each bid for freedom is read as an act of superstitious treachery, each act of resistance seen as irrational, evidence of the subject's continuing need for moral correction and for education into 'civilized' values.

At the 1988 Society for Education in Film and Television workshop I jointly ran with Cambridge Experimental Theatre and Cambridge AV Group,[1] the class of teachers concerned worked with us on the production of two different histories of Prospero's colonization. This was to be done by way of a sequence of theatre images; the group divided into two, one half to write Prospero's chronicle and the other to present Caliban's story. Each had to 'interpret' the same fragments of text from Act I Scene 2. One of these was Caliban's declaration 'I had peopled else/This isle with Calibans.' The two versions of this utterance were especially interesting. The Prospero account showed Miranda (represented by a man) giving birth to a whole string of Calibans, one after the other, each reproducing the same aggressive, robust, short-necked posture like a nightmare vision of the missing link. The voice of Caliban echoed down the emergent line like the crack of doom. In the Caliban account, all members of the group stood in line behind each other so that the 'audience' could see the front figure only. He sank to his knees like Al Jolson while, simultaneously, the head of each figure behind appeared fanned out in a variety of playful expressions. One had her mouth covered and eyes wide in mock horror; another was playing 'peek-a-boo'; a third had her tongue stuck out; a fourth was diddling his fingers behind his ears. We didn't fully debrief this exercise. If we had, I wonder whether we would have concluded that, though the second image was more 'positive' than the first, both actually presented stereotypes of the colonized native in white eyes? Possibly we would have reckoned that critical here is the distinction between the horrific sameness of Caliban's progeny for Prospero and its delightful difference for Caliban himself. Here, a sense of celebratory culture is emerging, rather than the Bosch-like, infernal fantasy of the usurped Duke's paranoia.

Prospero's obsessively detailed narratives to Miranda and Ariel, his attempts to write a total history of the island, are perpetually contradicted in action by Caliban. Caliban has no illusions about why he has been taught Prospero's language. It's so he knows his place. It identifies him as subhuman. But how was he 'seen' by Sycorax and Setebos? What position did he have in the culture of the island before Prospero's arrival? His own story, his version of the island's history, his knowledge and preoccupations, although only marginally represented in the manifest text, bubble irrevocably beneath the surface of the action. The amount of energy expended by Prospero in seeking to define Caliban's nature as that 'upon which nurture can never stick', in claiming his diabolical descent, his capacity for rape, murder and mindless violence, in mobilizing all his magical forces to quell the putative *putsch*, suggests a potential in Caliban which transcends any simple bestial description.[2]

Comparing *The Tempest* with *Othello* suggests some interesting parallels. As Caliban is lodged in Prospero's own cell, so Othello is admitted into the very bosom of European culture. Here, too, the privileged alien is seen getting uppity and trying to seduce a white girl. In both cases, the girl's father sees this as a violation of honour. Curiously enough, a very similar view is taken by Samuel Coleridge and the *Athenaeum* theatre reviewer in response to the performance of the Black actor Ira Aldridge in *Othello* at the Theatre Royal, Covent Garden, opposite a white actress. They had been used to Othello being played by a blacked-up white actor. Ruth Cowhig reminds us that Edmund Kean had 'made the part of Othello his own' (Cowhig 1985: 16) and established the convention of presenting the character as a 'tawny moor'. Ira Alridge's sudden appearance as a 'blackamoor' was evidently a rude shock to tender English sensibilities: 'it would be something monstrous to conceive the beautiful Venetian girl falling in love with a veritable negro' (Cowhig 1985: 20). Perhaps this gentleman suspected that Ira Aldridge had used foul charms on Ellen Tree. Samuel Coleridge was even more vehement: 'we protest against an interesting actress and a lady-like girl, like Miss Ellen Tree, being subjected by the manager of the theatre to the indignity of being pawed about by Mr. Henry Wallack's black servant' (Cowhig 1985: 17). One can imagine him leaping on to the stage, grabbing a torch and a sword and joining the squad of officers hired by Brabantio to arrest Othello.

The problem is that Othello is no Caliban. It's difficult now to grasp fully the radical significance of Shakespeare's characterization of Othello or the thoroughly disturbing impression that the original production must have had on its audience, albeit that the part would have been played by a blacked-up Burbage or Swanston. Caliban can be presented as the stereotypical 'native', an evil savage. Othello, though, seems culturally assimilated into white society, a Christian convert, a man of nobility. He is also the indispensable military leader whose job is to defend the Venetian state against the threat of another barbarous 'other', the Turk. Black is pitted against Black. Shakespeare's source for *Othello*, described by Kenneth Muir as a 'sordid, melodramatic tale of sexual jealousy' (1968: 7), is Italian – Giraldi Cinthio's *Hecatommithi*. Cinthio's leading character, simply called 'the Moor', undergoes a startling transformation in the hands of Shakespeare. Cassio, too – in Cinthio very much the Florentine libertine – is significantly ennobled. But no doubt the Italian associations would still have been triggered in a contemporary audience. Norman Sanders explains that Italy had a 'double image' (1984: 17) at the time. On the one hand, it was the birthplace of Ariosto, Petrarch, and Castiglione, 'the Renaissance model for less civilized northern lands'. On the other, it was 'the sump of sophisticated vice' (Florence, in particular, was identified with this cultural trait). Further (and here Venice was the paradigm):

It was the free state of Europe, a racial and religious melting pot which had successfully challenged the great European monarchies, and which gazed in two directions: towards civilized Christianity and towards the remote eastern world of pagan infidels, the Turks and the mighty power of Islam.

(Sanders 1984: 17)

115

For a time, Othello is à la mode in Venice. Just as Caliban was stroked and made much of by Prospero, so Othello is fêted and patronized by Brabantio. None of the characters in *Othello* have any problems with the idea of Othello as a distinguished soldier to be honoured as a guest in that particular role. The problems begin when he assumes a new and unexpected role – that of Desdemona's husband. Such a possibility is inconceivable to the patrician culture of Venice. Perhaps it is the very implicit prohibition on intimate relations between Black foreign soldiers and white aristocratic ladies that, paradoxically, permits the relationship between Desdemona and Othello to develop in the first place. They have to improvise, to make up rules of engagement as they go along. That the anxieties of the white, ruling elite extend beyond the question of their daughters' marriageability is made clear by Brabantio, who, told that the Duke is in midnight conference, resolves to take his grievance to his 'brothers of the state', thinking they will certainly be sympathetic to his view:

> For if such actions may have passage free,
> Bondslaves and pagans shall our statesmen be.
>
> (I.2.98–9)

What concerns Brabantio here are the possible consequences of Othello's marriage with Desdemona. He sees it as an implicit subversion of the whole Venetian social order; as paranoid an interpretation of this single act of transgression as anything imagined by Prospero.

Critical comments like those of Kenneth Muir, 'It is significant that only Iago and Brabantio seem to have any colour prejudice against Othello' (1968: 16), alert us to the need to engage our students in a process of active reading which considers the complexity of racism as an ideological force. Apart from the fact that Kenneth Muir has overlooked Roderigo's reference to Othello as the 'thick-lips', we should see 'colour prejudice' as not just a question of the conscious, overtly racist utterances of a Iago who, were he alive today, would quite possibly join the National Front; but far more as a matter of those unconscious utterances, unrecognized symptoms of an underlying culture of racism which propagates extreme racist attitudes and behaviour. The fact that traditional literary analysis of the play has avoided it and pursued such absurd irrelevances as whether or not Othello is truly noble or merely self-dramatizing is itself a sign that the culture of racism has been at work in the very heart of liberal humanism.

In my experience, the most intense debate focuses on utterances such as the Duke of Venice's throwaway comment to Brabantio:

> If virtue no delighted beauty lack
> Your son-in-law is far more fair than black.
> (I.3.286–7)

and Desdemona's apparently innocent remark:

> I saw Othello's visage in his mind.
> (I.3.249)

and there are particularly significant discussions to be had on such questions as how far Othello himself, as represented in Shakespeare's text, is self-oppressed, a victim of what Bob Marley calls 'mental slavery' (Owusu 1988: 5). Key textual moments here are:

> . . . Her name that was as fresh
> As Dian's visage is now begrimed and black
> As mine own face.
> (III.3.383–5)

or:

> . . . one whose hand
> Like the base Indian threw a pearl away
> Richer than all his tribe.
> (V.2.342–4)

or:

> . . . in Aleppo once
> Where a malignant and a turbaned Turk
> Beat a Venetian and traduced the state,
> I took by the throat the circumcised dog
> And smote him thus.
> (V.2.348–52)

Although there is considerable textual evidence to suggest that Othello has come to think like a Venetian about all those who are not Venetian, we can't ignore what indicates, on the contrary, that his own history and cultural identity are still strong within him. Just as Caliban defiantly reminds Prospero that he was his own king, so Othello quietly informs Iago:

> . . . I fetch my life and being
> From men of royal siege
> (I.2.21–2)

a fact which he has apparently not promulgated (or provulgated) but reserved to himself. His long speech to the emergency council of war in I.3, the report of his narrative to Desdemona, doesn't mention it, but does refer to his being 'sold to slavery'. What is especially interesting about this speech is its proximity to the tradition of travellers' tales and its strategic use of Christian vocabulary – 'redemption' and 'pilgrimage' are two key words. Othello is able to speak well the dominant language of Venetian culture (unlike Caliban, who can only curse) when this is necessary. Many critics have read his apparent conversion to Christianity as a negation of his original values and beliefs – but he seems to have brought very particular ideas about the sacred and the profane to his new beliefs which give his Christianity a special character.

Rather than seeing Othello's insistence on the sacred significance of the handkerchief passed on to him by his mother as a kind of tragic reversion to barbarism, we can recognize it as indicative of his own continuing identification with the culture and history that are the roots of his human being. In fact, the handkerchief, the butt of much white, male sarcasm since Thomas Rhymer, can thus be seen in its full significance. It appears to be the one object which has survived Othello's chequered personal history intact – the one symbol he has of his own cultural origins. It was, he tells Iago, his 'first gift' to Desdemona. Emilia lets us know how important it is to Othello's young wife:

> . . . she so loves the token,
> For he hath conjured her she should ever keep it –
> That she reserves it evermore about her
> To kiss and talk to.
>
> (III.3.290–3)

Desdemona seems to have fully entered into the spirit of the handkerchief's sacredness, to have accepted the value placed upon it by Othello. In this sense, it is difficult to believe that his description of it to her in III.4 is as new to her as her shocked incredulity appears to imply. Perhaps it is the tone rather than the content of what Othello says which provokes her bitter rejoinder:

> Then would to God I had never seen it!
>
> (III.4.77)

There has been much critical controversy about whether or not Othello 'knew' he was brushing away the handkerchief Desdemona offered him to soothe his headache – or realized that it had fallen to the ground (III.3.281–5). I don't see how this can be read other than recognizing that neither Othello nor Desdemona realize it has been dropped. This is, in itself, significant. The fact that both fail to 'see' it is indicative of the alarm and confusion which is already fracturing their relationship. But Desdemona's outburst, quoted above, is more significant, perhaps, than has so far been understood. It is, or it must seem to Othello like, a rejection of himself and his very cultural being, a confirmation of his worst fears. How are we, the audience, to read it? Is it the moment in the play when Desdemona's Venetian upbringing actually asserts itself for the first time as a force to separate her from him? Perhaps we are indeed seeing Desdemona, if only for a moment, 'reading' Othello as a barbarian. It is yet to be fully acknowledged what a radical act of sexual politics Desdemona's decision to marry Othello actually is. There has been a tendency for critics to take at face value what Brabantio says about his daughter:

> A maiden never bold;
> Of spirit so still and quiet that her motion
> Blushed at herself:
>
> (I.3.94–6)

without considering the obvious possibility that Brabantio actually knows very little about the Desdemona who has been in charge of his house for some time. We need to absorb the full significance of what she does. She marries Othello not only against her father's wishes but also against the conventional assumptions of Venetian society. This determination is expressed most remarkably when she openly declares her wish to travel with Othello to the war zone, involving a hazardous sea voyage and a possibly even more hazardous sojourn in Cyprus. She frankly tells the all-male assembly of senators:

119

JOHN SALWAY

> . . . if I be left behind
> A moth of peace, and he go to the war
> The rites for which I love him are bereft me,
>
> (I.3.253–5)

an assertion which seems to give the lie to such prim interpretations as Kenneth Muir's that 'Desdemona falls in love with his autobiography rather than with him' (1968: 33).

Last year, working with a group of trainee teachers on a PGCE workshop, I focused on the whole question of Desdemona's traditional representation in the theatre as an unlessoned and passive girl who has, in marrying Othello, exchanged one father for another. We had 'staged' the crucial scene I've just considered, paying special attention to the possible stage grouping of characters in the senate chamber, bearing in mind the question of their relative status and the ritual recognition of this. Most interesting of all, perhaps, was the group's decision to place Desdemona higher than Othello so that she was actually looking down on him as she spoke about her divided duty. She certainly wasn't stooping to conquer – in seeing his visage in his mind, she was recognizing his right to be her husband, to be on her level. From here we went on to improvise some scenes not actually written by Shakespeare, but certainly sanctioned by the text. The first was set in Brabantio's house and concerned Desdemona's management of the domestic affairs. We imagined the kinds of problem she might be involved in solving and the degree of confidence she would need in what we would now call 'management skills'. One involved, for instance, the decision about whether or not to dismiss a servant accused of embezzlement. From this we went on to plot the possible development of her relationship with Othello. We improvised the scene reported by Othello in his speech to the senate when Desdemona advised him to teach any friend that loved her how to tell his tale. We went on to speculate, in dramatic action, how they decided to defy Brabantio. It seemed clear to the group that Desdemona would be the moving force and Othello would be deeply anxious about his own position. In one very powerful improvised version, it was Desdemona who assured him most forcefully about his own indispensability to the Venetian state and therefore his safety from any possible retributive action by Brabantio. Far from being passive, she was the

120

moral leader in their decision to marry without Brabantio's consent.

The vast majority of white male critics seem to have shared both Brabantio's and Samuel Coleridge's (not to mention Iago's) disbelief that a 'lady-like' white girl could possibly find a 'veritable negro' sexually attractive. But, then again, there is in the play the contrary notion of the Black as 'lusty', as 'an old black ram', as possessing a sexuality highly dangerous to the secure nightcaps of white husbands, a paranoid complex most evident in Iago's salacious imagination. There is an irreconcilable duality in white ideas about Othello's attractiveness. He might have 'declined into the vale of years' but he is still an 'erring barbarian of here and everywhere', quite capable of 'making the beast with two backs', a figure of orientalist fantasy.

Othello has frequently been treated as a magnificent, atypical aberration, a kind of special racial case. Where attention is paid to his cultural background, it's nearly always coloured by orientalist fantasies of the kind described by Rana Kabbani (1986). References are made to barbaric superstition in apparent innocence of the fact that even renaissance Christendom was riddled with it. The problem of the white representation of a Black person is, as I've tried to argue, one that affects both literary criticism and theatrical production. It is a question of the invisibility to white eyes of Black people as agents of their own cultures and histories. What the theatre reviewers of 1833 were, in effect, denying to Ira Aldridge was his capacity to represent a Black character in white theatre. That, it was implicitly argued, could only be adequately done by a white actor. Ira Aldridge, the foreign, negro actor stepping into the all-white world of the Theatre Royal, Covent Garden and daring to touch, even symbolically, the body of Ellen Tree, was actually mirroring in social reality the predicament of Othello in the dramatic fiction being portrayed. Just as Roger Fry probably never questioned his capacity to interpret 'his' African mask, so Edmund Kean would never have dreamed of querying his ability to put on the mask of Othello.

But the far-reaching implications of Shakespeare's *Othello* cannot be unfolded unless the play, in reading and performance, is thoroughly informed by a Black presence in the role of Othello and charged with the experience of Black histories and cultures which throw important new light on areas of the text previously obscured or misunderstood. It is in that sense that we whites

JOHN SALWAY

(that is, most of us reading this book) are very much the problem when it comes to an adequate overstanding of *Othello*.

NOTES

1 I am indebted here to Charlie Ritchie of the Cambridge AV Group, and to Richard Spaul and Richard Fredman of Cambridge Experimental Theatre, as well as to the course members on the 'Making Shakespeare' workshop at Cambridgeshire College of Arts and Technology, June 1988.
2 For further development of these arguments, see Orgel (1987: 25–8) and Evans (1989: 71–8).

REFERENCES

Bhabha, Homi K. (1986) 'The other question: difference, discrimination and the discourse of colonialism', in F. Barker *et al.* (eds) *Literature, Politics and Theory*, London: Methuen.
Clark, Kenneth (1969) *Civilisation*, London: BBC Publications.
Cowhig, Ruth (1985) 'Blacks in English renaissance drama and the role of Shakespeare's Othello', in David Dabydeen (ed.) *The Black Presence in English Literature*, Manchester: Manchester University Press.
Evans, Malcolm (1989) *Signifying Nothing. Truth's True Contents in Shakespeare's Texts*, 2nd edn, New York and London: Harvester Wheatsheaf.
James, C. L. R. (1980) '*Othello* and *The Merchant of Venice*', in *Spheres of Existence*, London: Allison & Busby.
Kabbani, Rana (1986) *Europe's Myths of Orient*, London: Pandora.
Muir, Kenneth (ed.) (1968) *Othello*, The New Penguin Shakespeare, Harmondsworth: Penguin.
Orgel, Stephen (ed.) (1987) *The Tempest*, The Oxford Shakespeare, Oxford: Oxford University Press.
Owusu, Kwesi (ed.) (1988) *Storms of the Heart. An Anthology of Black Arts and Culture*, London: Camden Press.
Ridley, M. R. (ed.) (1958) *Othello*, The Arden Shakespeare, London: Methuen.
Said, Edward (1978) *Orientalism*, London: Routledge & Kegan Paul.
Sanders, Norman (ed.) (1984) *Othello*, The New Cambridge Shakespeare, Cambridge: Cambridge University Press.

FURTHER READING

General

Barker, Francis *et al.* (eds) (1985) *Europe and Its Others*, Colchester: University of Essex Press.
Brown, Paul, (1985) ' "This thing of darkness I acknowledge mine":

122

The Tempest and the discourse of colonialism', in Jonathan Dollimore and Alan Sinfield (eds) *Political Shakespeare. New Essays in Cultural Materialism*, Manchester: Manchester University Press.

Cartelli, Thomas (1987) 'Prospero in Africa: *The Tempest* as colonialist text and pretext', in Jean E. Howard and Marion F. O'Connor (eds) *Shakespeare Reproduced. The Text in Ideology and History*, New York and London: Methuen.

Drakakis, John (ed.) (1985) *Alternative Shakespeares*, London: Methuen.

Hill, Errol (1984) *Shakespeare in Sable: A History of Black Shakespearian Actors*, Massachusetts: University of Massachusetts Press.

Loomba, Ania (1989) *Gender, Race, Renaissance Drama*, Manchester: Manchester University Press.

Matthews, G. M. (1964) 'Othello and the dignity of man', in Arnold Kettle (ed.) *Shakespeare in a Changing World*, London: Lawrence & Wishart.

Okri, Ben (1988) 'Leaping out of Shakespeare's terror – five meditations on *Othello*', in Kwesi Owusu (ed.) *Storms of the Heart: An Anthology of Black Arts and Culture*, London: Camden Press.

Orgel, Stephen (1986) 'Prospero's wife', in Margaret W. Ferguson, Maureen Quiligan and Nancy J. Vickers (eds) *Rewriting the Renaissance: The Discourses of Sexual Difference in Early Modern Europe*, Chicago and London: University of Chicago Press.

Patterson, Annabel (1989) *Shakespeare and the Popular Voice,* Chapter 7, Oxford and Cambridge, MA: Basil Blackwell.

Ryan, Kiernan (1989) *Shakespeare*, pp. 51–8, 97–109, New York and London: Harvester Wheatsheaf.

Pedagogical issues and workshop practice

Shakespeare and Schools (*S&S* hereafter) is published termly, available on subscription of £5.00 p.a. to 'Shakespeare and Schools', Rex Gibson, Cambridge Institute of Education, Shaftesbury Road, Cambridge CB2 2BX (overseas subscribers £10.00 p.a., payment in sterling).

Bailey, Paul (1984) 'Not so Bard after all! Some approaches to Shakespeare', *2D* 4(1), Autumn.

Gibson, Rex (ed.) (1990) *Secondary School Shakespeare. Classroom Practice: A Collection of Papers by Secondary Teachers*, Cambridge, Cambridge Institute of Education.

Marshall, Sarah (1989) 'Behind the scenes', *2D* 8(2), Summer.

Peim, Nick and Elmer, Gerry (1984) '*Othello*: a drama approach to A-level English', *2D* 3(3), Summer.

Routh, Mike (1987) 'Active reading with the sixth form', *S&S* 3, Summer.

Salway, John (1987) 'Freezing the frame: using the tableau method', *S&S* 2, Spring.

—— (1987) 'All the world's a stage: or explorations in other spaces', *S&S* 4, Autumn.

—— (1988) 'This thing of darkness: anti-racist approaches to Shakespeare', *S&S* 6, Summer.

—— (1988) '*Othello* in black and white', *Dragon's Teeth* 31, Autumn.

——, 'Such shapes, such gestures and such sound: reading *The Tempest* in performance', *S&S* 8, Spring.

7

'My affection hath an unknown bottom': homosexuality and the teaching of *As You Like It*

Elaine Hobby

HOMOSEXUALITY AND THE CHANGING CURRICULUM

Under Section 28 of the Local Government Act 1988, a local authority shall not

(a) intentionally promote homosexuality or publish material with the intention of promoting homosexuality
(b) promote the teaching in any maintained school of the acceptability of homosexuality as a pretended family relationship.

It is too soon as yet to know what long-term effects on education this change in the law might have. There have been some widely publicized attempts to use the Section, most notoriously against various teachers who have been suspended for discussing homosexuality in the classroom. In April 1988, for example, Austin Allen, a supply teacher in Bradford, was reinstated after action had initially been taken against him for having, according to his headmaster, 'brought aspects of his personal life into his teaching which we do not expect to be brought in' (*The Times Educational Supplement*, 4 March 1988; *Gay Times*, April 1988). In Birmingham in October 1989, too, an attempt to dismiss the head of religious education at a Birmingham boys' school for 'promoting' homosexuality in his classroom was overturned at a tribunal (*Gay Times*, October 1989). Other gay teachers in Manchester, Essex, and London have been faced with similar attacks, but so far as I am aware, no one has yet lost their job. And there have been some significant defeats of attempts to use the existence of the Section to impose wider forms of censorship.

An article in *Gay Times* in June 1989 records, for instance, that two educational videos dealing with lesbian and gay lives made by ILEA have at last been released, despite fears that their suppression would be permanent; that the local educational authority in Strathclyde has withdrawn its threats to funding of lesbian and gay student societies after representations were made by the National Union of Students; and that Essex Local Education Authority has been persuaded to withdraw its ban on meetings of a lesbian and gay society at Colchester Institute of Further Education. Equally significantly, at its national conference in April 1988 the National Union of Teachers passed a motion that

> rejects all discrimination on grounds of sexual orientation . . . believes that it is part of the educative process to encourage pupils to develop unbiased attitudes about homosexuality . . . [and] condemns the Government's move to undermine the professional autonomy of teachers within the classroom and to restrict the range of texts which can be studied as well as the discussion of issues surrounding homosexuality.

The failure of the Section to restrict the freedoms of teachers and, in particular, lesbian and gay teachers, has not however been complete. As its opponents predicted, the existence of Section 28 is being used by homophobes as an excuse to attack homosexuals and homosexuality. In the summer of 1989, for instance, Peter Dawson, General Secretary of the Professional Association of Teachers, made a speech condemning the television programme *EastEnders* as 'a vile influence on the nation because it projects as normal wholly deviant forms of behaviour such as homosexuality, bad language, crime, infidelity and drunkenness'. Responding to a letter in the *Guardian* criticizing him, he asserted, 'If there is any active homosexual who thinks that his or her behaviour is normal, the sooner the idea is knocked on the head, the better. . . . Active homosexual behaviour is deviant. Anyone who teaches young people otherwise is an evil influence in the nation' (*Guardian*, 10 August 1989). In making such assertions, Dawson is quite in line with the statistics published in the fifth annual volume of *British Social Attitudes* in November 1988. This survey reveals that three out of four Britons then thought that homosexual relations are 'always/mostly wrong', and that 57 per cent of those questioned believed 'that it is wrong for a gay person to be allowed to teach in a school'.

Less publicized than such developments, though widely covered in the gay press, have been the more wide-ranging effects of the respectable face given to homophobic attacks by the Section. The numbers of gay men and women beaten up on the streets when leaving gay bars have increased dramatically, police anti-gay activity in the form of raids, entrapment, and abuse has escalated, and various pubs and clubs have closed their gay nights, reducing the available venues where people, especially young people, are safe to be open about their sexuality. In addition, the Section has been used as the excuse to ban meetings of some lesbian and gay student groups: the Principal of Kitson College, a further education college in Leeds, for instance, has refused to allow such a group to meet on college premises (*Pink Paper*, 23 December 1989).

It is also not yet clear how the fears aroused by the Section will alter what is taught in schools, or how material is dealt with, despite the fact that, as various eminent lawyers have repeatedly pointed out, the Section might prove useless for the purposes of legal enforcement, since the term 'promote' is so vague (and, more mischievously, any teaching of homosexuality other than as 'a pretended family relationship' – for instance the commendation of casual gay sex – is not mentioned by the Act at all!). Also important is the fact that, under the Education Act of 1986, sex education is no longer the responsibility of local authorities, but of school governors: the arena where homosexuality is most likely to be discussed in schools had been removed from the clutches of the Local Government Act before ever Section 28 was drafted. Despite this legal situation, the effects on classroom practices could be significant. Teachers might decide to play it safe – or might use the existence of the Section as an excuse not to recognize their own unconscious prejudice against homosexuality – and opt not to mention homosexuality in the classroom, and not to teach works by gay writers, or teach them but not mention the fact that the authors are gay. This alternative seems to me quite likely, given the fact that I am yet to meet an A-level student of English who has been told about Wilfred Owen's homosexuality, even though most have read his better-known poems at some point in their school career, and have been baffled in their attempts to make coherent heterosexual readings of some of his verses. Comparable extraordinary contortions are regularly made in my classrooms, and those of colleagues, by students denied knowledge of the fact that the majority of Shakespeare's *Sonnets* are addressed not to a mistress, but a young man. This silence about homosexuality is routinely continued in institutions of higher education.

This matters for many reasons, not only because it is symptomatic of an attempt to redefine homosexuality as a sickness, 'deviance' in a reprehensible sense, but also, and pragmatically, because some school students are being raised by lesbian or gay parents, and in our classrooms we have lesbian and gay students who are desperate for some affirmation that their existence, and right to work out their own meanings of their sexuality, are recognized and valued. In a survey of 416 individuals under the age of twenty-one who identified themselves as lesbian, gay, or bisexual conducted by the London Lesbian and Gay Teenage Group Research Project, it was found that 60 per cent of them had been verbally abused because of their sexuality, one in five had been beaten up for this reason, one in seven sent to a psychiatrist, one in five attempted suicide, and one in two had problems at school (Trenchard and Warren 1984). When asked what schools could do to help, the respondents' replies were analytical and constructive, including these suggestions from a nineteen-year-old:

> Prejudice and negative views against homosexuals should be viewed as racist remarks in that discrimination is factually unfounded and that it is the people making such prejudiced generalisations who are ignorant, not those on the butt end. Obviously schools should stock books about homosexuals, or with gay characters positively portrayed, as well as factual information about gay groups, etc.

These particular findings, of course, pre-date Section 28. It is to be feared that the situation has worsened since the Act was passed. What seems clear is that this attack on a homosexual lifestyle as 'a pretended family relationship' is part of a general policy of the present government to undo the progress made in various social fields in the 1960s and 1970s. In a speech made in 1982, Margaret Thatcher declared,

We are reaping what was sown in the sixties. The fashionable theories and permissive claptrap set the scene for a society in which the old virtues of discipline and self-restraint were denigrated.

(Quoted in Weeks 1985: 18)

The government, and the plethora of far-right 'moral' pressure groups that have its ear, appear to be setting out on a concerted attack on all forms of social allegiance other than those to nuclear family (and, presumably, to Party): on the agenda for destruction or control, therefore, are the unions and democratic control of local government, as well as 'alternative' living arrangements. The fact that what is at issue here, for all the nonsense that is talked about it by the Tories, is a tightening of government control over people's lives, and a reduction of autonomy, is demonstrated by the fact that this ideological onslaught is accompanied by the destruction of the practical and material supports necessary to both 'conventional' and 'unconventional' household structures: child benefits are held artificially low, nursing homes and hospitals closed down, and the NHS starved of cash. Insistence on the 'naturalness' and 'necessity' of the nuclear family has also encouraged the suppression of information about the widespread incidence of incest and violence against women, and Anne Winterton MP's recent attempt in a Private Member's Bill to outlaw artificial insemination for single women and lesbians. Through, in part, a sentimental appeal to a golden age of 'Victorian values', the family is to be reinstated as the locus of social stability, the arena where social control and law and order are maintained. This emotional and distorted evocation of the past is linked to the Tories' desire to reinstate the teaching of a particular version of history, one stressing Britain's 'greatness', celebratory of empire and keen to commemorate, for instance, the drubbing of nasty, uppity foreigners in the defeat of the Spanish Armada.

The leap from there to the teaching of Shakespeare is not a straightforward one, not least because thinking about the works of the Bard might seem an odd place to mount an attack on the uses made of the idea of 'family' by present-day government. In this chapter, none the less, I will examine the ways in which this centrality of the family can be explored, and in part challenged, when teaching a text that apparently resides quite comfortably within the core curriculum and notions of Shakespeare's 'greatness'. The reading of *As You Like It* that follows was developed through my teaching it to an A-level class in 1986–7.

HOMOSEXUALITY AND PRETENDED FAMILIES IN THE AGE OF THE FIRST ELIZABETH

From 1985–7 I taught A-level English at the Cambridgeshire College of Arts and Technology, an institution now reorganized and renamed, but then a mixed further and higher education college. My A-level students were all aged sixteen to nineteen, and in the first or second year of their A-level studies. They knew that I was a lesbian, because I told them; as far as I am aware, I was the only openly gay teacher any of them had been taught by, and indeed the first gay person that most of them had known they knew.

A key effect of my openness about my homosexuality was to prevent – sometimes with much hilarity – the trotting out of unanalysed assumptions about family structures, love and desire, the social roles of women and men, and the application of such 'truisms' to the study of literature. It is difficult to say 'everyone feels' or 'all women want' when the teacher sitting with you manifestly does not feel or want those things. This is significant because a great deal of what is studied at A level deals at least in part with family structures, with falling in love or with growing to 'maturity'. (Or perhaps more accurately, the focus of attention encouraged or permitted by the curriculum is on such issues, rather than on questions, for instance, of the material production of texts.) Limited, culturally specific assumptions about family, love, marriage, and gender roles of the kind promoted in the media, in teenage magazines, and by current government policies, can efface the specificity both of the students' own experiences (none of us really lives in the family imagined in dominant culture, although we are constantly exhorted to *want* to live like that, and perhaps many do), and force bland, homogenized readings of texts that bear little relation to the very different cultures within which they were written and first received. The pedagogic usefulness of being openly gay, and of encouraging classroom discussion of sexuality and gender construction, became clearest to me when teaching *As You Like It*, a play which I taught by bringing centre stage problems of family structure, the potential disruptiveness of sexual desire, and the arbitrary and stifling nature of gender roles.

The England in which Shakespeare was writing was intensely patriarchal. The monarch's power in the nation was likened to that of the father over the family: both, it was asserted, were appointed by God to ensure proper social stability (Graham 1989; Fraser 1984; Hill 1964). Men's control over their families, and the monarch's control of that larger family or amalgam of families, the nation, was as natural, and as necessary, as the head's control of the body. This link was asserted even and especially in the reign of a queen, Elizabeth, who spoke of herself not as a woman but a Prince (Heisch 1980; Montrose 1983). Reference was made to the Bible, God's Word, to instruct women and children in their proper subordination to their husbands and elders, a subordination also evident in men's legal and financial control over women, and in the system of primogeniture, whereby, in really wealthy families, and many lower down the social scale, inheritance passed from father to eldest son (Prior 1985; Stone 1977).

The social stability that this achieved was not, however, a permanent state: it was something that the powerful had constantly to reassert against resistance and the threat of disorder. Amongst the sources of disorderliness were uppity women, who could be punished by tortures including the ducking-stool and the scold's bridle (Fraser 1984); the playhouses, constantly associated throughout Elizabeth's reign with riot and immorality, and the continual object of censorship and other repression (Bristol 1985; Shepherd 1986; Patterson 1989); and sodomites, for whom the legal punishment, rarely enforced, could be death (Bray 1982; Licata and Petersen 1985).

Sodomites might seem a surprising part of this list but, as recent work on the history of homosexuality has shown, the possibility of sexual misconduct, and its relationship to other forms of social disorder, were much written about in renaissance England. The word 'sodomite' is not directly translatable into twentieth-century English, because the dominant sense of what sexuality is, where desire comes from and how it relates to society as a whole, have changed so radically (Foucault 1979; Bray 1982). Although the term 'sodomite' might be used simply to describe someone thought guilty of anal intercourse (then both a crime and a sin), it, and its adjectival form 'sodomitical', might be applied to almost any sexual act thought reprehensible and injuri-

ous to family order, including incest, adultery, pederasty, fornication, rape, oral sex, bestiality, and any form of homosexual
contact. All these activities, and others, were variously defined
as 'sodomitical' by the Catholic church's penitentials, guides to
sin and punishment that underpinned most European, including
English, legal attitudes to sexuality (Brown 1986). Crucial to our
understanding of the term 'sodomite' is the fact that the law and
church saw sodomitical activity as multifaceted and its dangers
as social and general. Anyone might be tempted to indulge in
any of these sins, and their existence was a result of the work of
the devil, a symbol and source of disintegration. Anyone participating in one of these activities – say, adultery – might also be
involved in another – say, homosexuality. (It is important to bear
in mind here, as most existing histories of homosexuality do not,
that what is being described is the *dominant* attitude to sodomites.
Those people actually enjoying such activities might not have seen
themselves in these same terms. This difference of perspective is
crucial to the writing of sexuality's history, but not pertinent to
the present discussion, since what is being examined is dominant
social myths about sodomitical activity.) At the most famous
seventeenth-century trial for sodomy, that of the Earl of Castlehaven, in 1631, the Attorney-General warned that the sodomitical
crimes Castlehaven was accused of (rape and homosexual anal
intercourse) were

> of that pestiferous and pestilential nature that if they be not
> punished will draw from heaven heavy judgements upon
> this kingdom. . . . By these abominations the land is defiled;
> and therefore the Lord doth visit this land for the iniquity
> thereof. That God may remove and take away his plagues,
> let this wicked man be taken away from among us.
>
> (Bray 1982: 29)

The state's anxiety about sodomitical activity and its supposedly
evil origins and pernicious effects were also specifically related to
the playhouses. The theatres were repeatedly attacked as pro-
moters of lust, not only because of the reputedly licentious
behaviour of their audiences, but also because they offered,
through the employment of boy actors playing women's parts,
alarming instances of courtship and sexual activity between men
and boys. (Jardine, 1983, quotes useful contemporary material on
this topic, though it must be noted that her use of it is anti-

132

homosexual in her attempts to be pro-feminist.) Around the time that *As You Like It* was first performed – 1600 – the employment of boy actors was a subject of particular concern, since in 1599 two companies comprised solely of boy actors, the Children of the Queen's Chapel and the Children of Paul's, were formed. The plays performed by them make frequent reference to the boys' sexual charms (Wren 1987). That the question of the roles of boy actors was also preoccupying Shakespeare might be indicated by his use of cross-dressing, gender confusion, and homoeroticism in *A Midsummer Night's Dream* (?1595), *The Merchant of Venice* (?1597) and *Twelfth Night* (?1601).

THE CASE OF *AS YOU LIKE IT*

In teaching *As You Like It*, I offered it to my students as a play centrally concerned with problems of order and disorder. It opens by presenting two parallel cases of conflict around male power and the structure of family and state. In his first speech, Orlando laments to Adam his ill-treatment by his elder brother Oliver, main heir to their late father's estate. He 'mines [undermines] my gentility with my education' (I.1.19–20), whereas 'my brother Jaques he keeps at school, and report speaks goldenly of his profit' (I.1.4–6). The language of class and money is no accident here, but runs throughout the subsequent exchange between the brothers, notably in the play around whether one of them is a villain/villein. Oliver, Orlando charges, is misusing his familial power under the rules of primogeniture, and thereby undermining Orlando's class status. As the scene proceeds, we learn of another case of discord between brothers, and its resultant destabilizing of social and economic power: 'the old Duke is banished by his younger brother the new Duke, and three or four loving lords have put themselves into voluntary exile with him, whose lands and revenues enrich the new Duke' (I.1.97–101). The ousted Duke Senior has taken to the forest (a frequent refuge for social outcasts and misfits (Hill 1972), as well as being a suitable setting for the play's exploration of pastoral convention, its only aspect much discussed in conventional literary criticism), soon to be joined there by the play's other victims of family breakdown, Orlando, Rosalind, Celia, and Touchstone.

The play's opening, therefore, clearly indicates the need for familial stability if social stability is to be maintained, whilst also emphasizing that the legal and conventional differentiations of status between older and younger brothers was a source of rebellion and rage. At the same time, the existence of such interdependence of family and state is shown in the play to be a major source of potential disruption and oppression. Repeatedly, questions of social alliance and personal identity are analysed in terms of their interrelationship with family structures: in I.2, Duke Frederick is disappointed to hear that the new champion, Orlando, is the son of an old enemy, and in the next scene Celia teases Rosalind by suggesting that Rosalind's supposed motive for loving Orlando – 'The Duke my father loved his father dearly' – means that Celia should by analogy hate him. A similar connection is drawn in III.1, when Duke Frederick justifies his seizure of Oliver's property on the grounds that he is angry with Orlando. The stability that the family is supposed to ensure is fragile and uncertain, something comically indicated in Adam's repeated attempts to find a vocabulary to refer to Orlando's family that does not include the words 'brother', 'son', and 'father' because of Oliver's murderous behaviour (II.3). Family structures are not really natural at all (any more than is the state they supposedly mirror and support), but social, ideological constructs ever open to disintegration. (For a related, extended analysis of the importance in the play of primogeniture, see Montrose 1981.)

For a lesbian and feminist reader/teacher such as me, however, the central focus of the play's concern with order is found in the character of Rosalind. (In specifying my politics and sexuality as the origins of this focus, I wish to draw attention to a wider issue: the fact that what interests us in texts is dependent not on the author's undiscoverable 'real intention', but on our own position as readers. There are more extended discussions of these issues in Belsey, 1980, and Batsleer et al., 1985.) Through Rosalind, we are presented with two interwoven challenges to the stability of gender. This is achieved through a juxtaposition of Rosalind's characteristics as young woman with her behaviour when playing the part of a young man; and through a series of jokes about the actual gender identity of the actor playing Rosalind/Ganymede's part.

In her first appearance, Rosalind is established strongly as female, as the archetypal witty woman not infrequently named Rosalind or Rosaline in writings of the period (Shepherd 1981, especially pp. 153, 164–6). Her most important relationship is with her cousin, Celia, and apparently everyone knows, in the words of Charles the wrestler, that 'Never two ladies loved as they do' (I.1.108–9). Neither woman has any time for men and marriage, their supposedly proper destination, but both are intelligent and bawdy: a bawdiness that Rosalind retains as Ganymede, for instance in her reference (III.2.334–5) to a 'cony that you see dwell where she is kindled' ('rabbit that you see dwell where she is born' or 'cunt/whore that you see dwell where she is enflamed with desire'). In the initial stages of the play it is Celia, not Rosalind, who is in charge in their relationship. In I.3, Celia tries to defend Rosalind against Duke Frederick's wrath, and when that fails it is she who plans their escape from the palace. The first act is closed with Celia's words. Once Rosalind is dressed as a man, however, it seems her prediction that assuming 'a swashing and a martial outside' (I.3.118) will change her is true. When the two cousins reappear (II.4) it is Celia who begs for rest – 'I can go no further' – Rosalind/Ganymede who boldly asserts 'I must comfort the weaker vessel, as doublet and hose ought to show itself courageous to petticoat.' As the action proceeds, Rosalind/Ganymede plays two parts, the one conventionally female, the other not. Rosalind moons around, lovelorn, or makes herself an object of Celia's teasing through her desperate desire for news of Orlando (III.2.163–248), whilst Ganymede needles and scolds Orlando (IV.1). She also speaks angry men's words to Phebe, berating her in terms like those of a renaissance love sonnet for not returning Silvius's love:

> 'Tis not your inky brows, your black silk hair,
> Your bugle eyeballs, nor your cheek of cream
> That can entame my spirits to your worship. . . .
> But mistress, know yourself. Down on your knees,
> And thank heaven, fasting, for a good man's love;
> For I must tell you friendly in your ear,
> Sell when you can, you are not for all markets.
>
> (III.5.46–60)

(Despising women for not acceding to male desire, or for prizing their beauties too highly, is a fundamental element in male love poetry in the period. Examples are legion, but most obviously include Spenser's 'Of this world's theatre in which we stay' (in *Amoretti*); Wyatt's 'Divers doth use, as I have heard and know'; Shakespeare's 'Two loves I have, of comfort and despair'; Daniel's

'I once may see when years shall reck my wrong' (in *Delia*). For a contemporary woman's analysis and rejection of this tradition, see Jane Anger, *Her Protection for Women* (1589) in Shepherd 1985.)

Rosalind/Ganymede's aspersions on women so enrage Celia, who has been forced, like the audience, to watch this near-caricatured acting out of women's inferiority to men, that she threatens her,

> You have simply misused our sex in your love-prate. We must have your doublet and hose plucked over your head, and show the world what the bird hath done to her own nest.
>
> (IV.1.192–5)

(Exactly what would be revealed by such a punishment is in fact ambiguous, since the play constantly foregrounds the fact, as I am about to indicate, that the actor is a boy.)

In the character of Rosalind/Ganymede, then, at this straightforward level, we see acted out the suggestion that differences between male and female behaviour are not natural but in some sense arbitrary, the result of social circumstance – clothing, or the beliefs and behaviour of those who surround us. In the words of Juliet Stevenson, who played the part of Rosalind/Ganymede in a Royal Shakespeare Company production of the play in 1985,

> I'd always suspected that there's a much more dangerous play in *As You Like It*. A subversive play, one that challenges notions of gender, that asks questions about the boundaries and qualities of our 'male' and 'female' natures.
>
> (Rutter 1988: 97)

Gender is a social construct, not a matter of essential nature.

Similar 'miraculous' transformations of character happen to both Duke Frederick and Oliver when they are confronted with changed circumstance: not only gender identity, but other aspects of identity as well, it is suggested, are open to radical change. These transformations should not be interpreted as 'radical' in all its meanings, however. These episodes happen off-stage, safely encapsulated as 'fable', and Oliver and Frederick are through them reabsorbed into a 'stable' family and state, with Duke Senior at its head. In Louis Montrose's words, 'paternity and fraternity are reaffirmed as spiritual bonds rather than as bonds of blood and property' (Montrose 1981: 45).

It is also relevant to note that in its presentation of the instability of gender identity, the play is not necessarily as progressive as my reading so far might suggest. Rosalind/Ganymede fights off tears (III.4) and faints (IV.3). She also reprimands Celia, 'Dost thou think, though I am caparisoned like a man, I have a doublet and hose in my disposition? (III.2.193–5); and 'Do you not know I am a woman? When I think, I must speak' (III.2.247–8). In addition, as Louis Montrose has pointed out, the play's ending of multiple marriages and the reimposition of family stability can be seen as the reimposition of patriarchal order in more ways than one, since 'the marital couplings dissolve the bonds of sisterhood [between Rosalind and Celia] at the same time that they forge the bonds of brotherhood' (Montrose 1983: 69).

It isn't necessary for a play to present these issues in an entirely liberal or progressive fashion to enable classroom discussion of the questions of gender roles and social structure, of course. The very fact of this closing down of options can in itself be a stimulating point of analysis. And it is also the case that Rosalind/Ganymede's gender ambiguity does not end with the question of whether she is, or could be, a he, despite Stevenson's assertions that the character is 'always only Rosalind', always to be seen and played as if truly female (Rutter 1988: 109). In choosing her pseudonym, Rosalind reminds the audience, should they have forgotten, that Ganymede was 'Jove's own page' (I.3.122). So he was; and Jove's lover. (See the opening scene of Marlowe's *Dido, Queen of Carthage* for a particularly outrageous and sexy demonstration of this.) The word 'ganymede', in fact, was one commonly used in the renaissance to refer to homosexuals (Bray 1982; Saslow 1986), and also and in particular to boy actors who played women's parts. (Other common terms included 'ingle' and 'catamite'.) In taking the name Ganymede, therefore, Rosalind is naming 'herself' a boy actor and a sodomite. This reference is not made only once in the play, but in a series of asides lost to the modern audience because the terminology and mythology commonly used to refer to homosexuality and to sexuality in general have changed. They have also been lost because of the impressive failure of modern editors of the play to point out such jokes to their readers, and because modern ways of performing the play, with a woman in Rosalind/Ganymede's part, efface the ambiguities once available. Reading the play alert to this issue, we might note, for instance, that the first words spoken by

Rosalind/Ganymede are 'O Jupiter!' (II.4.1); a foregrounding of the sodomitical origins of his/her name and the sodomitical associations of the boy actor's role.

This joke about Ganymede's relationship with Jove/Jupiter is repeated in various forms several times in III.2, the scene where Ganymede/Rosalind first meets Orlando. Having heard Celia's rendition of Orlando's abysmal love verses, Rosalind/Ganymede responds, 'O most gentle Jupiter! What tedious homily of love' (lines 155–6; this joke is missed by Albert Gilman, the editor of the Signet edition of *As You Like It*, who 'corrects' Jupiter to 'pulpiter'). When Celia describes how she found Orlando 'under a tree, like a dropped acorn', Rosalind/Ganymede responds 'It may well be called Jove's tree' (line 234). In the same scene, when accusing Orlando of not looking like the conventional lover his verses portray, s/he makes a well-worn joke about masculinity, forgiving Orlando for not having an untidy beard, 'for simply your having in beard is a younger brother's revenue' (lines 369–70). Rosalind/Ganymede himself, a boy actor, would not yet have had a broken voice or a beard, and jokes about beards were, as a result, a common source of bawdry on the stage. Then, in describing to Orlando how s/he once cured a man of love, s/he draws attention to the ambiguously related characteristics of women and boys:

> He was to imagine me his love, his mistress; and I set him every day to woo me. At which time would I, being but a moonish youth, grieve, be effeminate [unmanly *or* voluptuous *or* feminine; see *OED*], changeable, longing and liking, proud, fantastical, apish, shallow, inconstant, full of tears, full of smiles; for every passion something and for no passion truly anything, as boys and women are for the most part cattle of this colour.
>
> (lines 398–406)

A ganymede playing Rosalind plays Ganymede playing Rosalind. Continually through this scene, then, as the Rosalind/Ganymede ambiguity is played with on stage, the gender of the actor playing the part is also alluded to. The audience is offered this shifting identity as a source of humour, pleasure, and sexual titillation, in jokes that extend as well to Rosalind's lament to Celia, 'My affection hath an unknown bottom' (IV.2.198–9; for the common use of 'bottom' in bawdy humour to mean both arse and penis, see Patterson 1989: 65–9; and for a related discussion of images of anality and sexual and social transgression, Whigham 1988). A similar dig at the presence on stage of boy actors is also probably made in Rosalind/Ganymede's reflection to Silvius in III.5, 'You are a thousand times a properer man/ Than she is a woman.' Such references could be emphasized and embroidered with the use of gesture and knowing looks at the audience in any performance where Rosalind is acted by a boy.

It might be argued that this playing with gender and the consequent related destabilizing of social structure is only transitory in *As You Like It*, and that the end of the play settles down to a 'proper' ascription of gender and re-establishment of national authority. Such a reading would point out that the closure of the final scene is not limited to the fact, as I have already indicated, that the Duke is re-established as head of his people, and evil brothers reabsorbed into newly stable families. In addition, Rosalind becomes firmly female again, giving herself over as daughter and wife to Duke Senior and Orlando (V.4.116–17, 'To you I give myself, for I am yours'), her sexual ambiguity and social independence abolished. Phebe, furthermore, is apparently only too happy to marry the tedious Silvius rather than pursue a sodomitical fate and 'have a woman to [her] lord' (V.4.133–4; marriage to Silvius is 'appropriate' in class terms as well as gender ones, whereas the desired relationship with a Duke's daughter is certainly not). And Touchstone is respectably wedded to his Audrey, for all his earlier attempts to enjoy sex sodomitically: that is, outside marriage (II.4.44–61; see too his bawdy rewriting of Orlando's love poetry, III.2.101–12). Instability and sodomitical excess, then, are tamed.

But I prefer to point out that the very swiftness and artificiality of the ending of the play, which is achieved by the miraculous conversion of evil-doers and the descent of a god (Hymen, the god of marriage) from the skies, suggest that the conventional ending is exactly that: a convention, a masque or a mask. This interpretation of the play is strengthened by the fact that its closing words go to Rosalind – or rather, to a ganymede, the boy acting Rosalind – calling himself a lady, joking bawdily about needing no 'bush' (an advertising sign used by wine-sellers, and thus part of his/her metaphor here, but also a hairy part of the body, so perhaps 'cunt'), teasing the audience about their own flirtations with one another and offering to kiss the men, 'if I were a woman'. The play ends, then, with Ganymede's ambiguities, and with sodomitical desire, forefronted again. The stability of the end of Act V, the stability of the family and of the state, are temporary and an illusion.

In saying that this is what I prefer to point out, I want to bring this discussion back to its originating trajectory, a discussion of Section 28, pretended families, and homosexuality in the classroom. Attacks on deviant behaviour and beliefs have always been one of the ways in which oppressive regimes have sought to legitimize themselves. Indeed, as Jonathan Dollimore amongst others has demonstrated, one can learn a great deal about the structures of power and representation of the dominant order in any society by the fears and hatreds it reveals through what it attempts to outlaw or suppress (Dollimore 1986). Two connected targets of the Tories' present 'reforms' of our society are the family and school, as they attempt to force us into their straitjacket of pretended families. Through our practices as teachers, I believe, we can combat these attempts to police our lives and the lives of those we teach. Such an opposition can even be made when teaching Shakespeare.

I should like to thank, with love, for their part in helping formulate the arguments of this chapter, the students at CCAT with whom I discussed the play in 1986–7; Gill Spraggs, who generously gave me access to details of the work of the Lesbian and Gay Rights Working Party of City of Leicester NUT; Jim Friedman, Robin Hamilton, Deirdre O'Byrne, Simon Shepherd, Mick Wallis, Nigel Wheale, Christine White; and Tim Clarke, who first introduced me to *As You Like It* when I studied it for O level in 1971–2, although the reading we then developed bears little relation to the one offered here.

REFERENCES

Batsleer, Janet, Davies, Tony, O'Rourke, Rebecca and Weedon, Chris, (eds) (1985) *Rewriting English: Cultural Politics of Gender and Class*, London: Methuen.

Belsey, Catherine (1980) *Critical Practice*, London: Methuen.

Bray, Alan (1982) *Homosexuality in Renaissance England*, London: Gay Men's Press.

Bristol, Michael (1985) *Carnival and Theatre: Plebeian Culture and the Structure of Authority in Renaissance England*, London: Methuen.

Brown, Judith (1986) *Immodest Acts: The Life of a Lesbian Nun in Renaissance Italy*, Oxford: Oxford University Press.

Dollimore, Jonathan (1986) 'The dominant and the deviant: a violent dialectic', *Critical Quarterly* 28/1, 2: 179–92.

Foucault, Michel (1979) *The History of Sexuality. Volume 1: An Introduction*, London: Allen Lane.

Fraser, Antonia (1984) *The Weaker Vessel: Woman's Lot in Seventeenth-Century England*, London: Weidenfeld & Nicolson.

Graham, Elspeth, Hinds, Hilary, Hobby, Elaine and Wilcox, Helen, (eds) (1989) *Her Own Life: Autobiographical Writings by Seventeenth-Century Englishwomen*, London: Routledge.

Heisch, Allison (1980) 'Queen Elizabeth and the persistence of patriarchy', *Feminist Review* 4: 45–56.

Heron, Ann (ed.) (1983) *One Teenager in Ten: Writings by Gay and Lesbian Youth*, Boston: Alyson Publications.

Hill, Christopher (1964) *Society and Puritanism in Pre-Revolutionary England*, London: Secker & Warburg.

—— (1972) *The World Turned Upside Down: Radical Ideas During the English Revolution*, London: Maurice Temple Smith.

ILEA Learning Resources Branch (1986) *Positive Images: A Resources Guide to Materials about Homosexuality for Use by Teachers and Librarians in Secondary Schools and Further Education Colleges*, London: ILEA, Centre for Learning Resources, 275 Kennington Lane, London, SE11 5QZ.

Jardine, Lisa (1983) *Still Harping on Daughters: Women and Drama in the Age of Shakespeare*, Brighton: Harvester Press.

Lesbian and Gay Rights Working Party (1987) *Outlaws in the Classroom: Lesbians and Gays in the School System*, Leicester: City of Leicester Teachers' Association, 4 Rupert Street, Leicester, LE1 5XH.

Licata, Salvatore, and Petersen, Robert, (eds) (1985) *The Gay Past: A Collection of Historical Essays*, New York: Harrington Park Press.

Montrose, Louis (1981) ' "The place of a brother" in *As You Like It:* social process and comic form', *Shakespeare Quarterly* 32: 28–54.

—— (1983) ' "Shaping fantasies": figurations of gender and power in Elizabethan culture', *Representations* 1: 61–94.

Norris, Stephanie and Read, Emma (1985) *Out in the Open: People Talking about being Gay or Bisexual*, London: Pan Books.

Patterson, Annabel (1989) *Shakespeare and the Popular Voice*, Oxford: Basil Blackwell.

Prior, Mary (ed.) (1985) *Women in English Society 1500–1800*, London: Methuen.

Rutter, Carol (1988) *Clamorous Voices: Shakespeare's Women Today*, London: The Women's Press.

Saslow, James (1986) *Ganymede in the Renaissance: Homosexuality in Art and Society*, New Haven, CT: Yale University Press.

Shepherd, Simon (1981) *Amazons and Warrior Women: Varieties of Feminism in Seventeenth-Century Drama*, Brighton: Harvester Press.

—— (ed.) (1985) *The Women's Sharp Revenge: Five Women's Pamphlets from the Renaissance*, London: Fourth Estate.

—— (1986) *Marlowe and the Politics of Elizabethan Theatre*, Brighton: Harvester Press.

—— (1990) 'Promotional agencies, Section 28, law and education', *Text and Context* 4.

Stone, Lawrence (1977) *The Family, Sex and Marriage in England 1500–1800*, New York: Harper & Row.

Trenchard, Lorraine and Warren, Hugh (1984) *Something to Tell You . . . : The Experiences and Needs of Young Lesbians and Gay Men in London*, London: London Gay Teenage Group, 6–9 Manor Gardens, Holloway, N7.

Warren, Hugh (1984) *Talking About School*, London: London Gay Teenage Group, 6–9 Manor Gardens, Holloway, N7.

Weeks, Jeffrey (1985), *Sexuality and its Discontents: Meanings, Myths and Modern Sexualities*, London: Routledge & Kegan Paul.

Whigham, Frank (1988) 'Reading social conflict in the alimentary tract: more on the body in renaissance drama', *English Literary History* 55(2): 333–50.

Wren, Robert (1987) 'Pederasty in Elizabethan London', in *History Supplement: Papers of the 'Homosexuality, which Homosexuality?' Conference*, Amsterdam: Free University/Schorer Foundation.

8

The power of devils and the hearts of men: notes towards a drama of witchcraft

Sarah Beckwith

MAKING THE TEXT SOCIAL

The power of devils is in the hearts of men.

These are the words of George Gifford, nonconformist clergyman in Maldon, Essex; they are taken from his demonological treatise, *A Dialogue Concerning Witches and Witchcraft* of 1593.[1] Gifford's words locate two parallel readings of witchcraft. The first posits it as an externalized manifestation of metaphysical evil – 'the power of devils' – and the second places it in the 'hearts of men'. One view would seem to be part and parcel of a cosmological view which sees the religious, the moral, and the social as coterminous categories and where the consideration of human agency always occurs in a context which stresses divine attribution. And on the contrary the other view appears to offer a rationalist explanation of witchcraft as a problem of human community, human action. But it is crucial to Gifford's sense here that these two alternatives are by no means mutually exclusive. Indeed part of the structure of his aphorism is to break down such oppositions with their confident division between what can be accounted external and what internal, what the sphere of the devil, God, the supernatural, and what the social and humanly constructed sphere. Each he implies inheres in the other.[2]

Criticism of Shakespeare's *Macbeth* seems to have polarized around one or other of the poles of Gifford's analysis, ignoring the equivalizing, equivocating effect of that 'is'. Thus the witches are 'symbolic representations of the unconscious or half-conscious guilt of Macbeth himself' (Coles 1938: 196). Or, on the contrary, such a view is 'a wish to get rid of a mere external supernaturalism and to find a psychological and spiritual meaning in that which

143

the groundlings probably received as hard facts'.[3] But the 'is' of Gifford's quotation points to an area of radical instability in early seventeenth-century society, an instability which extended at the very deepest level to social identity. That instability was precisely a crisis in the attribution of responsibility, ensuing from changes in far-reaching and deep-rooted social relations; and since the self is itself a relational phenomenon, such changes necessarily involved profound changes to the structuring of identity and the self-perceptions of personalities. It involved a highly charged awareness of that which simultaneously separates people from each other, and that which connects them – an obsession with borders, margins, edges, or alternatively links, bridges, bonds. This demarcation of the relations between people encompasses the personal, the social, the economic, the religious and the political, and the relations between them. Any attempt to reduce the witches in *Macbeth* then, either to a figment of Macbeth's imagination, or indeed to a mere superstitious and erroneous outdated belief in the fiction of witches, misses the point, for the power of devils and the hearts of men are inextricably intermingled. *Macbeth* is an examination of that intermingling which has as its 'shaping form' 'a quite extraordinarily open interaction of social order and social disintegration' (Williams 1981: 157). One of the means of that examination is the phenomenon of witchcraft.

Witchcraft has often been seen as a crux, a problem of interpretation in the play, one which an older mode of historical criticism thought could be solved by locating some kind of ultimately grounding definition in a historical context which would find the answer to such problems by revealing that definitive meaning. 'If we could understand what witchcraft meant in the society that engendered *Macbeth*, then we could understand what it meant in the play *Macbeth* itself' is the story of this mode of criticism. One possible source for such 'contextualizing' would be, for example, the demonological treatises. But Stuart Clark, in an article which addresses witchcraft within the context of a discussion about the interrelation of the occult and scientific mentalities of the renaissance by means of a discussion of some of the demonological treatises, has emphasized the extent to which such treatises themselves constitute part of an 'epistemological debate' (Clark 1984: 368). Speaking of the analysis of 'demonic effects', he asks,

What were the criteria for distinguishing between their true and illusory aspects? Along what point on the axis from miracles through to natural wonders to ordinary natural contingencies were they to be placed? Tackling such questions involved making distinctions that were critical for any explanation of phenomena, whether demonic or not – distinctions between what was possible and impossible, or really and falsely perceived, and between both supernature and nature, nature and artifice.

(Clark 1984: 354)

Thus the line between where supernature ended and where human agency began was sometimes invisible, sometimes wavering, nowhere near as clearly delineated as the above quotations from Coles and Bradley imply, and it was certainly a line that was highly negotiable. The demonological treatises were one site, suggests Clark, of this historical negotiation, a place of struggle over meaning rather than a place where meaning can be fixed and safely laid to rest. The demonological treatises in Clark's illuminating handling of them do not simply provide a repository of knowledge *about* witchcraft which can then tell us *about* the depiction of witchcraft in the play. Thus if we are to seek help from history it can only be by locating texts such as the witch trials, the demonological treatises, the social history that mediates the phenomena of witch mania to us, as texts which do not themselves escape from the problems of interpretation. The point is that if we could understand the function of witchcraft in *Macbeth*, then we could understand the phenomenon of witchcraft in seventeenth-century society (although these are by no means identical phenomena), because both phenomena are part of the same 'signifying system' of culture, of institutions, practices, and works and the relations between them (Williams 1981: 208–9).

What this chapter seeks to do is to see not what use an understanding of 'witchcraft' is to the play, but what use understanding the play is for an examination of witchcraft. It seeks to reverse the priorities of literary criticism to posit the play as one *social text* among a series of others. In the agenda set out by a recent editor of essays on Shakespeare,

A course that attempts in this way to talk about plays in history and ideology will not 'cover' the usual array of literary texts. It will, instead, be investigating a range of social texts and practices against which to assess differen-

145

SARAH BECKWITH

tially, the specific function of the theater and dramatic representations, and it will be preoccupied with the grounds of
its own undertaking.

(Howard and O'Connor 1987: 8)

In doing so, it is clear that there can be no simple polarization
of background and foreground where historical texts can reveal
the meaning of fictional ones.[4] Thus an investigation of the play
may become not another addition to the Shakespeare hagiogra-
phy, but part of the much more difficult yet politically vital
task of investigating a crucial and determining moment in the
seventeenth century – its crisis in gender relations, its construction
of a new and massively influential masculine identity through and
around the birth of what has been termed the first 'political
ideology' – the ideology of witchcraft.[5]

The stage, as has been amply demonstrated by several recent
critics, is one forum for a complex investigation and construction
of identity, where histrionic versions of the self are pitted against
essentialist ones, and it is significant for the way in which it
is symptomatic not just of the culture of theatre, but of the
theatricalization of culture.[6] If the witch trials can be seen in the
play, then theatre and spectacle itself – the spectre of drama –
staging and 'production', also inhere in the very processes of the
witch trials themselves.[7] Ever since the discrediting of Margaret
Murray's thesis that there existed covens of witches (hidden and
secret pockets of subversion) conspiring against social norms,
historians have had to come to terms with the fantasized nature
of the crime, with its fictionality – which is not at all the same
thing as its non-existence.[8] Indeed it is evident that the necessity
to make sense of such phenomena has led to some markedly
interdisciplinary directions in conventional social history. A fully
historicized reading of *Macbeth* and a fully psychological social
history of witchcraft share at least one thing in common: both
need to account for the way history and fiction inhere in each
other.[9]

WITCHCRAFT AND IDENTITY

The more antithetical constructs (whose terms are mutually
exclusive, rather than dialectical or mutually relativizing) are

built into human relations, the more easily human beings can be dominated and ruled.[10]

Witchcraft, in the words of Christina Larner, one of the finest of the subject's historians, 'always began with the pointing finger extending away from the self'.[11] In doing so, it established the unstable boundaries of that self. It put a stop to the circulation of guilt that historians like Keith Thomas and Alan Macfarlane have seen as central to the phenomenon of witchcraft. These historians perceive witchcraft as a breakdown in 'communitas', in old values of neighbourliness put to extremities of strain by the violent polarization of levels of wealth in village life and the absence of any new structures which would accommodate the casualties of an increasingly market-oriented society. Influenced by functionalist anthropological accounts, they see witchcraft as one mechanism whereby those who most benefited from this increased social polarization could obviate claims that were made on their patronage. Their account links a nascent individualism, and therefore a different sense of the boundaries of the self, with an increasing differentiation from and in the community. Thus: 'Witchcraft is a means of effecting a deep social change – a change from a neighbourly, highly integrated and mutually interdependent village society to a more individualistic one' (Macfarlane 1970: 197).

Pointing out that many witch trials in England were initiated by refusals of charity, and observing that witches were statistically those at the bottom of the social pile – the old, the poor, women – they see the witch trials as evidence of the projection of the guilt of the newly rich on to those who have been most disadvantaged by the gaining of that wealth. It is an account which coheres with the kind of portrait offered in a play such as *The Witch of Edmonton*:

> And why on me? Why should the envious world
> Throw all their scandalous malice upon me?
> 'Cause I am poor, deform'd and ignorant,
> And like a bow buckl'd and bent together
> By some more strong in mischiefs than myself?
> Must I for that be made a common sink
> For all the filth and rubbish of men's tongues
> To fall and run into?
>
> (Dekker *et al.* 1983: II.1.1–8)

147

The play offers a portrait of a witch that simultaneously exemplifies her construction. Thus Mother Sawyer's words in the play.

> . . . Tis all one
> To be a witch as to be counted one.
> (II.1.113–15)

echo some of the sources Macfarlane quotes: 'half proofes are to be allowed, and are good causes of suspition' (Macfarlane 1970:16).

On one level it is 'the misery of beggary and want' that are the 'two devils' haunting the play (Dekker *et al.* 1983: I.1.18–19). It is the refusal of charity to Mother Sawyer that causes her to seek for revenge on those who have refused her patronage. And Sir Arthur Clarington, the man who palms off the maidservant he has seduced on to the impoverished Thorney, thinks she is a witch because she has located his secret of fornication. In the end the play accommodates simultaneously a version of witchcraft which sees it as socially constructed and engendered, but which nevertheless still sees Mother Sawyer as developing the power of witchcraft. An understanding of it as a social construction does not clash with its depiction as a cosmic drama (a point made by Dollimore 1984: 176–7). But when Mother Sawyer tries to circulate the guilt away from herself back to society, by asking the question, 'A witch, who is not?' and cites 'painted things in princes courts', 'city witches', and 'men of law' as the chief contenders, it is Clarington who observes, 'Yes, but the law casts not an eye on these' (IV.1.120). He reveals the way in which witchcraft is also the construction of a judiciary system which is acting in the interests of the ruling classes. And any analysis of witchcraft would have to examine the relationship between 'nation' and locality, between prince and people, between elite and 'popular' culture.[12] For witchcraft is not simply endemic to the community, spontaneously erupting as a result of local tensions. It is also part of a concerted political ideology, a concern not simply with the way people behave but also with the way people think. It is a state-enforced, national ideology, which 'identified the enemies of society with the enemies of God' (Larner 1981: 20). The legislation progressively involved a distinction between white and black magic, between *maleficium* and diabolism, the belief that witchcraft was the result of a demonic pact with the devil, and in the process it involved the sifting and examination of a whole set of animist beliefs which linked the sacred with the profane world. Peter Burke writes:

> . . . the reform of popular culture was more than just another episode in the long war between the godly and the ungodly, it accompanied a major shift in religious sensibility. The godly were out to destroy the traditional familiarity with the sacred, because they believed that familiarity breeds irreverence.[13]

As part of the reform of 'popular culture', witchcraft indeed has been described by one historian who sees the Reformation as the *first* attempt at a thoroughgoing Christianization of the peasantry, as 'an assault upon the animist mentality of the partly christianized peasant.' (Delumeau 1977: 170–2; also see Larner 1984: 65). And tied up with this severance of the sacred and the profane is a simultaneous appropriation of the sacred, a sacralization of sovereign authority, and an increasing separation of elite and 'popular' social groups. This is the period where an ideology of patriarchal kingship, of an absolutist notion of the divine right of kings, is in development. The persecution of 'witchcraft' constituted an attack on deviance which involved an increasing homogenization of the educated classes; indeed the developing judiciary was one of the very means of that homogenization, and one of the means by which the state strengthened its hold on the rural gentry. As Keith Wrightson puts it,

> The cohesiveness and sense of identity which the meetings of the quarter sessions had helped to develop at the level of the county, were complemented and expanded at the level of the nation by the experience of higher education.
>
> (Wrightson 1982: 192)

And as Christina Larner emphatically states, 'Witch-hunting was a ruling class activity . . . because any large scale pursuit and rounding up of categories requires official organization and administration' (1984: 2).

Stuart Clark, in a fascinating investigation of the demonological treatise of King James I, has noted the extent to which his *Daemonologie* functions simultaneously as an introduction of continental theories into England, a refutation of the notorious sceptic Reginald Scot, and a description of an ideal monarchy (Clark 1977). His active involvement with witch-hunting, as Clark

stresses, effectively ends with the North Berwick trials with
which he is crucially concerned as the supposed object of their
witching, and because as a result of this they are conducted as
treason trials.[14] The *Daemonologie* is the struggle carried on at
the ideological level. The marking out of the demonic is also a
sanctification of the sacral quality of kingship. So it is a short
step from,

> since the Devill is the very contrarie opposite to God, there
> can be no better way to know God, than by the contrarie –
> (Harrison 1966: 55)

to,

> the prince is a kind of likeness of divinity: and the tyrant
> on the contrary, a likeness of the boldness of the Adversary.
> (Erasmus 1936: 157, 174; also quoted in Clark 1977: 175)

Royal patriarchal absolutism is reinforced at the level of cos-
mology, and the enemies of society are made synonymous with
the enemies of God. Clark's essay stresses the extent to which
inversion is the topos through which order is categorized by its
binary opposite: disorder. The articulation of this particular political ideology, the ideology of patriarchal kingship, is expressed
through a gender divide. For as well as demarcating a new
relationship between citizen and state, a growing delineation of
the relations between private and public occurs in this period, a
division which will domesticate women, confining them to a
sphere which is deprived of political influence as that political,
public world is increasingly defined as masculine. The ideology
of witchcraft is crucially bound up with the patriarchal ideology
of femininity. For, 'where the Devill findes the greatest ignorance
and barbaritie, there assayles he grosseliest, as I gave you the
reason wherefore there was moe Witches of women nor men'
(Harrison 1966: 69).

The vast majority of witches were women. Where they were
not women they were usually accused of being witches because
they were witches by 'contagion' (witchcraft is a very contagious
disease) or because, as on the continent when the witch manias
reached their peak, men were caught up in their momentum.[15]
And witchcraft was closely related to a widespread criminalization
of women. The period when witch accusations reach their peak
is also the period when local court records disclose 'an intense

preoccupation with women who are a visible threat to the patriarchal system' (Underdown 1985: 119). The subordination of
women is the very principle of good government in family and
in the state, for, 'inferiours that cannot be subject in a family . . .
will hardly be brought to yield such subjection as they ought in
Church or Commonwealth' (Gouge 1985: 200).

Witches then are those women who are fantasized as the simultaneous subverters of the family and the state. In Middleton's *The
Witch*, for example, their spells are seen to parody the normal
role of feminine nurturing. Their dislocation of the organic body
in their subtle stews is bound up with incestuous relations
(especially Hecate with her son Firestone), with illegitimacy, and
with the destruction of fertility within marriages.[16] Renaissance
drama throughout the period uses the language of witchcraft and
of bewitchment to describe the unholy influence of women on
men. The language of 'possession' functions in a double sense; it
is the instability of women as 'possessions' which is radically
intertwined with the language of possession and self-possession.
To be in love in *Othello*, in *The Witch*, in *The Witch of Edmonton*,
in *The Duchess of Malfi* frequently *is* to be bewitched, and bewitchment is often, although not exclusively, something done to men
by women.[17] Thus witchcraft extends beyond the arena of the
courts to provide an extensive means of social control which runs
through all relations between women and men. In *The Subject of
Tragedy*, Catherine Belsey marks out the unstable subject position
assumed by men in this period, and adds that women, in comparison, 'both were and were not subjects'.[18] Post-Reformation ideology places a new emphasis on the notion of individual responsibility. Larner remarks how that new ideology renders the position
of women ambiguous. Until the witchcraft statutes (1542, 1563,
1604), the misdemeanours of women had been the responsibility
of their husbands and fathers, and punishments such as whip-
pings, which were appropriate to children, were deemed to be
an appropriate punishment for women too.

> As witches they became adult criminals acting in a manner
> for which their husbands could not be deemed responsible.
> The pursuit of witches could therefore be seen as a rearguard
> action against the emergence of women as independent
> adults.
>
> (Larner 1981: 102)

Peter Stallybrass talks of the 'ideological formation of the family and the state' as being 'staked out across the physical bodies of criminalized women' (Stallybrass 1986: 131). It would also be possible to add that it was a renegotiated 'masculinity' which was also being staked out in this way. Witchcraft is a testimony both to the viciousness and to the instability of those categories.

WITCHCRAFT AND STAGECRAFT IN *MACBETH*

Psychic experience is something inner that becomes outer and the ideological sign, something outer that becomes inner.

(Vološinov 1973: 39)

Therefore the topoi of disorder/order and the discourse of inversion which are the 'contrarieties' mapped out in the *Daemonologie* are not the stable oppositions which political theorists were sometimes concerned to make them. In *Macbeth* they are dangerously mobile categories, and the play is obsessed with borders: the borders of state (in this case England and Scotland), the borders of patriarchal kingship, and the borders of the masculine subject. For if witchcraft is one of the devices whereby the boundaries of society are delineated against the enemies of God, and if that delineation depends on the obvious externalization of guilt and the establishment of the scapegoat, then the very fact that it would be impossible to bring the witches in *Macbeth* to justice is of the utmost significance. For what this indicates is that the witches can function as *pure* embodiments (or disembodiments) of quintessential evil, their metaphysical essence – the *other* par excellence – untouchable by human society, and yet also that, as fantastic creatures, they are deeply interior to the imagination that they most closely inhabit.[19] There is in fact no unequivocal process of ejection in the play, for its drama opens up the arena of fantasy, the tenuous shadow area where it is not clear what is on the outside and what is on the inside. The witches in *Macbeth* can hardly stabilize boundaries, for they are neither inside nor outside, neither male nor female, neither culture nor nature, neither substantial nor immaterial, neither real nor merely apparent, neither inside the mind nor fully outside it. Their function is like one recent account of the patriarchal definition of femininity, acting both to edge off chaos, and to border on to it.[20] The

THE POWER OF DEVILS

witches are both marginalized to the wastelands of society, not fully individualized, speaking in 'improper' parody of the language of the ruling order, the fantasized projection of that society, and like all projections they are simultaneously deeply internal to the very workings of that society, effecting a disruption whose political name is tyranny. Their simultaneous existence inside and outside bespeaks a parallel splitting in Macbeth himself. His experience is increasingly one of a painful divorce between appearance and reality:

> . . . look like th'innocent flower.
> But be the serpent under't.
> (*Macbeth*, I.5.65–6)

> False face must hide what the false heart doth know.
> (I.7.84)

and allied with this a self-division,

> To know my deed 'twere best not know myself.
> (II.2.73)

This self-division is seen as a feminization in the play. Macbeth's tyranny is both brought on by the necessity of proving his masculinity, being the same in his own act and valour as he is in desire, and by the essential failure of that masculinity, tied up as it is with the feminine influence of the sisterhood of the witches and Lady Macbeth. In the last act the witches are seen to have mined Macbeth from within, to have 'cow'd' his 'better part of man'.[21] Those who will redeem the time in the society of *Macbeth* are those who are like Macduff, 'unborn of woman', or like Malcolm, 'unknown to woman' (IV.3.126). Masculine integrity, just like the integrity of the state, is based on the rigorous exclusion of women. Lady Macduff is slaughtered, Lady Macbeth goes mad, the witches simply disappear from the play. Masculine integrity in the drama must be based on a ruthless erasure of the relational nature of that identity.

At the end of the play Macbeth is left an empty cipher, and it is no accident that it is the image of the actor which he should use to give voice to his own nihilistic despair. The play has investigated another borderline phenomenon with a systematic rigour noticed by many critics. The clothes in the play are another interface between the public and the private: they simultaneously show the body forth to the world and hide the body from that world. They conceal and reveal. They are of course the very stuff of the actor's trade. In *Macbeth* the clothes imagery seems to point simultaneously to a histrionic version of the self, a self who makes himself, and who appears, and then also to an essentialist version of the self, one who is not made but pre-exists the social order. In the end Macbeth is the thief dressed in the borrowed robes of a giant; his disguise merely emphasizes how far he is from the grandeur of a king:

> . . . now does he feel his title
> Hang loose about him, like a giant's robe
> Upon a dwarfish thief.
>
> (V.2.20–2)

So on one level what is confirmed is a world where a king is obviously and self-evidently a king, and not a usurper, a tyrant (you can tell by the hang of his trousers . . .). It is a version of self which renders people present to themselves and to other people, transparently. In the end it is both witchcraft and stagecraft that must be eradicated within the play. For what both have in common is a version of the self which is not present to itself but which is fundamentally transforming, transformative, a self inhabited by others and which inhabits others. What they both share at different and unacknowledged levels is a sense of the boundary phenomenon of selfhood itself. Witchcraft is what happens to a society in flux when it cannot bear or articulate that flux. It is perhaps for this reason that witchcraft and stagecraft are frequently linked as metaphors in the works of the anti-theatrical pamphleteers: 'Do we not use (plays) to counterfeit witchcraft, charmed drinks and amorous potions and thereby to draw the affection of men and to stir them to lust?' (Munday 1986: 140, n.12)

In a brilliant article by Katharine Maus the suspicion of theatre and the suspicion of female sexuality are shown to be manifestations of the same anxiety. For, according to Maus, 'At the foundation of the anti-theatrical fear of histrionic display is a fear of losing male identity' (Maus 1987: 569). Women, witches, and actors are similar for they never show themselves to be 'such as indeed they are' – and if this duplicity can be identified as being in the realm of the 'feminine', then masculinity can maintain its own fictitious integrity, its own inviolate boundaries, the boundaries simultaneously of the self, of the state, of the body, and of the body politic (see Wiesner 1985). So it is no wonder that at the end of *Macbeth* the man who has been so emasculated should use the metaphor of the actor to describe himself, because he suspects that what he is describing is an empty fabrication, a duplicitous construction whose 'natural' names would or could be – the witch, the woman, the tyrant.

Macbeth in the last act describes himself as being 'tied to a stake' (V.7.11–12). The reference, as the editors note, is obviously to bear-baiting. But surely it is also an evident reference to the end of witches. Even though in England witches were hanged and not burned, the association of the witch and the stake was proverbial. But although on one level the play demonizes both witchcraft and stagecraft, its tragedy being in its attempt to articulate a world which is ceasing to be organic in organic terms (see Moretti 1983: 28), on another level it has shown the extent to which both are themselves a product of a world where the self is relational, but which cannot yet afford to recognize that. The anti-theatrical tracts locate the theatre as 'a site where anxieties about a changing social order were discursively produced and managed'.[22] Witchcraft could be said to be another means of managing the same anxiety. It is no coincidence that the anti-theatrical pamphlets die out at about the same time that witch accusations also diminish. Indeed both phenomena may be seen to be crucially bound up with the idea, not so much of *enchantment*, as of a disenchantment with whose effects we are still coming to uncomfortable terms.

I would like to end with a quotation which I have left deliberately unreconstructed. Its gender-blindness may in this case read as an insight. And at the same time it remains the best possible testimony to the self/other relation of the practice of teaching – Shakespeare or anything else:

> Man has no internal sovereign territory; he is all and always on the boundary; looking within himself, he looks in the eyes of the other . . . I cannot do without the other . . . I cannot become myself without the other; I must find myself in the other, finding the other in me (in mutual reflection and perception).[23]

ACKNOWLEDGEMENTS

Many thanks to both editors for their comments on this chapter. I would also like to thank David Aers for his characteristically informed and vigorous responses and in addition the participants at the History Workshop conference in Brighton 1988 for theirs. This material is based on a course that I have taught for two consecutive years at the University of East Anglia. The course goes under the 'hold-all' title of 'Representations of Women in Renaissance Drama'. In the past two years its focus has been on the construction of witchcraft and its relations to the discourse of inversion in renaissance practice. I would like to thank all the students who have participated in those seminars. This chapter is for them.

NOTES

1 *A Dialogue Concerning Witches and Witchcraft* (1593, this edition 1843) pp. 22–3, quoted in Muir *Macbeth*. (1984: lv). Also see Macfarlane's essay on Gifford (Macfarlane 1977). Macfarlane describes Gifford as a ' "Puritan" by most definitions', whose work 'is one of the most humane and rational attacks on current belief about the evil power of witches' (1977: 145). Excerpts from the *Dialogue* are reprinted in Haining (1974: 76–111).

2 See Peter Stallybrass's comment here on a similar point, 'But it would be misleading to interpret this overdetermination as a *conflict* between supernatural and natural modes of explanation, since, within the cultural context, there was no necessity to choose between those modes' (Stallybrass 1982).

3 Bradley (1961: 290). I am grateful to students for drawing my attention to these passages.

4 It perhaps still needs saying, however, that this is because of the historicity of fiction rather than because of the fictionality of history, as some depoliticized readings have it.

5 'The christianity of the early modern period with its emphasis on personal accountability was therefore Europe's first political ideology' (Larner 1981: 194).

6 There is by now an ever-growing body of 'new historicist' literature on renaissance theatrical culture, but see especially, Greenblatt (1980), Orgel (1975), Tennenhouse (1986), and Montrose (1980). For an excellent review of such approaches see Wayne (1987). For a feminist critique see Jardine (1986).

7 The body of the witch was very much on display, from the evidence of the witch's mark, to the ducking ceremonies, formal or informal, which were enacted to test whether the woman was a witch, through

to the execution itself. See especially Matthew Hopkins, *The Discovery of Witches* reproduced in Haining (1974: 175–86).

8 See Murray (1921) and Larner's essay, '*Crimen Exceptum?* The crime of witchcraft in Europe', in Larner 1984 (35–69) for a useful criticism of Margaret Murray. The confusions of inner and outer reality evinced in the phenomenon of witchcraft itself make it a site where the inadequacies of a naively empiricist approach, or conversely but complementarily, a psychologizing approach, become blatantly apparent.

9 I am thinking particularly of the uses of anthropological models in the social history of Macfarlane (1970) and Thomas (1971).

10 Theweleit (1987: 378). The whole book is strongly recommended.

11 Larner (1981: 135). There were of course women who proclaimed themselves witches. Some of the tensions and difficulties of definition, attribution, and self-ascription are minutely handled in Thomas Dekker, John Ford and William Rowley's *The Witch of Edmonton* edited by Simon Trussler and notes by Jacqui Russell (Dekker *et al.* 1983).

12 For the 'acculturation' thesis of witchcraft, which hinges on changing relations between popular and elite culture, see Muchembled (1978) and for a useful critique of the academic terminology of 'popular' culture see Richard Trexler, 'Reverence and profanity in the study of early modern religion', in vòn Greyerz (1984).

13 Burke (1978: 211–12). And see Bob Scribner, 'Cosmic order and daily life: sacred and secular in pre-industrial German society', in von Greyerz (1984): 'There is no sudden shift from one form of belief to another; rather the sacred is no longer regarded as a workable means of effectively ordering the profane world.'

14 It is worth observing here that Christina Larner points out: 'James was relatively uninterested in demonology until 1590, intensely interested from the sorcery trials of 1590 until the publication of his *Daemonologie* in 1597, and slightly embarrassed and anxious to make the least of his former enthusiasm thereafter' (Larner 1984: 5).

15 See Midelfort (1972) and for the relation between 'woman-hunting' and witch-hunting see Larner (1981). For a systematic account of the witch-hunts as a means of social control of women, see Hester (1987). Hester's account makes a welcome intervention in a critical arena which increasingly sees issues of gender as mere allegories for masculine power and the masculine body.

16 See *The Witch* I.2.97–8. Hecate to her son Firestone, 'You had rather hunt after strange women still/ Than lie with your own mothers' (Middleton 1964).

17 The language is so common as to be ubiquitous throughout the range of renaissance literature, but familiarity and conventionality should not blind us to the kinds of connection that are being suggested here.

18 Belsey (1985: 150). Othello is himself notoriously accused of witchcraft (I.2.63) because in the eyes of Brabantio it is only witchcraft – a supernatural transgression of the 'natural(ized)' social hierarchy – which could seduce a socially superior white woman to be the bride

SARAH BECKWITH

of a Black and socially subordinate man. Witchcraft accusations in
this play at least are hence an important site for the displacement of
racist as well as sexist anxiety, here directed against a man subordi-
nated as a result of his ethnic identity. See Karen Armstrong, 'And
wash the Ethiop white: femininity and the monstrous in *Othello*', in
Howard and O'Connor (1987: 143–62).

19 Reactions to the witches are carefully differentiated in the play, so
that it is made obvious the extent to which reaction to them is
fundamentally interactive and reciprocal. See Thomas Middleton's
The Witch, where Hecate says, 'Call me the horrid'st and unhallowed
things/ That life and nature trembles at, for thee/ I'll be the same.'
(I.2.200).
20 See Moi (1985: 166–7): 'if patriarchy sees women as occupying a
marginal position within the symbolic order, then it can construe
them as the *limit* or borderline of that order. From a phallocentric
point of view, women will come then to represent the necessary
frontier between man and chaos; but because of their very marginality
they will also seem to recede and merge with the chaos of the outside.
Women seen as the limit of the symbolic order will in other words
share in the disconcerting properties of all frontiers: they will be
neither inside nor outside, neither known nor unknown.'
21 V.8.18. Terry Eagleton (1986: 2) talks of the witches as 'catalysing
the region of otherness and desire in Macbeth'.
22 See Jean Howard, 'Renaissance antitheatricality and the politics of
gender and rank in *Much Ado about Nothing*', in Howard and O'Connor (1987: 163). The article is highly relevant to the kinds of argument
outlined here.
23 Mikhail Bakhtin, *Problems of Dostoevsky's Poetics*, Appendix II, ed.
and trans. Caryl Emerson, Minneapolis, 1984, quoted in Todorov
(1984: 96).

BIBLIOGRAPHY

In addition to the books cited in the text I have listed a few of the works
from the vast literature on witchcraft which I have found particularly
useful for teaching.

Belsey, Catherine (1985) *The Subject of Tragedy, Identity and Difference in
Renaissance Drama*, London: Methuen.
Bradley, A. C. (1961) *Shakespearean Tragedy*, London.
Burke, Peter (1978) *Popular Culture in Early Modern Europe*, London:
Temple Smith.
Clark, Stuart (1977) 'King James's *Daemonologie*: witchcraft and king-
ship', in Sydney Anglo (ed.) *The Damned Art: Essays in the Literature
of Witchcraft*, London: Routledge & Kegan Paul, pp. 156–82.
—— (1980) 'Inversion, misrule and the meaning of witchcraft', *Past and
Present* 87 (May): 90–127.
—— (1984) 'The scientific status of demonology', in Brian Vickers (ed.)

Occult and Scientific Mentalities in the Renaissance, Cambridge: Cambridge University Press.

Coles, B. (1938) *Shakespeare Studies: Macbeth*, New York.

Currie, Eliot P. (1973) 'The control of witchcraft in renaissance Europe', in D. Black and M. Mileski (eds) *The Social Organization of Law*, New York and London: Seminar Press, pp. 344–67.

Dekker, Thomas, Ford, John and Rowley, William (1983) *The Witch of Edmonton*, ed. Simon Trussler and Jacqui Russell, London: Methuen.

Delumeau, J. (1977) *Catholicism between Luther and Voltaire: A New View of the Counter-Reformation* London: Burns & Oates.

Dollimore, Jonathan (1984) *Radical Tragedy: Religion, Ideology and Power in the Drama of Shakespeare and his Contemporaries*, Brighton: Harvester Press.

Eagleton, Terry (1986) *Shakespeare*, Oxford: Basil Blackwell.

Easlea, Brian (1980) *Witch Hunting, Magic and the New Philosophy: An Introduction to the Debates on the Scientific Revolution 1450–1750*, Brighton: Harvester Press.

Erasmus, Desiderius (1936) *The Education of a Christian Prince*, trans. L. K. Born, New York: Columbia University Press.

Garrett, Clarke (1977) 'Women and witches: patterns of analysis', *Journal of Women in Culture and Society* 3: 461–70.

Gouge, William (1985) *Of Domesticall Duties: Eight Treatises* (London, 1634), quoted in Susan Amussen, 'Gender, family and the social order, 1560–1725', in A. Fletcher and J. Stevenson (eds) *Order and Disorder in Early Modern England*, Cambridge: Cambridge University Press.

Greenblatt, Stephen (1980) *Renaissance Self-Fashioning: From More to Shakespeare*, Chicago and London: Chicago University Press.

Haining, Peter (ed.) (1974) *The Witchcraft Papers: Contemporary Records of the Witchcraft Hysteria in Essex 1560–1700*, London: Robert Hale.

Harrison, G. B. (ed.) (1966) *James I, King of England (and VI of Scotland) Daemonologie*, Edinburgh: Edinburgh University Press.

Hester, Marianne (1987) 'The witchcraze in sixteenth and seventeenth-century England as a means of social control', lecture given in the 'Women in Context' lecture series at the University of East Anglia (June).

Howard, Jean E. and O'Connor, Marion F. (eds) (1987) *Shakespeare Reproduced: The Text in History and Ideology*, New York and London: Methuen.

Jardine, Lisa (1986) ' "The Moor, I know his trumpet": problems with New Historicist readings of women in Shakespeare', paper presented to the Berlin Shakespeare Conference.

Kieckhefer, Richard (1976) *European Witch Trials: Their Foundations in Popular and Learned Culture 1350–1500*, London: Routledge & Kegan Paul.

Larner, Christina (1981) *Enemies of God: The Witch-Hunt in Scotland*, with a foreword by Norman Cohn, London: Chatto & Windus; Baltimore, MD: Johns Hopkins University Press.

—— (1984) *Witchcraft and Religion: The Politics of Popular Belief*, edited with a foreword by Alan Macfarlane, Oxford: Basil Blackwell.

159

SARAH BECKWITH

Macfarlane, Alan (1970) *Witchcraft in Tudor and Stuart England: A Regional and Comparative Study*, London: Routledge & Kegan Paul.

—— (1977) 'A Tudor anthropologist: George Gifford's *Discourse* and *Dialogue*', in Sydney Anglo (ed.) *The Damned Art: Essays in the Literature of Witchcraft*, London: Routledge & Kegan Paul.

Maus, Katharine (1987) 'Horns of dilemma: jealousy, gender and spectatorship in English renaissance drama', *English Literary History* 54/3 (Fall).

Middleton, Thomas (1964) *Collected Works*, 8 vols, ed. A. H. Bullen, New York.

Midelfort, H. C. Erik (1972) *Witch Hunting in Southwestern Germany 1562–1684: The Social and Intellectual Foundations*, Stanford, CA: Stanford University Press.

—— (1982) 'Witchcraft, magic and the occult', in Steven Ozment (ed.) *Reformation Europe: A Guide to Research*, St Louis: Center for Reformation Research.

Moi, Toril (1985) *Sexual/Textual Politics: Feminist Literary Theory*, London: Methuen.

Montrose, Louis (1980) 'The purpose of playing: reflections on a Shakespearean anthropology', *Helios* n.s.7: 51–74.

Moretti, Franco (1983) 'The soul and the harpy: reflections on the aims and methods of literary historiography', in *Signs Taken for Wonders*, London: Verso.

Muchembled, Robert (1978) *Culture populaire et culture des élites dans la France moderne (XVe–XVIIIe siècles)* Paris: Flammarion.

Muir, Kenneth (ed.) (1984) *Macbeth*, The Arden Shakespeare, London: Methuen.

Munday, Anthony (1986) *A Second and Third Blast of Retrait from Plaies and Theaters* (London, 1580), quoted in Laura Levine, 'Men in women's clothing: anti-theatricality and effeminization from 1579 to 1642', *Criticism* 28/2 (Spring).

Murray, Margaret (1921) *The Witch-Cult in Western Europe: A Study in Anthropology*, Oxford: Clarendon Press.

Orgel, Stephen (1975) *The Illusion of Power: Political Theater in the English Renaissance*, Berkeley, Los Angeles and London: University of California Press.

Potts, Thomas (1971) *The Trial of the Lancaster Witches*, ed. G. B. Harrison, London. Facsimile of proceedings originally published in 1613.

Rosen, B. (ed.) (1969) *Witchcraft*, Stratford-upon-Avon Library, vol.6, London: Edward Arnold.

Stallybrass, Peter (1982) '*Macbeth* and witchcraft', in John Russell Brown (ed.) *Focus on Macbeth*, London: Routledge & Kegan Paul.

—— (1986) 'Patriarchal territories: the body enclosed', in Margaret W. Ferguson, Maureen Quilligan and Nancy J. Vickers (eds) *Rewriting the Renaissance: The Discourses of Sexual Difference in Early Modern Europe*, Chicago: Chicago University Press.

Tennenhouse, Leonard (1986) *Power on Display: The Politics of Shakespeare's Genres*, New York and London: Methuen.

Theweleit, Klaus (1987) *Male Fantasies*, Cambridge: Polity Press.

Thomas, Keith (1971) *Religion and the Decline of Magic*, London: Weidenfeld & Nicolson.

Todorov, Tzvetan (1984) *The Dialogical Principle*, Manchester: Manchester University Press.

Underdown, David (1985) 'The taming of the scold: the enforcement of patriarchal authority in early modern England', in A. Fletcher and J. Stevenson (eds) *Order and Disorder in Early Modern England*, Cambridge: Cambridge University Press.

Vološinov, V. N. (1973) *Marxism and the Philosophy of Language*, Cambridge, MA: Seminar Press.

von Greyerz, Kaspar (ed.) (1984) *Religion and Society in Early Modern Europe 1500–1800*, London: German Historical Institute.

Wayne, Don E. (1987) 'Power, politics, and the Shakespearean text: recent criticism in England and the United States', in J. E. Howard and M. F. O'Connor (eds) *Shakespeare Reproduced: The Text in History and Ideology*, New York and London: Methuen, pp. 47–67.

Wiesner, Merry (1985) 'Women's defense of their public role', in Mary Beth Rose (ed.) *Women in the Middle Ages and the Renaissance*, Syracuse, NY: Syracuse University Press, pp. 1–27.

Williams, Raymond (1981) *Culture*, London: Fontana.

Wrightson, K. (1982) *English Society 1580–1680*, London: Hutchinson.

Wrightson, K. and Levine, David (1979) *Poverty and Piety in an English Village. Terling 1525–1700*, New York: Academic Press.

9

'His majesty the baby': a psychoanalytic approach to *King Lear*

Val Richards

PSYCHOANALYSIS AND LANGUAGE

Psychoanalysis, originating with the work of Sigmund Freud (1856–1939), developed from confirmation, through clinical practice, of the age-old belief that the human mind appears to function on several levels, from the wholly conscious, to the deeply, yet powerfully active, unconscious. Freud and his successors found that the surface disturbances of patients, their presenting symptoms, were often precipitated by the persistent harmful effect of early experiences, forgotten but unresolved. The main objective of psychoanalysis is to bring to consciousness this 'cut-off' material; to heal, in some measure, the split between conscious and unconscious – a direct consequence of human language – and to arrive at a fuller, though necessarily partial, realization of the whole self.

The process of self-discovery occurs in the context of a special therapeutic relationship, in which the disclosures of the patient, under the normally detached, but sensitive, attention and tactful interventions of the analyst, lead to the building of new meanings, perspectives, and patterns. It is thus primarily through speech that psychoanalysis, referred to by an early patient (Freud with Breuer 1895) as the 'talking cure', is conducted. The rhetorical structures, juxtaposition of points, the silences, the dialectic between present, past, and future, in the analytic discourse, are all means by which therapist and patient together reconstruct the patient's story. Apart from feelings and problems related to present situation, conscious memories, and concerns for the future, the therapeutic process also depends on the involuntary products of dreams and free associations, which may form an important vehicle for the patient's unconscious communications.

Central to the process are the dual aspects of the relationship between analyst and analysand (patient). Firstly, there is the 'reality' relationship or 'working alliance', which is concerned with the practical management of a meeting between two adults, who may have a high regard for each other (Greenson 1969). Inseparable from this, though on a different level, is the transference/counter-transference relationship. This is the projection on to each other by patient and analyst of roles and images belonging to earlier relationships. The intense feelings of love and hate often aroused in the patient towards the analyst are the raw material, the 'butterfly in the net', with which the analyst works.

So the psychoanalytic encounter can involve more participants than two, with 'ghosts' or 'images' from the past of each richly complicating the interaction, while, always, it is what is happening 'now', at the moment of the meeting, that is the source of meaning and psychic healing. 'Psychotherapy must remain an obstinate attempt of two people to recover the wholeness of being human through the relationship between them' (Laing 1967).

This account of psychoanalytic practice conforms closely to the approach of Freud and his contemporaries. Unfortunately, there is not space to include the distinctive ideas of Freud's subsequent antagonist, C. G. Jung (1875–1961) whose profound vision of the structure of the human psyche and the nature of the psychoanalytic encounter influences most forms of current psychotherapy. For the purposes of this study, though, it is important to demonstrate how psychoanalysis has also been affected by the discoveries of Melanie Klein (1882–1960) and D. W. Winnicott (1882–1960).

Instead of the 'normal' neuroses treated by Freud and focusing on the relatively late Oedipal stage of development, Klein and Winnicott have demonstrated that many patients suffer from more psychotic disturbances deriving from an earlier stage: the oral. This is associated with the first weeks and months of life and is centred on the mother's breast (Little 1985). Because of some failure to graduate from the infant's innate destructive/self-destructive fantasies (Klein 1975), and/or because of defective environmental care (Winnicott 1987), or because of a narcissistic crisis at the Mirror stage (see p. 164, and Lacan 1977a), unresolved primal fantasies impinge on later life, and a false self is constructed for the protection of the original, wounded true self (Rycroft 1968).

In analytic psychotherapy, these insights have led to the facilitating of patients' regression to infantile dependence on the analyst as a nurturing figure, able and willing to 'hold' the patient, with a 'mirroring' of the patient's words preferred to analytic interpretation, until s/he can form a 'normal' transference (Winnicott 1987).

In the first weeks of life, then, at the oral stage, all the infant's emotions and desires, both loving and hostile, are centred on the part-object, the breast (or bottle). If all goes well, the mother's (carer's) giving of sustenance coincides with the hungry infant's hallucinated creation of its provision. This sense of its own omnipotence applies until the first glimmerings of differentiation. But the same privileged object, the breast, is not only desired; it is also dreaded, alternating as the perceived source of all good and of all bad. Unable to reconcile these opposed feelings, the infant reacts with cannibalistic fantasies of introjecting all the bad from outside into itself, and of projecting on to the breast its own inner contents. So the erstwhile loved object becomes terrifying and dangerous.

Coupled with this intense relationship with the mother through the breast is the primal terror of separation and abandonment, which, if actualized beyond a bearable limit, causes intolerable anxiety 'worse than rape or being eaten alive' (Winnicott 1987). This stage of experiencing in extremes of black and white is termed the 'schizoid position' and is both paralleled and superseded by a gradual sense of differentiation between infant self and mother, with an ability to acknowledge its own bad feelings, and to achieve an attitude of ambivalence towards the breast as simultaneous source of good and bad. Referred to by Lacan (1977a) as the Mirror stage, this transition is the culmination of a baby's fusion with its mother in the Imaginary stage. On first seeing its own reflection in the mirror, it 'misrecognizes' it for the ideal Other. This mirror moment, supported by the constant mirroring of the infant by the mother, implies a healthy narcissism and prepares for the awareness of real 'difference', which is associated with the Oedipal crisis, described by Lacan as the 'Law-of-the-Phallus' or the 'Father', that initiates the child into the symbolic order or linguistic system. The Oedipal crisis is Freud's name for the unconscious, apparently incestuous desires of young children for the parent of the opposite sex, and of rivalry with the parent of the same sex.

For the purposes of my discussion of *King Lear*, it is important to emphasize that these theories of Lacan, who was popularly known as the 'French Freud', concerning infant development, are an attempt to 'rewrite Freudianism in ways relevant to all those concerned with the question of the human subject, its place in society and, above all, its relationship to language' (Eagleton 1983).

Invoking the structuralist/poststructuralist claim that the individual is constructed by the language and culture into which s/he is born, Lacan adopts and adapts the description devised by the Swiss linguist, Ferdinand de Saussure (1857–1913) of the relationship between language and reality, with its key terms: sign, signifier, and signified (Saussure 1974). A sign (unit of language) consists of two parts: the signifier, which is the physical sound or shape of the sign; and the signified, which is the concept or image conjured up by the signifier. Words or names, therefore, do not directly represent or express 'reality'. Indeed, their very utterance points up the discrepancy between the sign and what it stands for. For example, the name 'cat' describes not the observed creature, but the *concept* of 'cat', as opposed to, say, 'rat' or 'car'. For signifiers possess meaning only by virtue of their difference from other signifiers in the total system (language, 'langue'). The relationship between particular groups of sounds and letters and what they designate is arbitrary and the actual world of objects and the internal world of feelings and thoughts are articulated along a culturally determined spectrum.

While, for Saussure, the status of language as a structure was determined by the tight bonding between each signifier and signified – CAT = cat – and their difference from all other signifiers in the structure, poststructuralists point to the instability of that bond. For each signified is also a signifier, immediately activating a new signified. Meaning, therefore, is not single, but overdetermined, multiple, and ultimately elusive – 'an incessant sliding of the signified under the signifier' (Lacan 1977a).

This, then, is the structural, linguistic model appropriated by Lacan in his elucidation of the two infant stages – the Mirror stage and the (Oedipal) access to the symbolic order. In Lacan's view, the Mirror stage represents the point at which the infant's image, seen as the signifier, is for a moment perfectly fused with

165

the reflection, seen as the signified. Now there is an exact marriage of word and meaning and not yet any distinction between conscious and unconscious. But with the subject's initiation into the symbolic order, and the accompanying repression of illicit desire, this bond between signifier and signified is severed, the gratifying narcissistic equation broken. For, henceforth, there will always be a gap between signifier and signified, between the sensation of desire and its definition. And it is the gap between word and meaning, signifier and signified, which, according to Lacan, constitutes the human unconscious, itself structured like a language.

Evolving from the concept of the Mirror stage and the subject's approaching access to the symbolic order (negotiation of the Oedipal stage) is Lacan's formulation of the scopic drive. This is no less basic than the other drives and encompasses the entire spectrum of 'loving to look' and being looked at, since the eye is the conductor of desire. But the subject's initiation into language causes a gap between what is gazed at with desire, and the object of desire, in the unresolvable paradox of separateness.

In my discussion of *King Lear* I propose that light is shed on Lear's internal development and the structure of the drama in its received, traditional form, by viewing it as the dramatization of a primal crisis at the Mirror stage, resolved through the shifting play of the scopic drive. (Current scholarship finds that the text of *King Lear* underwent a process of quite drastic revision over a period of time, and psychoanalysis might well draw conclusions from the nature of revisions made, though this is not part of my considerations here.)

This review of the connection between psychoanalytic and linguistic theory prepares us now for the examination of the relationship between psychoanalysis and literary criticism.

PSYCHOANALYSIS AND CRITICISM

Although recent psychoanalytic criticism has developed the notion of essential cognitive factors in the process of artistic creation (Roland 1978), Freud's pioneering venture saw art as 'regression in the service of the ego' (Kris 1964). His (as he later acknowledged) simplistic analysis of texts sought to identify the underlying neuroses of their authors and reflected closely the preoccupation of nineteenth-century literary criticism with the biographical material of writers. This approach is now seldom employed. A second psychoanalytic approach then became concerned with the analysis of possible primal fantasies in particular fictional characters, which might interfuse disturbing and mystifying surface action (Jones 1949). As will be seen in my discussion of *King Lear*, not only does this approach shed light on individual motivation, with the figures viewed, for practical purposes, as 'real people', but it becomes possible, simultaneously, to recognize their *function* in the basic structure of the work. Characters thus analysed emerge as elements in a partly concealed pattern, which is further exposed by attention to rhetoric and imagery as vehicles of the fantasy undergoing disclosure.

In poetic drama, particularly, a concern with rhetoric and imagery involves the identification of recurring themes, of contrasts and oppositions, of parallels and mirrorings, and this suggests a link between psychoanalytic and formalist/structuralist approaches, as these, too, concentrate on the structure, design, and rhetoric of a work, in a search for 'meaning' and concealed patterns. A psychoanalytic approach is valuable not least because the language of Shakespeare's drama is so richly complex, with a multi-layering that includes levels of both infant development and myth. This is especially so when, as in the case of Lear, the discharge of passion seems to exceed all the given and implied circumstances of the drama. Perhaps this is another way of saying that psychoanalysis addresses itself to Eliot's idea of a 'deficient objective correlative', as applied to Hamlet (Eliot 1919).

In relation to dramatic performance, rather than mere literary analysis, a director, or the actor of a Shakespearean part, may benefit from psychoanalytic insights, as in, for example, Antony Sher's account of his acclaimed Richard III (Sher 1985). Apart from understanding how his/her 'character' forms one integral element in the overall pattern, for a successful dramatic realization the actor may seek an underlying working coherence, an overriding desire that subsumes the shifting moment-to-moment impulses. This desire is defined by Stanislavsky (1980) as 'superobjective' and implicitly encompasses primal fantasies which may pervade the manifest contradictions and successive masks, especially, perhaps, in the most complex and seemingly inconsistent dramatic portraits.

This notion of the 'superobjective' relates to Stanislavsky's concept of 'sub-text' – that is the 'unconscious' of the text – and to a third psychoanalytic approach to texts, which can be only briefly mentioned. That is the analysis not of author nor, primarily, of individual characters, but rather of the total text as psyche or patient. This approach, in its dynamic interaction of 'analyst' and text, points to the provisionality of any single interpretation, while, nevertheless, yielding ideas for a particular production. Similarly, Stanislavsky's 'sub-text' refers to all that is found to be implicit within a play, which may be realized in a given production, 'like a musical score awaiting performance' (Benedetti 1982). Again, there can be no question of a definitive production since all depends on the effect of the raw material on the particular participants. Both the notion of 'sub-text' and the third approach accord with the emphasis of current research on the inseparability of surviving play texts from the performance constraints of their own age and from the accretions of subsequent scholarship. Hence, any quest for the original text, unveiled in all its purity, or for an ultimately 'whole' text, is held to be misconceived.

So far, then, this discussion has moved from the suggestion that the rich ambiguity of poetic drama renders it susceptible to psychoanalytic criticism to a recognition that a text remains always in some sense potential, except when embodied in particular performances and actors. This provisional equivalence of text and performance is seen by some poststructuralist theorists as a fruitful variant of the signifier/signified relationship, in its Lacanian instability and fracture: a site of more dynamic deconstructive operations than that of purely literary signs, as in the novel or poetry. A 'revised theory of representation' has been proposed 'based on the theatrical sign, "the wounding, healing, affectional power of the performed word" ' (Ritchie 1988: 112, quoting Robert Weimann). Since the province of psychoanalysis is the split between conscious and unconscious, or (in Lacanian–Saussurean terms) between signifier and signified, this emphasis on work-in-performance is a further inducement to the psychoanalytic reading of drama texts, leading now to a consideration of the 'wounded, healing, affectional power' of *Lear* or 'The Lac/King'.

THE LAC/KING

This psychoanalytic approach to *King Lear* was developed in Shakespeare seminars with BA (humanities) polytechnic students; in a 'one-off' A-level revision session with sixth-formers, drawn from numerous schools; and with polytechnic drama students. All groups were interested in performance aspects.

The following is a reconstruction, based on ideas explored with these students, for whom a stimulating foretaste proved to be Freud's mythological interpretation of the play, with Cordelia, the loved daughter, seen as the disguised goddess of Fate and Death (Freud 1913). Found to be less palatable was Freud's later account, in terms of Cordelia's guilty Oedipal love (Freud 1934) and F. L. Lucas's alternative Oedipal reading (Lucas 1970). But most students were excited and convinced by the pre-Oedipal emphasis pursued, by the theories involved and, particularly, by the notion of the submerged mother.

Reflections on Lear's unfathomability raised questions as to how readers and performers of the role might get closer to the intensity of pain, masked by his overt reactions. 'What might Lear deeply fear and desire?', 'What could be the source of such fury?', 'What light is shed on his internal state by the dominant imagery and rhetorical structures of his discourse?', 'Who and where is the mother in *King Lear*?' were the main issues explored, in the hope of testing Lacan's contention that the formulations of speech reflect the structures of unconscious desire. The following psychoanalytic discoveries emerged. (All quotations are taken from *The Tragedy of King Lear*, the Folio Text, *The Complete Works*, ed. Stanley Wells and Gary Taylor, Oxford 1988. All italics within quotations are my own.)

It was noticed first that when Lear demands:

> . . . Tell me, my daughters . . .
> Which of you shall we *say* doth love us most . . .
> . . . Goneril,
> Our eldest born, *speak* first.
>
> (I.1.48–54)

he is insisting on a sign of love, to be expressed orally. The vehicle is privileged above the meaning:

> . . . what can you *say* to draw
> A third more opulent than your sisters? *Speak.*
>
> (I.1.85–6)

> . . . Mend your *speech* a little . . .
>
> (I.1.94)

169

Not only does Lear invite a distasteful correlation between love and avarice, but by assigning this supremacy to the verbalization of love he has forged for himself what proves to be a fatal equation between 'tongue' and 'heart'. So he becomes trapped in a private symbolism at odds with the general signifying practice of his adult companions. Such is the force of this equation (paralleled equally disastrously by that of Gloucester between *'sight'* and 'heart' – 'Let's see. Come, if it be nothing I shall not need spectacles' (I.2.35–6)) that one way of examining Lear's subsequent agony is to trace the effects of successive assaults upon both this equation and on a second, still more catastrophic: 'King equals power minus responsibility.'

> . . . Only we shall retain
> The name and all th'addition to a king.
>
> (I.1.135–6)

It is with the splitting apart of these two equations that, on the manifest (adult) level, Lear becomes utterly deprived and denuded.

At a more primal level this material invites a psychoanalytic reading. For Lear's extreme privileging of the verbal in relation to his daughter's affections can be seen as a displaced enactment of the oral stage. The infantile lack of differentiation between self and 'mother' is reflected even in the actual syntax, with an odd switch from self-address (first person) to second person in that first question:

> Which of you shall *we* say doth love us most . . .
> . . . Goneril,
> Our eldest born, (you) *speak* first.
>
> (I.1.51–4)

Speech and hearing, by association with mouth and therefore with sucking, are substitutions (displacements) for the latter (and can be observed acting with similar force in *Macbeth* and *Othello*).

It becomes clearer why Cordelia's 'nothing' proves so persecuting to Lear. Her soliloquized resolve, 'What shall Cordelia speak? Love, and be silent.' (I.1.62), when put to the test, is violated, becoming a clearly voiced: 'Nothing, my lord.' (I.1.87), which, like the proffering of a milkless nipple, bears a far greater emptiness than pure silence, for that can be fullness still withheld, laden with promise, a mere deferring of the desired sustenance (words).

Thus Lear, actively deprived of the expected food which, it will be recalled, the omnipotent infant hallucinates as its own creation – 'Whom shall *we* say?' – erupts into a destructive fury.

In this demand for verbal nourishment, in assuming equivalence between love and its expression, and secondly, between 'King and Power (minus responsibility)', Lear is unwittingly yoking each signifier to a false signified, 'misrecognizing' the bonding as a true match. In a similar manner, at the Mirror stage, the infant at first misrecognizes its reflection as the ideal Other. That Lear might be seen as fixated at the narcissistic Mirror stage is equally implied by his idealization of Cordelia as the already observed chief source of oral satisfaction. She is the nurturing 'mother' 'on whose kind nursery' he 'had hoped to set his rest', when, in the imagery of infancy, he would 'crawl unburthen'd to the grave'.

As Coppélia Khan (1986) points out, although, in the play, the father is presented as 'the only source of love and power', the mother insists on her presence by Lear's 'repressed identification with her'. And the enormity of his need is highlighted by regarding as a 'given' of the drama the maternal deprivation suffered by royal (and other) infants, who were farmed out from birth to twelve or eighteen months with a wet-nurse. Khan comments that, whether with wet-nurse or with the mother, the infant's primary bond is with a woman, and a feminist interpretation attributes the harsh patriarchal values of Lear's kingdom (espoused inevitably by the 'woe-men', Goneril and Regan) to the violent severing of a boy from his early bond for the sake of forging a masculine identity, in antithesis to the feminine. The girl need undergo no such traumatic rupture. So the 'actual' mother of Lear, in her marginalization to the point of non-existence, theoretically constitutes Lear's great lack and the play's underlying dynamic.

Cordelia, as the transferred 'mother', by offering 'nothing', becomes immediately dangerous in Lear's terrified primal realization that she might not be part of him. His hitherto 'good object' must now be projected, exiled. And it is Cordelia's *danger* to Lear that could be brought out in a sensitive performance. The actor might portray not only rage, but also terror, lingering tenderness, and wistful longing, thus conveying a greater emotional range and inwardness than, for instance, the recent bellowings of Anthony Hopkins at the National Theatre. This psychoanalytic dimension could lend a special poignancy, for example, to Lear's injunction:

VAL RICHARDS

Thou hast her, France. Let her be thine, for we
Have no such daughter, nor shall ever see
That face of hers again. Therefore be gone,
Without our grace, our love, our benison.

(I.1.262–5)

Yet no sooner has Cordelia, the 'bad mother', been expelled
than Lear undergoes a typical primal swing from projection to
introjection in a fantasy of indirectly devouring the bad object:

. . . The barbarous Scythian,
Or he that makes his generation messes
To gorge his appetite, shall to my bosom
Be as well neighboured, pitied, and relieved
As thou, my sometime daughter.

(I.1.116–19)

Cordelia, like Lirope, the mother of Narcissus (in one of the
numerous Narcissus legends), who would not reflect her son in
her own eyes (McDougall 1986), has refused to reflect to Lear
the short-circuiting image of himself, and refused to support the
preservation of this prized equation, which would imprison him
in the Mirror stage. But, unlike Lirope whose son was trapped
in *her* gaze for ever, Cordelia, resisting the role of imaginary
'mother', seeks instead to initiate him into the symbolic order,
the world of adult language.

Goneril and Regan, however, colluding at first with Lear's
insatiable demands, exalt speech in the act of deprecating it:

Goneril: Sir, I love you more than words can wield
            the matter;
            . . . A love that makes breath poor and
            speech unable.

(I.1.55,60)

and Regan: . . . In my true heart
I find she names my very deed of
love –
Only she comes too short, . . .

(I.1.70–2)

After Cordelia's expulsion Goneril and Regan become the bearers
of the primal mother role, which will imprison Lear in the Mirror
stage, until they also choose to defy Lear's elected equation. Like

172

Cordelia's denials, their ensuing assaults on Lear also provoke in him fantasies of their expulsion and introjection. To Goneril's repeated subversion of the equation, 'King equals Power minus responsibility', and her stripping of Lear to his naked self, 'What need one?', Lear reacts by reducing the 'mother' to a diseased excrescence inside himself:

> But yet thou art my flesh, my blood, my daughter –
> Or rather a disease that's in my flesh,
> Whit I must needs call mine. Thou art a boil,
> A plague-sore or embossed carbuncle
> In my corrupted blood.
>
> (II.2.394–7)

No less crucial a step in the reduction of Lear's status is the insupportable spectacle of Kent in the stocks, which induces an internalization of the 'bad mother' in her entirety (reflecting the ancient belief that hysteria is a female malady caused by movement of the womb):

> O, how this mother swells up toward my heart!
> *Histerica passio* down, thou climbing sorrow;
>
> (II.2.231–2)

There is the 'mother', safely inside the 'infant', but simultaneously, such are the delusions of terrified omnipotence that Lear also fantasizes the expulsion of both 'mother' and her procreative functions for ever from the natural world:

> Hear, nature; hear, dear goddess, hear:
> Suspend thy purpose if thou didst intend
> To make this creature fruitful.
> Into her womb convey sterility.
> Dry up in her the organs of increase,
> And from her derogate body never spring
> A babe to honour her.
>
> (I.4.254–60)

In apostrophizing Nature, Lear projects upon this 'dear Goddess' the role of supreme 'mother', 'feeding' her ears with words, as he had sought to be fed. So orality – what issues from mouth to ear, even in Lear's reversed position – retains supremacy, and under the continuing sway of the omnipotent fantasy he confidently commands the blighting of the rejected 'mother' – 'Suspend thy purpose' – 'dry up in her' – 'convey sterility' – while relish is evident in the syntax as Nature's action is visualized. '*Into* her womb convey sterility', reinforced by the tautological 'Dry up in her the organs of increase.' But a weakening of the omnipotent stance occurs, as the subjunctive replaces the imperative, command shading into mere desire:

> And from her derogate body *never spring*
> A babe to honour her.

A transition to the conditional tense signals a further note of doubt: '*If* she must teem, Create her child of spleen.'

In a single trope, the fantasy has swung from an eternal expulsion of the 'bad mother' to her begrudging reincorporation into the primal scenario, where any subsequent offspring – 'siblings' – will be (in accordance with Melanie Klein's model) objects of destructive envy in the infant's unconscious fantasy.

> . . . If she must teem,
> Create her child of spleen, that it may live
> And be a thwart disnatured torment to her.
> Let it stamp wrinkles in her brow of youth,
> With cadent tears fret channels in her cheeks,
> Turn all her mother's pains and benefits
> To laughter and contempt, that she may feel –
> That she may feel
> How sharper than a serpent's tooth it is
> To have a thankless child.
>
> (I.4.260–9)

The image of a tooth evokes a picture of the infant biting the breast, instead of sucking, while the very violence of Lear's abuse conjures up an opposite image – of a tender mother, perhaps one who has 'given suck' and 'know[s] how tender 'tis to love the babe that milks me'? (*Macbeth* I.7.54–5). Hence, the intensity of Lear's disavowal becomes an almost explicit affirmation of the maternal function.

Far from staying buried in the labyrinth of Lear's unconscious, after successive rejections in its oral, narcissistic form, by Cordelia, Goneril, and Regan, this fantasy is reclaimed in its post-Oedipal mode and vested in the disguised persons of Kent and the Fool, to re-emerge, transformed, in the end, by Cordelia. But, before any restoration, Lear must undergo a psychotic regression, in which the self, no longer secure in its fantasy of fusion with either 'mother' or mirror image, experiences a sense of splintering; its 'going-along' is disturbed. With the shattering of the equations, or of the 'mirror', Lear's inner turmoil is increasingly externalized in imagery of sight, the act of seeing and being seen.

In his adoption of the 'mother' mask, Kent, like Cordelia, has attempted to act as Oedipal 'father'. It is his 'See better, Lear' and his 'father' function of challenging the infant to divert its gaze from the 'mother's' eye and break the narcissistic bond, 'Let *me* be the true blank of thine eye', that provokes Lear to banish him from his field of vision in a thundering 'Out of my sight'. The 'father' function of Kent, as well as of Cordelia, is repudiated and only in disguise, as nurturing 'mother', can Kent's gaze, like that of the Fool, be faced by Lear, as they continue to 'hold' him through his oral regression, until his emergence from psychosis. Reacting to Goneril's erosion of his once secure narcissism and doomed adherence to power, as well as uttering a stream of execrations, Lear undergoes a personal and visual disorientation, paralleling the infant's dawning awareness of itself as *object* of others' vision, rather than pure subject. Blindness is preferable to the loss of his reflection in the 'mother's' eyes:

> Old, fond eyes, . . . I'll pluck ye out.
> (I.4.281–2)

– a *fantasy* of blinding, that the offending agent may be obliterated, to be *actualized*, in the case of Gloucester, after the fracture of his own equation between 'heart' and 'sight'.

Lear's own eyes, detached from their self-rejection, are dangerous to him, while the 'burning' eyes of Goneril signal, despite the incipient psychosis, a further awareness of the 'other'. The acute sense of Lear observing himself being observed enacts Lacan's formulation of the scopic drive and its contradictions: 'The gaze I encounter is not a seen gaze, but a gaze imagined by me in the field of the other' (Lacan 1977b). It is as though Lear steps across the footlights to join the spectators in watching the 'other' watching his plight:

> You see me here, you gods, a poor old man
> As full of grief as age,
> (II.2.446–7)

175

VAL RICHARDS

But eyes may also 'comfort', and the 'wash'd', tear-filled eyes of
Cordelia, of necessity, resist the narcissistic self-reflection of the
infant's gaze. Hence they become the ultimately healing agent,
when Cordelia returns to replace the ministrations of Kent and
the Fool. Disguised, their gaze (and that of Poor Tom) can be
borne, but Lear's first direct perception of a figure without disguise is of the *blinded* Gloucester. Perhaps, at the primal level, a
first recognition of the true 'other' can be better endured if the
gaze is not returned: 'You never look at me from the place from
which I see you' (Lacan 1977b).

And Lear will 'by no means yield to see his daughter', at least
until his eyes have been permitted to close in a healing sleep. In
encountering her tear-filled eyes, instead of again delegating the
burden of his own tears to his 'mother' Nature ('I'll not weep'
having signalled the onset of the storm), Lear can now weep,
showing the narcissistic infant to be freed from the binding spell
of the Mirror stage. Tears reflect tears. His gradual perception of
both himself as separate and of Cordelia as post-Oedipal
'm/other', balances and contrasts with his earlier sense of fragmen-
tation and psychosis. Now the visual is privileged above the oral:

> Where have I been? Where am I? Fair daylight?
> I am mightily abused. I should ev'n die with pity
> To *see* another thus. I know not what to say.
> I will not swear these are my hands. Let's *see*.
> I feel this pin prick.
>
> (IV.6.45–9)

and enables Lear to obey Cordelia's: 'O! Look upon me, sir'
(IV.6.50) identifying both himself and her as separate beings:

> . . . Do not laugh at me,
> For as I am a man, I think this lady
> To be my child, Cordelia.
>
> (IV.6.61–3)

At the climax of the tragedy, Lear's entry bearing Cordelia's
body, the pressure of the primal fantasy begins to fall away, as
the (now adult) Father (however ironically) enfolds his (child)
Daughter in his arms. This action brings together again the
elements which, once falsely fused, had to be split apart in the
service of Lear's purgation: 'heart', 'tongue', and 'eyes', and Lear

176

now projects on to Nature the fantasy of shattering which he has undergone internally:

> Howl, howl, howl, howl! O, you are men of stones.
> Had I your tongues and eyes, I'd use them so
> That heaven's vault should crack.

(V.3.232–5)

This inaugurates the exorcism of the Mirror stage fantasy, to be completed by its full externalization when Lear takes a real looking-glass, not for self-contemplation, but to detect signs of breathing in Cordelia. As at the beginning, 'nothing' issues from her mouth. But this time it is true silence and not the teasing of sound without substance, the *absent* breast rather than the *empty* breast. Lear now faces up fully to the pain of weaning, albeit a weaning from life itself:

> . . . She's gone for ever.
> I know when one is dead and when one lives.
> She's dead as earth. Lend me a looking-glass.
> If that her breath will mist or stain the stone,
> Why then she lives.

(V.3.234–8)

From this attention to Lear's discourse in relation to an unresolved primal fantasy, the figure of the 'mother' emerges as a central unifying principle, who in the surface text is merely either an unmentioned, but insistent ghost (Lear's 'real' mother), or entombed (the mother of the three sisters), or gamesome in Gloucester's bed (the mother of Edgar and Edmund), or Nature herself. Revealing the structural functions of the principal dramatic figures, the 'mother' mask flits from face to face, determining the issue of events, leading, in the surface tragedy, to psychotic breakdown and restoration; and, in the primal fantasy, to progression from the earliest stages of fusion and narcissism to the beginnings of self-differentiation.

This psychoanalytic level of reading a fragment of so huge a text may shed a little light on the nature of Lear's anguish, and on why the pain of the tragedy is somehow supportable: in psychoanalytic terms, the suffering and deaths of Cordelia and Lear are a metaphor for individuation and developing life.

177

REFERENCES

Benedetti, Jean (1982) *Stanislavsky: An Introduction*, London: Methuen.

Eagleton, Terry (1983) *Literary Theory: An Introduction*, Oxford: Basil Blackwell.

Eliot, T. S. (1919) 'Hamlet', in *Selected Prose of T. S. Eliot*, ed. Frank Kermode, London: Faber (1975).

Freud, S. with Breuer, J. (1895) *Studies on Hysteria*, Harmondsworth: Penguin (1981).

— (1913) 'The theme of the three caskets', in *The Standard Edition of the Complete Psychological Works of Sigmund Freud*, vol. XII (1911–13), trans. fron the German under the general editorship of James Strachey in collaboration with Anna Freud. London: The Hogarth Press in association with The Institute of Psycho-Analysis (1958).

— (1934) letter to James S. H. Bransom, in Ernest Jones, *Sigmund Freud. Life and Work*, 3 vols, vol. III, *The Last Phase 1919–1939*, London: The Hogarth Press (1957).

Greenson, Ralph (1969) 'The non-transference relationship in the psychoanalytic situation', in *Explorations in Psychoanalysis*, New York: Indiana University Press.

Jones, Ernest (1949) *Hamlet and Oedipus*, London: Gollancz.

Kahn, Coppélia (1986) 'The absent mother in *King Lear*', in Margaret W. Ferguson, Maureen Quilligan and Nancy J. Vickers (eds) *Rewriting the Renaissance: The Discourses of Sexual Difference in Early Modern Europe*, Chicago: University of Chicago Press.

Klein, Melanie (1975) *Love, Guilt, and Reparation, and Other Works 1921–1945*, Introduction by R. E. Money-Kyrle, London: The Hogarth Press.

Kris, Ernst (1964) *Psychoanalytic Exploration in Art*, New York: Schocken Books.

Lacan, Jacques (1977a) *Ecrits: A Selection*, London: Tavistock.

— (1977b) *The Four Fundamental Concepts of Psychoanalysis*, London: Peregrine.

Laing, R. D. (1967) *The Politics of Experience, and The Bird of Paradise*, New York: Pantheon Books.

Little, Margaret (1985) *Winnicott: A Personal Record*, London: Free Association, issue 3.

Lucas, F. L. (1970) 'On *King Lear*', in M. D. Faber (ed.) *The Design Within: Psychoanalytic Approaches to Shakespeare*, London: The Hogarth Press.

McDougall, Joyce (1986) *Theatres of the Mind: Illusion and Truth on the Psychoanalytic Stage*, London: Free Association.

Ritchie, Charlie (1988) review, in Edward E. Esche (ed.) *Ideas and Production. 8: Drama in Theory and Performance*, Cambridge: Anglia Higher Education College.

Roland, Alan (ed.) (1978) *Psychoanalysis, Creativity and Literature: A French-American Inquiry*, New York: Columbia University Press.

Rycroft, Charles (ed.) (1968) *Psychoanalysis Observed*, Harmondsworth: Penguin.

Saussure, Ferdinand de (1916) *Course in General Linguistics*, trans. Wade Baskin [1959], London, Fontana (1974).

Sher, Antony (1985) *Year of the King: An Actor's Diary and Sketchbook*, London: Chatto & Windus/The Hogarth Press.

Stanislavsky, Constantin (1980) *An Actor Prepares*, London: Methuen.

Wells, Stanley and Taylor, Gary (eds) (1988) *The Tragedy of King Lear* [The Folio Text] in *William Shakespeare. The Complete Works*, Oxford: Clarendon Press.

Winnicott, D. W. (1987) 'Primary maternal preoccupation', and 'Withdrawal and regression', in *Through Paediatrics to Psychoanalysis*, London: The Hogarth Press.

FURTHER READING

Adelman, Janet (1978) Introduction to *Twentieth-Century Interpretations of 'King Lear'*, Englewood Cliffs, NJ: Prentice-Hall.

Belsey, Catherine (1980) *Critical Practice*, London: Methuen.

Culler, Jonathan (1982) *Saussure*, Glasgow: Fontana.

Hawkes, Terence (1977) *Structuralism and Semiotics*, London: Methuen.

Holland, Norman (1975) *Five Readers Reading*, New Haven, CT: Yale University Press.

Jorgensen, Paul A. (1967) *Lear's Self-Discovery*, Berkeley: University of California Press.

Rose, Jacqueline (1985) 'Sexuality in the reading of Shakespeare: *Hamlet* and *Measure for Measure,'* in John Drakakis, (ed.) *Alternative Shakespeares*, London: Methuen.

Rothenberg, Alan B. (1973–4) 'Infantile fantasies in Shakespearean metaphor: II Scopophilia and fears of ocular rape and castration', *Psychoanalytic Review* 60.

Schwarz-Salant, Nathan (1982) *Narcissism and Character Transformation*, Toronto: Inner City Books.

Segal, Hannah (1979) *Melanie Klein*, Glasgow: Fontana.

Sinfield, Alan (1976) 'Lear and Laing', *Essays in Criticism* 26: 1–16.

Skura, Meredith Anne (1981) *The Literary Use of the Psychoanalytic Process*, New Haven, CT and London: Yale University Press.

Sturrock, John (1979) *Structuralism and Since*, Oxford: Clarendon Press.

Winnicott, D. W. (1985) *Playing and Reality,* Harmondsworth: Penguin.

Wollheim, Richard (1982) *Freud*, Glasgow: Fontana.

Wright, Elizabeth (1984) *Psychoanalytical Criticism: Theory in Practice*, London: Methuen.

Plate 1 Miching mallecho: filming the Player King and Queen. Olivier's
Hamlet (GB 1948). Production still supplied by the National Film
Archive, London, and reproduced by courtesy of the Rank Organization.
Production stills are promotional images, and are not necessarily an
accurate record of what we see in the final edited version of the film
concerned.

Plate 2 Innokenti Smoktunovski as the Prince in Grigori Kozintsev's *Hamlet* (USSR 1964), in front of the players' cart: a cryptic reference to Kozintsev's involvement during the 1920s with agit-trains and FEKS (Factory of the Eccentric Actor)? (Collick 1989: 140). Production still supplied by the National Film Archive, London, and reproduced by courtesy of Sovscope Films.

Plate 3 The army of Fortinbras: men dressed in the clothes rather than the costumes of war: Kozintsev's *Hamlet* (USSR 1964). Production still supplied by the National Film Archive, London, and reproduced by courtesy of Sovscope Films.

Plate 4 'I don't think that she was ever quite so good again': Michael Powell on the eighteen-year-old Jean Simmons's performances as Kanchi in Powell's and Pressburger's *Black Narcissus* (GB 1947), and (here) as Ophelia in Olivier's *Hamlet* (GB 1948) (Powell 1986: 579). Production still supplied by the National Film Archive, London, and reproduced by courtesy of the Rank Organization.

Plate 5 God hath given you one face but the Director will make another: Laurence Olivier prepares Jean Simmons's Ophelia for muddy death, *Hamlet* (GB 1948). Production still supplied by the National Film Archive, London, and reproduced by courtesy of the Rank Organization.

Plate 6 '. . . a potent and obsessive figure in our cultural mythology.' (Showalter 1985: 78): John Everett Millais, 'Ophelia' (1852), oil on canvas, 30 × 40 inches. Reproduced by courtesy of the Tate Gallery, London.

Plate 7 Anastasia Vertinskaya as Ophelia in Grigori Kozintsev's *Hamlet* (USSR 1964). Ophelia performs a solitary, robotic dance to the old woman's eerie lute accompaniment; scoring by Dmitri Shostakovich. Shostakovich wrote four different orchestrations for *Hamlet*, from 1932 to 1963: Shostakovich, *Film Music from 'Hamlet', 'King Lear' and 'Five Days and Five Nights'*, RCA Victor CD RD87763. Production still supplied by the National Film Archive, London, and reproduced by courtesy of Sovscope Films.

10

Unlocking the box: Shakespeare on film and video

Peter Reynolds

To make effective use in the classroom of the ever growing library of video and film productions of Shakespeare's plays will require many teachers to overcome two ingrained cultural prejudices. The first involves attitudes to the medium of film, and especially television, whilst the second concerns the phenomenon of performance. The act of reading continues to carry high status in contemporary culture despite its near eclipse as a leisure activity among many young people. Watching television, especially in comparison to watching 'live' performance, is a low-status activity despite the fact that the skills required to respond critically to it are quite as complex as those required for reading books or watching plays.[1] The products of television (and to a lesser extent film) are seen, at best, as entertaining or diverting, and at worst as potentially harmful, especially to the young. Television is rarely, if ever, recognized as an appropriate forum for the transmission of serious ideas. Thus although televised schools programmes are increasingly used in the curriculum, they tend to be confined either to junior school, or used very selectively, usually with so-called 'non-academic' students in the secondary streams. A teacher who screens a video of a Shakespeare play as part of a teaching strategy preparing, for example, students for public examinations, will inevitably be seen by some colleagues (and perhaps also by him/herself) to be taking an easy option: an option perceived as inherently of less value, certainly given far less time, and supposedly requiring considerably less work from both teacher and students, than the activity of reading the text. It is part of my argument that watching Shakespeare on television or on film is a valuable but under-used alternative to reading him on the page. It does not *replace* the act of reading, but is

189

complementary to it, and deserves a commensurate degree of time and attention in the curriculum.

Watching a performance of Shakespeare, whether it is live or recorded, can engender a second, equally firmly held prejudice: the fear that, by exposing impressionable young minds to an immediate and powerful theatrical impact, there is a risk of their confusing a *director's* text (or 'concept' as it is pejoratively labelled) for *the* text. The classic example of this, and one frequently cited in order to prove the point, is Roman Polanski's film of *Macbeth*. At one moment in the action he has the camera follow Macbeth into Duncan's bedchamber and shows the audience the horror of those bloody and unnatural acts. Many a school student writing about the play for GCSE has been tripped up by this into supposing that Polanski's text and Shakespeare's are the same thing. But of course the fault lies not in the film, but in the way in which the film has been used to teach the play. Polanski's decision to add a scene only described by Shakespeare should have been highlighted and used as a basis for discussion.

Performances of Shakespeare recorded on film/video can prove a stimulus to discussion, and therefore to good teaching, by continually challenging students to make their own connections between the words on the page and the images on the screen. Like printed texts, recorded performances on video can be reread as often as necessary, and, more effectively than printed texts, they can be used graphically to demonstrate that there are no 'right' answers, and no such thing as a 'definitive' production. The teacher using them, far from taking an easy option, serves the interests of students by posing open questions that require an *active* not a passive response. Watching Shakespeare re-produced can stimulate active reading, both of the images on the screen and of those conjured in the theatre in the mind's eye, and can produce a productive debate concerning, amongst other things, textual fidelity and the construction of meanings. Nor is language neglected; in fact, being required to make connections between what is seen and what is heard rejuvenates language. Far from being a poor substitute for reading the plays, the experience of watching *and* listening to them on film/video can motivate a student to return time and again to the printed text.

One of my most vivid memories of school was the day we were allowed out of it and taken *en masse* to the local cinema – the Regal – for a matinée screening of Laurence Olivier's film of

Richard III (1955). That classic film, together with Olivier's *Hamlet* (1948), is now part of a cheap video library of films of Shakespeare.[2] But, in addition to the availability of feature films on videotape, the last decade has also seen the production of video recordings of some of the plays as staged by the Royal Shakespeare Company, and the BBC/Time–Life recording of the complete dramatic works of Shakespeare is also available. Uneven in quality, all this material none the less represents a potentially valuable teaching resource.

Although copyright problems probably prevent the showing of some televised Shakespeare in schools or colleges, one of the developments of the decade has been the availability of video recorders in the majority of households. There is nothing to stop, and everything to encourage home taping by students of such material. However, once they have taped it they have to be taught how to make the best use of these performance texts. Students have to be encouraged not only to *watch* Shakespeare on television, but to look at it *critically*. To do this they need to be made aware of the issues and critical debates that make the whole phenomenon of Shakespeare in performance (including performances recorded on film and video) very much a 'live' critical issue. Immediately performance is considered, in whatever form, it makes real to students the need continually to make interpretive decisions when thinking about any Shakespeare text. It brings home to them the inescapable fact that Shakespeare is incomplete and partial without the added dimension of performance, whether that performance is on stage, film, or taking place in the theatre of the mind's eye. In adding that dimension they must also consider the range of legitimate interpretation open to the reader.

There is a lengthy stage history of cutting, adapting, and rearranging Shakespeare's texts for performances which is not simply confined to the work of Nahum Tate and Derek Jarman. There is a good deal of historical evidence to support those who argue that directors and actors can and should be free to work on a Shakespeare text in any way that suits their fancy. After all there are no manuscripts of Shakespeare's plays, and therefore the authority for all the modern editions we now have is ultimately editorial not authorial. (See Ann Thompson's chapter in this book). We do not know, and *cannot* know exactly what Shakespeare intended; perhaps he didn't know himself until he saw the plays as the players performed them. In any case the business of running an Elizabethan/Jacobean theatre never centred around the work of any one writer: it was much more of a collective operation in which the writer's role, though important, was only one of many equally necessary to the continuing survival of the company as a whole. This decentring of the author by current criticism and scholarship, and its alternative focus on a more collective artistic process of generation, has been hard to accept for many critics, especially those reared in an age that reveres individual achievement over collective endeavour. As far as today's students of Shakespeare are concerned, they need to be reminded, and perhaps reassured, that *any* performance is *a* text and not *the* text, and that the really important question is not whether this or that version is closer to what Shakespeare might have written 400 years ago, but rather to ask what is being attempted in the performance and how successful in intellectual, emotional, and aesthetic terms is the result.

One of the arguments against making use of filmed versions of the plays is that it takes far too long to show them and requires a complicated revision of the timetable. But to discuss issues of textual fidelity, and indeed to make effective use of filmed versions of the plays as a teaching resource, it is rarely necessary to show the whole performance through at one sitting. This may prove a useful introduction to the subsequent study of the play on the page (and perhaps inevitable if a hired film is the only option), but it is often more useful for students to allow them to compare the treatment of one scene or incident in the play as seen by two or more directors, or simply to focus attention on one scene and to show it several times. To do this effectively it helps to use a video recording rather than a 16mm film.

I mentioned my own childhood memory of watching Olivier's exciting film of *Richard III;* another classic Olivier film of Shakespeare, made before *Richard III* but, like it, also now widely available on video, is *Hamlet*, made in 1948. Like his *Richard III*, a screening of *Hamlet* will also raise interesting and complex issues of fidelity to the original text and therefore of interpretation on the part of the director. Olivier omitted the characters of Voltimand, Cornelius, Reynaldo, second gravedigger, Rosencrantz and Guildenstern and, even more significantly, made no room for any mention of, or appearance by, Fortinbras and his army. The obvious issue for discussion is why were they omitted, and what is lost/gained as a result?

Olivier explained the omission by saying that he wanted to concentrate on the story of the Prince ('This is a story about a man who could not make up his mind' the opening credits say) and exclude all so-called extraneous material. Olivier had read Ernest Jones's Freudian account of the play (Jones 1949) and accordingly his film became an attempt to explore the psyche of Hamlet. In addition to its famous Oedipal emphasis on the relationship of the Prince and his mother, it is also a highly romantic view of Hamlet as heroic individual. As with Olivier's Duke of Gloucester, his Hamlet is also a man set apart by fate from ordinary people. He is isolated and adrift in an apparently meaningless universe. From the labyrinthine setting which suggests the complexities of the human mind, to the Oedipal suggestiveness of casting in the role of Gertrude an actress (Eileen Herlie) who looked no older than her supposed son, and by the inclusion of a large bed and a wet kiss in the closet scene (III.4), Olivier's interpretation is resolutely apolitical: it is the personal tragedy of a man, not a Prince. The potential for a political reading of the play is entirely and deliberately avoided by Olivier. However, another film of the play admirably demonstrates how such a reading can be made to work, and much discussion can be provoked by comparing Olivier's *Hamlet* with that of the Russian diretor, Grigori Kozintsev, made in 1964.[3]

Olivier was almost exclusively concerned to use his film to explore Hamlet's personality, but Kozintsev's lens shows a broader focus on the issues and ideas raised in the play as a whole. He also made highly effective use of the talents of the composer Dmitri Shostakovich to create an atmospheric score (Olivier used the British composer William Walton), and employed Boris Pasternak to rewrite Shakespeare. Despite having the potential mobility provided by shooting on film, Olivier mainly avoided location shooting, preferring instead to shoot in the studio on the set. In doing so he chose to emphasize the metaphorical qualities of the design and also kept the action isolated and separated from any connection with a social world outside Elsinore (Plate 1). Olivier's camera focuses a great deal on the face of the Prince, registering the actor's signalling of his character's continual changes of mood, and creating a sense of intimate contact between the observer and the observed. Kozintsev cut at least as much of the written text as Olivier, but used the screen to create a visual narrative of great subtlety and significance.

Students of Shakespeare on film and television can benefit from considering not only what is omitted from the printed text, but also what has been added to it by the director. In his film of *Richard III* Olivier added the character of Jane Shore (only alluded to by Shakespeare) to the action. In his *Hamlet* Kozintsev added some telling images rather than additional characters. His camera moves outside the castle walls and, shooting on location, creates a social context for what happens to Hamlet in a realistic world of work. Some of the film's most articulate images are not of Hamlet at all but show, for example, a team of peasants turning a heavy capstan to wind up the drawbridge to admit the returning Hamlet to the castle of Elsinore; Claudius walking down a long corridor followed by anxious courtiers (as he moves the camera pulls back slightly to reveal that at his side walk two guards, both armed with hideous blunderbusses); a soldier on horseback whipping away a small group of peasants who have strayed too close to the furtive burial of Ophelia. Thus Kozintsev uses his camera to set the story of Hamlet in a very real social context rather than in an abstract metaphorical location (Plate 2). The use of a realist convention creates a powerful narrative showing not only the deeds of powerful men, but also offering an audience the opportunity of placing them in an historical and therefore a political context. Kozintsev does not undermine the importance and centrality of the character of Hamlet, but arguably he does make a more balanced film of the play than Olivier.

One especially powerful scene demonstrating how Kozintsev uses film to highlight the politics of *Hamlet* comes when he chooses to show the army of Fortinbras marching along a desolate sea-shore to be confronted by the questioning Prince. This scene (IV.4) does not show some half-dozen men dressed in highly polished armour straight out of the costume store (this is the unfortunate impression given by Rodney Bennett's production for the BBC/Time–Life Shakespeare Series). There is no half-hearted attempt at pageantry, but instead the audience are shown men dressed in the clothes rather than the costumes of war (Plate 3). The exchange between Hamlet and the Captain – cut by Olivier – has little to do with a Hamlet played as a kind of universal Everyman figure, or as a troubled soul full of existential Angst, but everything to do with a man who is also a Prince, and therefore a political animal, capable of wielding enormous power over other people. Kozintsev's army reminds the spectator of the contrast between Hamlet's fate and that of these ordinary men. The soldiers are expected, when commanded, to die for nothing, but *Hamlet* is conventionally dramatized, by Olivier and others, to celebrate its hero's equivocation.

Both Olivier and Kozintsev use the camera to frame a narrative about Ophelia. Olivier chose to *show* the drowning woman floating on the river whilst using Gertrude's description of the event as a voice-over (Plate 4). Plate 5 also shows the film crew gathered round Jean Simmons, who is trying hard not to look too uncomfortable in this publicity shot. Olivier is leaning over her, apparently adjusting her make-up. The photograph is interesting in that it reveals the amount of work and effort that obviously went into constructing this particular visual fiction. Olivier was clearly trying to reproduce as exactly as possible Millais's painting of Ophelia (Plate 6). The whole effect, both of Millais's original image and Olivier's reproduction of it, is to romanticize the suicide, and to distance it from the reality of 'muddy death'. It makes Ophelia into an icon, and removes her conveniently from the circumstances – and the individuals – that led first to her madness, and then to her death. Kozintsev does not show Ophelia's death. What he does show are two images that offer an audience the chance not simply to empathize with Ophelia's plight, but to go some way towards understanding it. In the first a dancing lesson is in progress (Plate 7). The only sound used is that of the musical accompaniment to the dance played by the old woman in black. It is a sharp-toned repetitious tune to which the appropriate movements are puppet-like. The image suggests that Ophelia is schooled to dance to a particular tune, a tune requiring the suppression of her individuality. The second image follows the death of Polonius. The camera shows us anxious black-clad women fussing about Ophelia and dressing her in funeral black. Underneath her heavy dress, and supporting it, is a metal frame that encloses almost the whole of her torso. She is buckled into it, creating a visual metaphor for a young person constrained and shackled by the dictates of her class and society (Showalter 1985). In Kozintsev's film Denmark is shown to be a prison for more people than Hamlet.

A good choice for a more detailed comparative analysis of both films would be each director's handling of the closing action. Olivier, having no Fortinbras, ends his film with the body of the Prince being carried aloft to the top of a tower surrounded in mist on which the camera looks down from a great height. The image (which was also used at the beginning of the film) emphasizes Hamlet's uniqueness and isolation from other people. Kozintsev, like Shakespeare, does not end the action with Hamlet's death. He shows the troops of Fortinbras occupying the castle, literally illustrating that, despite a stage littered with the bodies of great and powerful men, including the King of Denmark and his heir, there will be no power vacuum, and that order rapidly replaces any threat of chaos and anarchy. There is never a time in which the deaths of those with power can open up the possibility of a change in the social order.

So far we have looked at the issue of textual fidelity largely from the point of view of the written text, and have also looked at how, by comparing selected episodes from the films of different directors, we can open up discussion. But although the fidelity we have discussed concerns the words written to be spoken by actors, there is another language, already briefly touched on, that communicates ideas and emotions and, especially in the cinema and on television, is of equal if not more significance than spoken language: the visual text. To be able to read such visual texts with the same degree of attention that we give to their spoken equivalent we have to know not only what a particular image is trying to say, but also how it has been constructed and why.

A priority for any teacher considering the use of filmed and/or televised Shakespeare material must be to ensure that, as far as possible, their students possess basic visual literacy. They have to be able to read *consciously* at least some of the signs and signals generated subconsciously through the consumption of visual images; to be able to decode what the designers/producers of images have encoded in them. Second, students need a basic awareness of the grammar and syntax of television and film, so that at the very least when watching the projection of a film of a Shakespeare play they are aware that they *are* fictions and that they have been deliberately constructed in a particular way for a particular reason.

To help achieve this students could usefully spend a few moments on one or two evenings watching televised advertisements and, if they have a VCR, recording one or two. They need to be reminded to ask not only what the advertisement is selling, but how it goes about it. To whom is it designed to appeal: young/old; male/female, etc? Is a lot of money required to obtain the product? What is the setting? Is there a narrative? What is the relationship of the images to the spoken text? Does it feature a well-known personality, and if so why? In addition to the content, encourage students to become aware of the form. For example, at the cutting from shot to shot and at how many times in, say, 15 seconds, the camera's focus changes. (Use a stop-watch or the second hand to actually time it). Where is the camera looking from: inside a building looking out, low level looking up and elongating figures/buildings over the shoulder? When is a close-up replaced by a distance shot and how is the transition accomplished? How and when does the director focus attention: is the camera on a character who is talking or on the reaction of a listener(s)? or does the director make use of point-of-view shots, for example when the camera is used as if it is looking out through the eyes of a particular character? Can an educated guess be made at how many cameras are being used?

There is no necessity for the student to be able to deconstruct an advertisement completely, any more than you can reasonably expect them to be able to deconstruct a fictional narrative completely. Nor is it necessary for them to spend an inordinate amount of time looking at how these fictions are made. The exercise serves as an *aide mémoire*, vital if subsequently the student is to remain aware of how illusions are constructed to represent reality, and that this critical awareness is brought to bear on versions of Shakespeare made for film and/or television. This is the key to unlocking the box and creating an active and exciting *critical* response to Shakespeare.

Teachers also need to prompt their students to consider some of the ways in which film and/or television reproductions of Shakespeare plays differ from stage performances. Perhaps the most significant difference between 'live' and recorded performance is the degree of control exercised over the experience of watching it. The individual member of a theatre audience ultimately chooses where to focus his or her attention, a choice that may be influenced by his or her position in the auditorium and its relationship to the stage/acting area. Although theatre audiences may have been encouraged to focus in a particular direction at a certain moment by the staging of the director, or the gesture of an actor, it is always possible to look elsewhere, to decide, for example, to concentrate not on the actor who is speaking but on a small group of minor players listening. In any performance listening is an expressive act and any actor who can be seen by an audience signals something to them that contributes in some way to the general discourse of the performance text.

In the theatre, seats with a restricted view are sold at a discount, for everyone is assumed to want to be able to see simultaneously the whole of the acting area and every performer using it. Directors stage plays in the knowledge that audiences will construct their own meanings from what they see as well as from what they hear and that this will include *everything* that is visible on the stage. But, in televising a Shakespeare play, or making a film of one, the audience is never in the position of being able to define its own field of view. The director chooses where the audience will look and continually changes their focus. In doing so, when for example showing a close-up of an actor's face, the viewer may be denied the reactions of the person or persons to whom this discourse is addressed. In Shakespeare's dramas this is particularly significant because they are essentially rhetorical: everything spoken was designed to be overheard by the audience and usually by actors on stage as well. Nor is this simply a technical matter of the limitations of the medium; it is a matter that affects the way in which the viewer interprets the action. For example, one of the most dramatic scenes in *Hamlet* is the encounter between Hamlet and Ophelia immediately following the 'To be or not to be . . .' soliloquy (III.1). In a performance of the play on stage the audience will always be watching and aware of both performers (and perhaps too of the presence of Claudius and Polonius behind the arras) even though it is Hamlet who has most of the spoken text. In Rodney Bennett's production of the play for the BBC Shakespeare series, the camera is used in this scene in such a way as to focus the viewer's attention almost exclusively on Hamlet. Although the presence of Ophelia is registered throughout the televising of the scene, the actress is often filmed from behind, the camera looking over her shoulder towards Hamlet. The viewer invariably cannot see her full-face. Even when her face is shown in close-up, it is in profile and the image blurred in order that the primary focus remains the Prince. Consciously or not, the director's use of the camera makes Hamlet the subject of this scene. We watch his reactions to what is happening, he is the active, dynamic force, she is presented as passive. The scene thus constructed becomes almost exclusively a further extension of Hamlet's narrative, his crisis, his betrayal, whilst those of Ophelia are marginalized. The irony here is that when the BBC/Time–Life consortium set out to televise the whole of Shakespeare they initially tried to avoid directors who might create what the producers saw as 'fashionable' productions, that is, programmes overtly offering a reading of the text. Instead they chose men [sic] who would attempt to reproduce faithfully the text of Shakespeare, thus guaranteeing, as they saw it, programmes that would not date and would, in the industry's own jargon, have a long 'shelf life'. What my example demonstrates is that there can never be a performance of Shakespeare that is not at the same time an *interpretation* of Shakespeare. Bennett's interpretation of the play is not overt, but, as this scene reveals, his camera-work is covertly constructing a text that highlights Hamlet at the expense of Ophelia.

The conventions of film and television are not identical, but, even more than the theatre, both are highly contrived media. There is almost no 'live' television drama, and of course no such thing as 'live' film. All Shakespeare productions on film/video have been pre-recorded and edited. But the illusionistic conventions of television (and that of most stage productions of Shakespeare) do not draw attention to this artificial process of generation, but attempt to kid the viewer into accepting the illusion that the action unfolding is real. Ironically such illusionist conventions are the opposite of those employed on the unlocalized stages of the Elizabethan/Jacobean theatres. Jonathan Miller, one of the producers of the BBC/Time–Life Shakespeare series, has said that 'televising Shakespeare forces the director to adopt an illusionistic idiom . . .' (Miller 1986: 65). Whether or not this is true is beside the point. What is irrefutable is that most television directors work in that way. That is to say their recordings are made in such a way as to conceal the artificiality of the process of their genesis. Although that process is highly artificial and contrived, it is eventually transmitted not as art, but as life. Action that may have been recorded over a number of days or months, and shot out of sequence, will be edited so as to ensure its eventual representation as a seamless whole. The means of producing this illusion – the lights, the cameras, the film crew – are likewise hidden: they are all outside the frame. Not only do the audience not see the mechanics that produced the image, illusionism is also used to encourage an emotional identification and involvement with the action.

Although film and television are two distinct media possessing their own distinctive conventions, they are united in constructing Shakespeare illusionistically. Their material is inevitably made in such a way that it always appears as if it is the viewer's eye looking at the action, just as it does in the theatre, switching its focus from individual to group, from face to face. But in reality it is a point of view selected not by the individual spectator, but fixed previously by the director and camera operator. Television in particular focuses attention on small groups, head and shoulder shots, and especially on close-ups of the face. This capacity to foreground facial expressions, in which the attention of the audience flickers continually from mouth to eyes, places the interpretive interest inevitably on the psychology and personality of the individuals subjected to such close scrutiny. Actors in leading roles, or roles given such a high focus, develop a minimalist acting style in which they strive for psychological naturalism. In the BBC Shakespeare series (with one or two notable exceptions from Jane Howell) there is almost no concentration on anything other than character, from the point of view both of the actors and of the directors. As a consequence although the BBC text of *Hamlet* has few cuts, and Fortinbras and his army are shown, their potential for making a political reading for example, is unfulfilled because of the director's preoccupation with creating identification and sympathy with individuals, rather than inviting a more reflective consideration of the totality of the events in which those individuals are caught up.

The consumer of such fictions is entertained by experiences and sensations – of fear, tension, laughter, sentiment – but usually remains unaware of the craft that produced them. This is of course true of most contemporary art, but with a novel or poem, or with the printed text of a play, although not part of the process that initiated it, the reader *is* part of the process of producing the meaning by the act of reading it. And, unlike conventional performances in cinemas and theatres, s/he has a choice whether or not to decide to reread a page, go back to the beginning, or even to ignore the given structure of the book and start by reading the conclusion first before deciding whether to proceed with the rest.

All this presents a formidable obstacle to the student of Shakespeare in performance. Directors working in an illusionist convention construct their text in such a way as to eliminate contradictions, not to highlight them. It is not necessary to be a disciple of Brecht to accept that emotional identification and involvement in a situation can make thinking about it more difficult. So a priority for any teacher who wants to use these products to stimulate debates about what they mean is to try to distance students from illusionistic representations of Shakespeare in order that they can see (and therefore criticize) the basis on which they have been constructed.

You cannot reread a 16mm film as you can a book, but you *can* reread a videotape as often as you like. Therefore, in order to challenge and resist illusionist conventions and the lure of ready-made answers to complex questions of interpretation, however sympathetic they may seem, and to learn to recognize that the known and familiar isn't always the *only* way of seeing, students must learn not only to look, but to look critically. If you can use a video to study the narrative and to explore how meanings have been manufactured, you can control the screening rather than letting the screening control you. That means being able to stop or 'freeze' the image, to slow down the action, and to rewind the tape in order to look at a section of it again. Ideally (but by no means always) it also means running two video recorders and using two monitors so that you can literally compare films frame by frame.

I would argue that to teach Shakespeare on film with the same degree of attention to close analysis that you use in reading a printed text you have to have the material on videotape, and need to keep your finger continually on the pause button, for the whole thrust of the illusionist convention is to give the impression of continual motion, to avoid breaking up the action, and to drive the viewer inexorably forward in linear progression: beginning, middle, end. In a continual screening (as in a theatrical perform-ance) there is little opportunity to pause and reflect, and the viewer is rarely invited to stop and consider how the images have been joined together or why. It is very difficult, unless you have been previously alerted to it, to notice, say, how Rodney Bennett's camera-work in *Hamlet* constructs one meaning whilst excluding others, or how and why an image from Kozintsev works.

At a time when there is a good deal of interesting critical material forthcoming which deals with issues and arguments concerning Shakespeare on film and television (Donaldson 1990;

Collick 1989; Bulman and Coursen 1988; Davies 1988; *Shakespeare Survey* 1987) it is mildly depressing if not entirely surprising to find that the most recent prestigious editions of *Hamlet*, for example, restrict their editorial commentary to the history of the plays on stage (Edwards 1985; Hibbard 1987). But at least there *is* a commentary on staged performances; not too long ago even this would have been considered irrelevant or inappropriate. For despite what apparently happens in the English department of the grammar school in Stratford-upon-Avon, where the Bard's works as performed by the RSC were recently (1989) declared out of bounds because too 'trendy', Shakespeare is part of a *changing* curriculum. One of the changes that must surely come is that increasingly his plays will be effectively studied not only as literary texts (or literature that walks on a stage), but also as films and videos – material of equal status and interest to the printed text, and no less full of interesting and relevant critical issues.

NOTES

1 See the evidence cited by Nigel Wheale in Chapter 11.
2 For a small sum (1990: £5.00 members, £9.50 non-members) teachers can obtain an invaluable booklet listing all currently available video/film material on Shakespeare from the British Universities Film Council, 55 Greek Street, London W1.
3 Kozintsev's *Hamlet* (Sovscope/Lenfilm 1964; unfortunately unavailable on video) is a very useful film to show not only because of the directorial skill of Kozintsev but also because the actors speak in Russian, making the audience much more conscious than is usual of the quality of the visual text.

REFERENCES

Bulman, J. C., and Coursen, H. R. (eds) (1988) *Shakespeare on Television. An Anthology of Essays and Reviews*, Hanover and London: University Press of New England.
Collick, John (1989) *Shakespeare, Cinema and Society*, Manchester: Manchester University Press.
Davies, Anthony (1988) *Filming Shakespeare's Plays: The Adaptations of Laurence Olivier, Orson Welles, Peter Brook and Akira Kurosawa*, Cambridge: Cambridge University Press.
Donaldson, Peter (1990) *Shakespearean Films/Shakespearean Directors*, London: Unwin Hyman.
Edwards, Philip (ed.) (1985) *Hamlet, Prince of Denmark*, by William Shakespeare, Cambridge: Cambridge University Press.

Hibbard, G. R. (ed.) (1987) *Hamlet* by William Shakespeare, Oxford: Oxford University Press.

Jones, Ernest (1949) *Hamlet and Oedipus*, London: Gollancz.

Miller, Jonathan (1986) *Subsequent Performances*, London: Faber & Faber.

Powell, Michael (1986) *A Life in the Movies. An Autobiography*, London: Heinemann.

Shakespeare Survey (1987) vol. 39, 'Shakespeare on film and television', Cambridge: Cambridge University Press.

Showalter, Elaine (1985) 'Representing Ophelia: women, madness, and the responsibilities of feminist criticism', in Patricia Parker and Geoffrey Hartman (eds) *Shakespeare and the Question of Theory*, New York and London: Methuen.

11

Scratching Shakespeare: video-teaching the Bard

Nigel Wheale

I

Oh 'tis most sweet
When in one line two crafts directly meet.
(*Hamlet* [Q2] III.4.210–11; Edwards 1985)

Scratch video is every viewer's revenge on televisual banality: tape your least favourite politician in full flow, link up your VCR with a second one borrowed from a fellow scratcher, then proceed to invert the broadcast meaning through copying and transposing sentences, repeating edits, and cutting in with the voice-over borrowed from a cat-food ad.

Scratch effects were developed by independent video artists during the early 1980s, and have attained broadcast status because of their incorporation into sharp adverts and pop promos, as well as through the hilariously disrupted speech patterns of a mega-personality like Max Headroom. It is another (small) example of how innovation at the periphery is taken up and into the voracious, technocratic centre; what began as attack upon media-tized meanings ends up by being co-opted to the universal sales drive. Scratch in its purer format as a critique of broadcasting conventions has been seen on the national airwaves in occasional programmes such as Gorilla Tapes' *Invisible TV* (Bode 1988), but by definition it is an off-limits form because it begins with piracy (Armes 1988: 198–9). Scratchers steal the hugely expensive productions which are broadcast materials by taping them off-air, and they then proceed to deface, invert, and satirize. Coca Cola would not be pleased; Coca Cola would reach, indeed, for the lawyers.

Shakespeare is another hugely expensive multinational product, imbricated in many different kinds of complex structure: the tourist industry, broadcast entertainment industry, the National Curriculum, and then more diffusely in a variety of kinds of discourse: the languages of cultural value, heritage, spiritual insight . . . and the politics of nationalism (Dollimore and Sinfield 1985; Holderness 1988). Bringing together 'Shakespeare' and 'video' in our teaching allows us to put this traditionally sanctioned body of writing into provoking new relations with contemporary technology, and more than this, with our students' inherent sprightliness (for which read irreverence/sass/critical intelligence, and delete as appropriate). The interaction of videotape and renaissance drama as a component of the curriculum presents us as teachers and students with many opportunities: a technology which is often very familiar to pupils, and which contributes to a significant part of their leisure interests, which intrigues and involves them in its processes, can be actively used to elicit interest in writing, which for many of them is full of difficulty and remote from their experience. The combination need not be spurious; it's not a question of smuggling in a forbiddingly academic subject by coating it with technological allure (Lusted 1988). Videotape recording animates the dramatic texts, allows them to be acted and assessed in performance. They can be directed, edited, and viewed within a context of active production – all of these being functions which are implicit in the plays as dramatic pre-texts. The inert page which is read only as a phenomenon of print (those disappointing essays where the pupil discusses the 'book' or – alas – the 'novel' *Hamlet*) can through video activity be legitimately studied in performance and collaboration.

Simultaneously, the means by which this work is done – the television camera, monitor and editing facility – are themselves an implicit part of the learning. Effective media studies develop the kinds of attention which are paid to the possibilities and constraints of the transmitting form (Masterman 1985: 24–37). In this application they can focus questions about the nature of the original performances of Shakespeare's plays, issues which may otherwise remain mute and covered over by unexamined assumptions when texts are studied only through reading and discussion. The study of Shakespeare is enshrined atop some of the highest summits of academic achievement and the demanding expectations of certain kinds of literacy; this status is now under active question from a number of quarters (Gibson 1986, 1990; Holder-ness 1988). The highly anomalous fact that the texts were written only to be consumed by audiences at performance has been elided through the emphasis on reading alone, now the dominant means of approaching Shakespeare for study. Video practice can exploit this productive contradiction: when 98 per cent of homes possess one or more television receivers; when the household may spend on average 20–25 hours a week in viewing, with an average daily total of 3 hours 8 minutes, including breakfast television (BARB 1988), and when 20 per cent of a child's week may be passed in construing television, perhaps it is time to act, direct, and scan the plays with this medium, rather than continuing to commune alone with them in the study-bedroom.

Involving pupils in video production helps to dispel the prevail-ing assumption that televisual culture necessarily induces a gen-eralized passivity in its audience because the consumption of its product is somehow 'thoughtless'. Recent research argues differ-ently:

> children's response to television is typically a complex cogni-tive act, not the enemy of reading and thought as so widely feared, but so closely akin that it makes good sense to talk of 'reading' television. Allied to this is a conception of children as not solely passive and helpless in this transaction, but active as well, creating and using meanings in their own lives, for their own purposes.
>
> (Hodge and Tripp 1986: 3)

If this is true of watching programmes, then it will be even more so in producing them: the explicit assumption of this chapter is that the students' own highly developed 'cultural capital' derived from their active viewing ('reading') of television can be called on as a resource and confidence when working with video, and that this can be done in relation to texts about which most students understandably feel defensive. This approach calls for a range of skills and offers a spectrum of learning possibilities, which also suits it to classes containing differentiated abilities. Arguments for the active incorporation of media studies in the curriculum as a way of broadening and redefining literacy as such can be followed conveniently in publications of the British Film Institute's Education Department (*Television and Schooling*, BFI

1985; BFI/DES National Working Party on Primary Media Education papers; Bazalgette 1988).

An example: it isn't just the graduate seminars and the international academic conferences that have new perspectives to offer us. I think of the 240 primary school children attending 'Shakespeare Day', a culminating event in the 'Shakespeare and Schools' project (Gibson 1986–; 1990). Each group offered a well rehearsed and carefully considered extract from one of half a dozen plays, and throughout the six hours this was watched with absorbed and critical attention by everyone else. Scenes were performed collectively, with speeches delivered in choric style, obviating the need for a star system, and this returned the dramatic speaking to its origins in group delivery. One class of ten-year-olds offered a sensitively edited version of *Titus Andronicus;* they were inspired by their teacher, who had seen Deborah Warner's extraordinary production at the Swan Theatre, Stratford 1987. This was a fine example of stage-to-school transfer. The class took the political conflict of the play and turned it into a *News at Ten* spoof report on the Roman elections, including a nervous interview with Saturninus and Tamora, all choreographed, together with three cameras, studio manager, anchorman, and weather report. Here the children of Icknield School were animating the Shakespearean text through an ironic use of communications technology, with numerous lessons to be learnt about the renaissance version of Rome, and the cynicism of media hype, media manipulation. This kind of adaptive exercise can be purely extrinsic to the play text itself, but it was clear in watching the preparations and the final version of Icknield School's performance that the children were being encouraged to consider closely the implications of *Titus Andronicus* through these inventive scenarios.

The uses of videotape for this kind of teaching can be grouped under three headings: (1) watching film adaptations of the plays and exploiting the differences between theatrical and film realizations of the text (Holderness 1985; Wheale 1987; Collick 1989; Peter Reynolds Chapter 10 of this book); (2) using videotapes prepared for educational contexts, where the specific audio-visual qualities of the medium are drawn on; (3) in-class production of taped materials where the end product is only one element in the process of exploring text and technology in a mutually interactive way. What follows will concentrate on examples of the second kind of activity. As regards the first category, there is now a developing literature which usefully analyses Shakespeare as filmed and televised (Wells 1987; Bulman and Coursen 1988; Collick 1989); and no one needs to be given examples of what might be done with a class and a camera, since good practice will endlessly generate its own ideas.

Video materials for teaching Shakespeare already exist in growing profusion (McLean 1980; Terris 1986) but by and large they offer a conventional window-on-the-world programme treatment of their subject, and very few incorporate what we may term the Scratcher's Perspective, that is an active sense of the interaction of late twentieth-century electronic format and early modern dramatic pre-text. I will now describe two examples of this more conceptually developed video work.

II

systems invented to record the world become systems of *representation* when used to create fictional or documentary works.

(Armes 1988: 137)

The Cambridge Experimental Theatre's *Hamlet* (1987) cuts down the cast list to Gertrude and Ophelia, Claudius and Polonius; these four roles are taken by two female and two male actors, who then play the role of the Prince, fairly equally distributed between them. Without benefit of props or scenery, Roland Kenyon's carefully collaged version of the *Hamlet* text receives the viewers' full attention as the site of all activity. CET draw on twentieth-century traditions of 'impoverished spectacle' in the theatre by way of a reduction through concentration of effect which recalls the original staging and its fluid, open playing area. The non-naturalistic qualities of early seventeenth-century theatre are also summoned through CET's use of mask and 'gestic' playing, formalized speaking and movement within the unadorned space of the TV studio. Speeches are often shared, or delivered in chorus, so that we can rehear soliloquies that have become too familiar, and be distanced from possessively psychologized versions of the roles: much contemporary criticism focuses on the nature of characterization in these early modern dramas, usually in an attempt to set aside assumptions developed by audiences who are usually more accustomed to naturalistic conventions. So in

CET's performance, verse rhythm becomes a kind of contagion which spreads or is delegated to the rhythmicized gestures of the bodies in group orchestration. Finally, the tight framing of the poetry is given an additional patterning through the dramatic cutting produced by camera angle and editing facility. The CET *Hamlet* continually snags its viewers through audio-visual device – freeze-frame, dissolve, montage, multi-tracking – and plays off our awareness of what is being said against the means of saying itself. Acting, camera work, and editing are equally part of our viewing attention.

CET's Prince is shared between the four players, a strategy which dis-locates the singularity of the role. There are three good reasons for employing this device: first, the play itself puts into question the nature of human identity and the ways in which we attempt to know each other. Every familial, political, and affectionate relationship in *Hamlet* is under severe tension, or is rendered inscrutable; resolving these enigmas is fundamentally the process of the tragedy. Second: it is a mistake to think that late sixteenth- and early seventeenth-century assumptions about human personality and its personation (a word invented during Shakespeare's career) on the stage coincide exactly with our own expectations, and this is particularly the case with the representation of women. Therefore CET's stylized acting interposes itself between the text of the play and our conventional expectations as to how it might naturalistically be performed. Third: many debates in our own period, deriving from philosophy, psychoanalysis, linguistics, and cultural theory have investigated those aspects of self-identity which might be broken down into separable and not necessarily reconcilable elements of the person. CET's *Hamlet* displays fragmented identity suffering the crises of language, authority, and division which the early modern drama so effectively articulates.

There is a balance of gender within the CET company, and the roles are evenly shared between the sexes. The Elizabethan and Jacobean theatre, however, was an exclusively male institution, from the writers, actors, and owners, through to the audience itself, where women were only present as it were by permission of the men whom they accompanied. Shakespeare's plays confine their womenfolk closely, the parts are notoriously underwritten, so that the symbolic females become the mute focus of intense attentions, whether of desire, jealousy, possessiveness, or hatred, and in the tragedies they are very unlikely to survive the unfolding of the action (Tennenhouse 1989). The CET strategy of disseminating the roles more equally overcomes this confinement, and adds subtle inflections to the tensions of gender and representation in the play. A moving example is the use of the 'feminized' Hamlet-character to debate with Gertrude during the closet scene, so that the dialogue at one level becomes an externalized playing out of the mother's hidden conscience.

CET's production of *Hamlet* theorizes a performance and a reproduction of the play; Cambridge AV Group's *Making Shakespeare* uses the audio-visual resources of video to situate *Othello* within a history of performance and a history of criticism. Independent educational video production takes place outside schools and colleges, and within the interstices of educational institutions (Marshall 1979; Hines 1987; *Independent Media* throughout). The work of the CAVG and CET is described here as examples of the best kind of independent sector production, using an extra-institutional base as a way of making new kinds of reading of Shakespeare and exploring new kinds of pedagogical practice.

Videotape's mode of address is different from that of the cinema and of television proper (Ellis 1982); Roy Armes describes it as 'a positive communal form' which interests and unites small but committed audiences who have a particular investment in the content of the specific tape that they are watching and discussing: 'video has shown that it has the potential to become the communal mode which television never gave us, with tapes shown to an intimate (but non-family) audience which has gathered specifically to see them' (Armes 1988: 133). But this does not mean that video is only a form of special-interest home movie. Because independent videotapes are non-broadcast and are therefore narrowcast in exactly this way, they do not need to conform to the conventions of nationally networked programmes, and can attempt to put into question the generalized modes of operation of broadcast material by drawing on their more communal liaison with the audience.

How do programmes lay claim to authority? How do students learn from televised programmes? Are there techniques within programmes that can be exploited to stimulate student response in ways which classroom discussion and printed texts cannot follow? And how are televised materials best incorporated within all the other kinds of learning which go on? Different kinds of presentation can be used within alternative tapes so as to put into tension the various arguments being made, and simultaneously prompt the viewer to reflect on the structure of conventional programmes. A presenter, or voice-over, is an obvious linking narrative which gives credibility to materials in television; another is the 'talking head' or expert. Both of these elements are unproblematically reproduced by conventional programming as its content and truth; alternative tapes encourage a greater awareness of the medium itself and the ways in which it endorses what it carries; the visual and aural textures of the tape become intrinsic to the construction of the sequential argument. And precisely because video is a technologically eclectic medium (Armes 1988: 152) it can be used to pick n' mix among the forms and assumptions of the media it follows – cinema, radio, television. In this way formal tensions are created which are also opportunities for critical insight (Jameson 1987).

Cambridge AV Group consists of three individuals (see Acknowledgements) who have committd their (spare-time) video production to making programmes which can be of use to secondary-school, sixth-form, and first-degree-level students. This range of audiences is specifically addressed in order to cross the boundaries between secondary and tertiary groups, and this allows approaches that have been developed in graduate and undergraduate teaching to be introduced at an earlier stage of the educational process. Simultaneously, media education practices encourage the kinds of 'learning by doing' more usually associated with lower school work, but carry these forward into the secondary and tertiary sector, with all their advantages in terms of practically applied intelligence and collaborative activity.

The Video Group's first tape, *D. H. Lawrence and the Culture Industry*, provided some trenchant social/industrial and political contexts for the study of Lawrence: but the programme is more than a conventionally thematic discussion of the Great Author because it also considers the kinds of representation and dissemination which the novel (and biography) have undergone through film, television, and syllabuses. The 'alternative' element in such a treatment emphasizes the processes of reproduction and inevitable rescription to which any text is subject within the majority systems that circulate information: an 'independent' tape should by definition be in a more favourable position to articulate some of the silences, elisions, and underemphases in the accounts of texts

211

made through established formats, precisely because it is pos-
itioned in a different relation to the conventions of representation
and discourse that are uniformly at work elsewhere. Given wit
and skill, the resulting tape should be usefully provocative as a
pre-text for discussions, and the nature of audio-visual rhetoric
should become clearer through the devices of the programme.

Making Shakespeare sets into relation a number of approaches
to *Othello* through film excerpts, archive materials, student discussion classes, and interviews with directors, designers, and academics who have been closely involved with some of the recent
debates on the nature of English studies in general, and teaching
renaissance drama in particular. *Othello* is chosen because of its
well established place in the examination lists, but also because it
is marked by some of the questionable aspects of 'Shakespearean
tragedy' which are not usually part of discussion within schools
or colleges.

Making Shakespeare, in common with the other critical
approaches explored here, focuses on the *kinds of construction* which
we as audience or students place on Shakespeare's plays. And
precisely because of the singular status of the idea of Shakespeare,
an icon which represents English-literature-as-such to so many
people, then very generalized constructions may be made at the
expense of more historically specific understanding. The tape aims
to make us aware of the constructedness of the Shakespearean
reputation by presenting changes in theatre convention, audience
response, and literacy between 1600 and our own period.
Changes, but also parallels which can help us study the plays:
this first mass urban, commercial entertainment anticipated in
significant ways the wide appeal of our own broadcast media.

Raymond Williams is the first critic to present arguments on
the tape, and this is appropriate because his particular kind of
cultural materialist reading of literature is one that informs the
video's overall approach (Williams 1983); tragically, Williams's
contribution was one of his last teaching activities before his
untimely death in 1988. He draws attention to the diversity of
the original audience's social and therefore linguistic competence,
and the way in which this allowed scenes to be 'multivocal',
addressing different issues and varying social interests. And classroom practices which 'flatten' the plays through a grinding process of close reading, to the exclusion of a sense of the social
'gradients' present between the different kinds of speaking, can

do an enormous disservice to the dramas. The pervasive influence of print culture and mass literacy may have made us less responsive to the aural and socially embodied signals of the period stage. (But yes, of course, we must still have a lively sense of what the words precisely mean.) In one of its continuously inventive visual metaphors, *Making Shakespeare* graphically dramatizes these arguments with the advance of The Text, tied to a chronometric beat, against which 'flattened' figures play out extracts from *Othello* II.1.

Williams has argued elsewhere that the attention given to plays by the pre-modern audience was necessarily non-naturalistic, concentrating less on character traits, and was consequently more fluid; a significant generality in the dramatic verse was able to articulate a wide range of concerns across classes. Because it was less focused on questions of character, the switching of audience attention from monologue to dialogue, and from scene to scene, would not have psychologized character in the way that twentieth-century readings are tempted to do, to the exclusion of more discursive kinds of meaning:

> Thus there is no formal equivalence between presumed psychological content, of a subjective kind, and a mode of writing centred on a single and isolated speaker. The 'soliloquy', to put it another way, is not 'inner speech' in any defining or exclusive sense.
>
> (Williams 1983: 55)

This kind of perspective releases *Othello* for more socially based readings, rather than intensively psychological interpretations made at the expense of context and history.

The sexual and racial gradients in *Othello* are peculiarly severe, and the opening of Act II Scene 1 is offered as a passage which conventional critical interpretations have misread, exactly as a 'flat text' – M. R. Ridley, editor of the Arden edition, commenting on II.1.109–66, finds it 'one of the most unsatisfactory passages in Shakespeare' (Ridley 1965: 54). A critic like Ridley is presumably unsettled by Iago's offensive display of laborious wit, made at Desdemona's expense. But his chivalrous and prudish reading misses the point of the violence being offered by Iago's 'homely' speaking (Cassio's comment on him, line 165); it is an assault which does Iago no credit as he attempts to implicate Desdemona in his obscene play through a vindictive parody of Cassio's more Florentine (for which read 'cultivated') dalliance with Emilia.

Raymond Williams's discussion of the Shakespearean text and its social moment is implicitly a demotic, or even democratic position: he discusses the dramas as 'unusually open writing, at several different levels' – an openness to different kinds of social speaking, to which we must attend, as here. However the next critical perspective to be put is one which goes on to question the nature of the game being played in this scene. Lisa Jardine is a feminist literary critic whose scrupulously detailed historical research in the daily conduct of renaissance public and private spheres finds that the dramas limit and confine their female characters through highly repressive conventions, the cumulative effects of which are time and again to reinforce images of predation on, and violence against women in the period. Professor Jardine in voice-over to the actors performing II.1 argues that this 'beach scene' plays out a scenario in which the assumptions of Desdemona's society would require her not to participate at all – as she defines her own delicacy at lines 122–3:

> I am not merry, but I do beguile
> The thing I am, by seeming otherwise:

The social dynamic of this scene effectively harasses the female character, but it is only a verbal prelude to the physical violence of Act V. Feminist readings of Shakespearean tragedy note the persistent confinement of female characters within very straitened roles, and the pervasive suspicion of women which is articulated through male character: Hamlet, Lear, the insufficient husband Mr Macbeth. Lisa Jardine's reponse to a student's wish to read Emilia's speech 'Let husbands know/Their wives have sense like them . . .' (IV.3.93ff.) as a proto-feminist statement is provocative: she argues that the plea is made by the least powerful character involved in the action, and the context in which it is made, a preparation for bed, is erotically charged. Any attempt to produce this dialogue as a strongly 'feminist plea' would be mistaken, because what follows is then perceived as the vengeful male destruction of a shrewish virago. This is an absolute limit of interpretive possibility, she argues, which is dictated by the period-bound assumptions of the early modern play.

An effective way of countering the play's biases, omissions, and distortions is to rewrite the text, and contemporary critics are increasingly interested in the potential mobility to be created with Shakespeare as pretext, and for three good reasons: first, because twentieth-century textual criticism is progressively uncovering the evidence of revision and patching within the plays themselves (see Ann Thompson's chapter in this collection); second, because production history shows how the plays have been more often performed in radically altered forms than in the scrupulously 'restored' texts currently in use; and third, because there are so many vigorous arguments conducted with Shakespeare now by authors who are adapting or rewriting his aged scripts wholesale. Work can be done in the classroom on different versions of the plays as textual scholarship is re-editing them: for example, Stanley Wells and Gary Taylor's edition of *The Complete Works* (Oxford 1986) gives the Folio and Quarto *Lear* (and see Taylor and Warren 1983); Philip Edwards's edition of *Hamlet* (Edwards 1985) clearly lays out the arguments and options in the text for possible revisions made to the play. Or passages and whole plays can be offered as instances of modern commentary-by-rescription: Georg Büchner's *Danton's Death* (in Howard Brenton's translation) as a revolutionist's appropriation of Shakespearean histories and tragdies; Günter Grass's *The Plebeians Rehearse the Uprising* as a counter-*Coriolanus;* Aimé Césaire's *Une tempête*, with Derek Jarman's *Tempest* (Wheale 1988); Edward Bond's *Lear* against either or both of Shakespeare's pitifully botched attempts at political tragedy (Sinfield 1982). . . .

In not attempting to reconcile Raymond Williams's approach with that of Lisa Jardine, *Making Shakespeare* expects its audience to develop their own constructions, and explore the potential disagreement: from the position of the female roles and a female spectator/reader, *Othello* is only 'multivocal' in a quite closely circumscribed way, only 'open and interactive writing' in particular, gendered senses.

In the early seventeenth century the part of Desdemona, in common with all the women's roles, was taken by a youth – who might be so convincing that a spectator in Oxford, 1610, could write that the boy 'moved us especially in *her* death when, as *she* lay on her bed, *her* face itself implored the pity of the audience' (Sanders 1984: 38). That counterfeit has become unacceptable to our own conventions, yet the imitation of a Black prince by a white actor has not become problematic in the same way. Why should this be? *Making Shakespeare* provokes this kind

215

of question about the conventions of representation by rehearsing the changes in fashion which the role has undergone during the last 200 years. Production history is not usually included in the study of Shakespeare in schools, partly because of the necessary emphasis on the students' interaction with the text before them, and partly because of the difficulty of resuscitating the narrative of a play's history (this is a Resource Question): nothing so dusty as old playbills and empty costumes (but see the chapters by Simon Shepherd and John Salway in this collection for workshop-based strategies to explore historical difference in productions). Videotape can present recorded performances and so reconstruct a more lively argument about production history. *Making Shakespeare* asks us to consider the stage history of *Othello* so as to demonstrate the changing expectations which have been brought to the playing of the Moor's role.

The tape establishes a history of racial misrecognition as mediated through the character of the Moor of Venice by citing Court records and attitudes from the early seventeenth century. These already demonstrate a conflicting mixture of assumptions: Moor as heathen threat, as attractively exotic, as racially invasive. Therefore, it argues, there was already a potent and 'unstable' set of assumptions about Moorishness which Shakespeare's play drew on. The authorial intention is irrecoverable, but we have an eloquent sequence of productions which articulate changing attitudes to the relationship of Othello and Desdemona.

Europe's colonial involvement in Africa added new dimensions of prejudice to the play. Influenced by Edmund Kean's performance of Othello as a light-skinned Arab in 1814, and reinforced by S. T. Coleridge's distaste at the prospect of 'this beautiful Venetian girl falling in love with a veritable negro', nineteenth-century English critics were reluctant to accept the power of the interpretation given by the Black actor, Ira Aldridge. *Making Shakespeare* offers a concise biography of Paul Robeson, the greatest twentieth-century Black interpreter of Othello, showing how he turned his performance into a powerful statement against bigotry in our own period. Robeson's courageous political activism led to the destruction of his career and his persecution during the McCarthy trials; this history can also be called on in our interpretation of the play's changing meanings.

Several speakers on the tape – students, a critic, a director, an actor – describe the insidious appeal of Iago, able to implicate the audience, however consciously unwilling, in his racist point of view. And this shameful effect is explored via ideology, the most abstract critical concept discussed in *Making Shakespeare*. Jonathan Dollimore and Alan Sinfield describe 'the ideological' as the kinds of narrative constructed by characters about each other, and supremely by Iago of Othello. Iago draws on a sympathetic resonance of suspicion that is harboured within Venetian society towards the Moor and uses this to destroy both him and his wife.

Dollimore and Sinfield stress the crucial role of ideas in the early modern period, when they were used as a form of social control to be exercised through an imposed consensus of beliefs and attitudes; this was necessary, they argue, because the physical apparatus of state power and coercion with which we are familiar – surveillance, security, deterrence – was utterly lacking. And this goes some way to account for what must seem to us the strangely pervasive presence of religion and theological belief in so many aspects of renaissance life. On this description, Othello himself becomes a demonstrable case of how the personality is only socially constructed; his identity is thoroughly 'scripted' by Iago's insinuations. For example, in III.3 when Othello returns, driven to madness by Iago's distorting narrative, the link he makes between Desdemona's 'infidelity' and his social being is shockingly explicit:

> And, O you mortal engines, whose rude throats
> Th'immortal Jove's dread clamours counterfeit,
> Farewell! *Othello's occupation's gone.*
>
> (III.3.361–3)

Dollimore and Sinfield argue from a developed critical position which is committed to material, anti-humanist readings of literature (Dollimore and Sinfield 1985; Dollimore 1989). Situated simultaneously at the margin and the centre of its society, performed on the South Bank as well as in the Court, Shakespeare's plays were in contradictory relation to the values of their period. What forms of identification and social endorsement were actively at work in that theatre, ostensibly a ritual of distraction, but perhaps finally a process of reinscription within the conventional? Here again *Making Shakespeare* sets out critical positions which are implicitly at odds with each other, leaving the video-reader to resolve contradictions for her/himself: how, for example, does this non-essentialist description of Othello's character as 'an effect

217

of language' compare with Paul Robeson's lifelong exploration of, and – according to Sam Wanamaker – complete identification with the role as one which was able to contest vicious social clichés?

The final sequence in the video raises issues about representation, and this implicates the format of the programme itself: as viewers we are *watching* argument – rather than following abstract ideas through reading, as we would be in the narrower band of literate attention. But in this context debate is visually structured, and our reception of the tape's ideas is inflected by the sound and imagery in which they are conveyed. This is a dense form of argument, made from a commitment to the audio-visual medium as one capable of bearing complex ideas on its own terms. Renaissance drama within its original institution was a spectacle of ideas, layered with visual conventions which inflected the script; video technology allows us to dramatize the distance between those original conventions and our contemporary forms of spectacle, forms of argument. And in the classroom video can actively encourage us to appreciate/enjoy/question/turn to our own uses, these near-and-distant plays.

ACKNOWLEDGEMENTS

Many thanks to all the following whose work is described in this article: Rod Macdonald of the Media Production Division, Anglia Higher Education College [hereafter AHEC]; Ed Esche, AHEC, for liaison with the Royal Shakespeare Company, Shakespeare Institute and Shakespeare Centre at Stratford; Brian Musgrove, Charlie Ritchie, and Paul Allitt, of Cambridge AV Group; Richard Spaul, Roland Kenyon, Richard Fredman, Melanie Revill, Tricia Hitchcock, and Alan Wilson of Cambridge Experimental Theatre; Rex Gibson and John Salway of the 'Shakespeare and Schools' Project, Cambridge Institute of Education, and all the teachers and pupils attending the 'Shakespeare Day', 12 July 1988, at Long Road Sixth Form College; Cathy Pompe, Sean Cubitt and everyone involved in the 'Media School' weekend, the Society for Education in Film and Television national conference, 2–3 July 1988 at AHEC; Sorley Macdonald, Arts Cinema, Cambridge; my evening class, A-level and degree students at AHEC where many of these arguments and approaches have been tried on and out.

RESOURCES AND REFERENCES

The tapes described can be obtained from:
CET/CCAT *Hamlet*, Media Production Division, Anglia Higher Education College, East Rd, Cambridge CB1 1PT. VHS and US format, plus teaching guide, £25.

Making Shakespeare, Cambridge AV Group, 10 Latham Rd, Cambridge CB2 2EQ. VHS format, plus teaching guide, £20.

Armes, Roy (1988) *On Video*, London and New York: Routledge.

BARB [Broadcasters' Audience Research Board] (1988): average daily viewing levels for four weeks ending 16 June 1988. In *Audits of Great Britain Limited*, BARB.

Bazalgette, Cary (1988) ' "They changed the picture in the middle of the fight . . .": new kinds of literacy?', in Margaret Meek and Colin Mills (eds) *Language and Literacy in the Primary School*, Lewes: Falmer Press.

BFI/DES National Working Party on Primary Media Education, papers available from BFI Education, 81 Dean St, London W1V 6AA.

Bode, Steven (1988) 'Seen . . . and not seen', an interview with Tim Morrison of Gorilla Tapes in *Independent Media* 77: 2–4.

Bond, Edward (1983) *Lear*, London: Methuen.

Büchner, Georg (1982) *Danton's Death*, A new version by Howard Brenton, from a translation by Jane Fry, London: Methuen.

Bulman, J. C. and Coursen H. R. (eds) (1988) *Shakespeare on Television. An Anthology of Essays and Reviews*, Hanover and London: University Press of New England.

Collick, John (1989) *Shakespeare, Cinema and Society*, Manchester: Manchester University Press.

Dollimore, Jonathan (1989) *Radical Tragedy: Religion, Ideology and Power in the Drama of Shakespeare and his Contemporaries*, 2nd edn, Brighton: Harvester Press.

Dollimore, Jonathan and Sinfield, Alan (eds) (1985) *Political Shakespeare. New Essays in Cultural Materialism*, Manchester: Manchester University Press.

Edwards, Philip (ed.) (1985) *Hamlet, Prince of Denmark* by William Shakespeare, Cambridge: Cambridge University Press.

Ellis, John (1982) *Visible Fictions. Cinema: Television: Video*, London and New York: Routledge.

Gibson, Rex (ed.) (1986–) *Shakespeare and Schools*, The Newsletter of the 'Shakespeare and Schools' Project, Cambridge Institute of Education, Shaftesbury Road, Cambridge CB2 2BX, tel: 0223–69631.

—— (ed.) (1990) *Secondary School Shakespeare. Classroom Practice. A Collection of Papers by Secondary Teachers*, Cambridge: Cambridge Institute of Education.

Grass, Günter (1972) *The Plebeians Rehearse the Uprising. A German Tragedy*, with an introductory address by the author. Trans. Ralph Manheim, Harmondsworth: Penguin.

Hines, Sylvia (1987) 'Independent distribution. Changes for the 80s', *Independent Media* 72: 9–11.

Hodge, Robert and Tripp, David (1986) *Children and Television. A Semiotic Approach*, Stanford, CA: Stanford University Press.

Holderness, Graham (1985) 'Radical potentiality and institutional closure: Shakespeare in film and television', in J. Dollimore and A. Sinfield (eds) *Political Shakespeare. New Essays in Cultural Materialism*, Manchester: Manchester University Press.

—— (ed.) (1988) *The Shakespeare Myth*, Manchester: Manchester University Press.

Independent Media, monthly, is 'devoted to the concerns of independent media makers and users . . . covers in detail questions of distribution, exhibition, and education'. Available from The Media Centre, South Hill Park, Bracknell, Berkshire RG12 4PA, tel: 0344–427272. Publishes a 'Directory of Facilities and Training' annually.

Jameson, Frederic (1987) 'Reading without interpretation: postmodernism and the video-text', in Derek Attridge, Nigel Fabb, Alan Durant, and Colin MacCabe (eds) *The Linguistics of Writing: Arguments Between Language and Literature*, Manchester: Manchester University Press.

Lusted, David (1988) 'Media education in an age of uncertainty', *Initiatives* 9: 12–18.

Marshall, S. (1979) 'Video: from art to independence', *Screen* 26/2: 66–71.

Masterman, Len (1985) *Teaching the Media*, London: Comedia.

McLean, Andrew M. (1980) *Shakespeare. Annotated Bibliographies and Media Guides for Teachers*, Illinois: National Council for Teachers of English.

Ridley, M. R. (ed.) (1965) *Othello* by William Shakespeare, London: Methuen.

Sanders, Norman (ed.) (1984) *Othello* by William Shakespeare, Cambridge: Cambridge University Press.

Sinfield, Alan (1982) '*King Lear* versus *Lear* at Stratford', *Critical Quarterly* 24: 5–14.

Taylor, Gary and Warren, Michael (eds) (1983) *The Division of the Kingdoms. Shakespeare's Two Versions of 'King Lear'*, Oxford: Clarendon Press.

Television and Schooling (1985), London: British Film Institute.

Tennenhouse, Leonard (1989) 'Violence done to women on the renaissance stage', in Nancy Armstrong and Leonard Tennenhouse (eds) *The Violence of Representation. Literature and the History of Violence*, London: Routledge.

Terris, Olwen (ed.) (1986) *Shakespeare. A List of Audio-Visual Materials Available in the UK*, British Universities Film and Video Council, 55 Greek St, London W1V 5LR.

Wells, Stanley (ed.) (1987) *Shakespeare Survey* 39: 'Shakespeare on film and television', Cambridge: Cambridge University Press.

Wheale, Nigel (1988) 'SCREEN/PLAY: Derek Jarman's "Tempest" as critical interpretation', *Ideas and Production*. 8: 'Drama in theory and performance', Edward J. Esche (ed.), Cambridge: Anglia Higher Education College.

Willems, Michele (1987) 'Verbal-visual, verbal-pictorial or textual-televisual? Reflections on the BBC Shakespeare series', in Stanley Wells (ed.)

Shakespeare Survey 39: 'Shakespeare on film and television', Cambridge: Cambridge University Press.
Williams, Raymond (1981) *Culture*, London: Fontana.
—— (n.d.) [1983] *Writing in Society*, London: Verso.

Index

All page numbers in italics refer to illustrations

INDEX

McLean, Andrew M. 208
McLuskie, Kathleen 24, 38, 101
Mahabharata, The 4
marginalization 99–102; of
drama 104
Marley, Bob 117
Marlow, Christopher, *Dido, Queen
of Carthage* 137
Marshall, S. 210
Marxism 64, 65, 66; and
drama 104; and response 43
master symbols 65–6
Masterman, Len 205
Maus, Katherine 154
meaning, importance to text-
centred commentaries 103;
layers of in structuralist
theory 165; Shakespeare as
negotiated set of 103–4
Measure for Measure 37, 80
media studies, as academic
subject 205, 206–7
Merchant of Venice, The 93, 95, 101,
103, 133
Michelangelo 67
Middleton, Thomas 80; *The
Witch* 151, 157, 158
Midelfort, H. C. Erik 157
Midland Examining Group,
guidelines for choice of texts 32
Midsummer Night's Dream, A 30,
36, 45, 92, 133
Millais, John Everett,
'Ophelia' *186,* 195
Miller, Jonathan 38, 199
Milton, John, *A Masque presented
at Ludlow Castle* 23
Mirror stage of human
development 163, 165–6, 171,
172, 176, 177
Mitterand, François 64
modernism 59
Moi, Toril 158
Montrose, Louis 131, 134, 136,
137, 156
Moore, Charles 5
moral tradition and 'master
symbols' 65–6
Mosley, Lady Diana 4

Much Ado About Nothing 98
Muchembled, Robert 157
Muir, Kenneth 115, 116, 120
Mullaney, Steven 20
multivocality 212–13, 215
mummery approach to
representing Shakespeare 47
Munday, Anthony 154
Murray, Margaret 146, 157
music for Shakespeare in
performance 187, 193

National Curriculum 8, 9, 11, 41,
205; and drama 104; and
English language teaching 46;
English Working Group 36;
Key Stages 32–8; and media
studies 206–7
National Foundation for the Arts,
Warwick University 51
National Theatre of Brent 67
National Union of Teachers, and
homosexuality 126
nationalism 26–7, 63, 115–16, 205;
and English curriculum 5–7;
and National Authors 4
naturalism 208–99, 213
New Bibliograph 82
New Criticism 82, 95
new historicism 9, 14, 81, 95, 156
New Left 59
normalization of racist
language 111–12
Norris, Christopher 74, 82
'nurturing mother' in *King
Lear* 169–77

O-level courses 30–1, 34, 43, 47–8
Oedipal emphasis, in Olivier's
Hamlet (q.v.) 193
Oedipal stage of development 163,
164–5, 166, 174–5
Olivier, Laurence, film version of
Hamlet 3, 16, *181, 184, 185,*
191, 192–6; film version of
Richard III 190–1, 192, 194
open texts 45; and *Othello* 214
oral stage of development 163, 164
Original-Spelling Edition 76

228